Book 1

OCR GCSE

Jill Carter
Annabel Charles
Garrett O'Doherty

English Language

Developing the skills for Component 01 and Component 02

OXFORD
UNIVERSITY PRESS

OXFORD
UNIVERSITY PRESS

Great Clarendon Street, Oxford, OX2 6DP,
United Kingdom

Oxford University Press is a department of the University of Oxford.

It furthers the University's objective of excellence in research, scholarship, and
education by publishing worldwide. Oxford is a registered trade mark of Oxford
University Press in the UK and in certain other countries

British Library Cataloguing in Publication Data

Data available

ISBN 978-019-833278-7

10 9 8 7 6 5 4 3 2 1

Printed in Great Britain by Ashford Print and Publishing Services, Gosport

Introduction from OCR

GCSEs are changing from 2015; GCSE English Language will have no controlled assessment, no tiers in the exams, and the qualification is linear, so the first assessment will be in June 2017. At OCR we are very aware of the challenges that these changes create and we are doing everything we can to support teachers and students in the transition to the new GCSE English Language.

We have worked closely with Oxford University Press to produce this lively, high-quality text book which will help support teachers in their delivery of an engaging and relevant GCSE curriculum, which is tailored toward preparing students for the new OCR exams.

OCR's GCSE English Language has two exams, which both assess Reading and Writing. Paper 1 focuses on reading and writing non-fiction, including a short 19th Century text. In Paper 2 students read modern literary prose and produce their own creative writing. We use engaging, authentic unseen texts, to provide a rich curriculum that can be effectively integrated with our GCSE English Literature course. Speaking and listening is central to English teaching and learning, and ideas and activities are embedded throughout this book to support students' preparation for the spoken language endorsement, as well as helping to develop their reading and writing skills for the exams.

Hester Glass

OCR Curriculum Leader for English

Contents

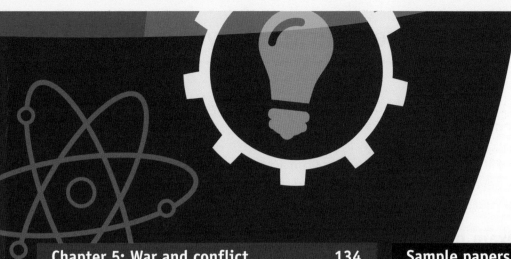

OCR GCSE English Language sepcification overview

You are studying for a GCSE English Language qualification from OCR. The OCR GCSE English Language specification has been designed to help you explore communication, culture and creativity. You will have the opportunity to read a wide variety of literary and non-fiction texts from across a range of genres and time periods, developing your independent and critical reading skills and helping you to develop your voice as a writer.

The exam papers

The grade you receive at the end of your OCR GCSE English Language course is entirely based on your performance in two exam papers. The following provides a summary of these two exam papers:

Exam paper	Reading and Writing questions and marks	Assessment Objectives	Timing	Marks (and % of GCSE)
Paper 1: Communicating information and ideas	**Section A: Reading information and ideas** Exam text: • Two unseen non-fiction texts, including a text from the 19th century Exam questions and marks: • One short-answer question (1 x 4 marks) • Two medium-answer questions (1 x 6 marks and 1 x 12 marks) • One extended question (1 x 18 marks)	Reading: A01 A02 A03 A04	2 hours	Reading: 40 marks (25% GCSE) Writing: 40 marks (25% GCSE) Paper 1 total: 80 marks (50% of GCSE)
	Section B: Writing for audience, purpose and impact • Writing original non-fiction for different audiences and purposes Exam questions and marks: • Choice of two extended writing tasks (24 marks for content, 16 marks for technical accuracy)	Writing: A05 A06		
Paper 2: Exploring effects and impact	**Section A: Reading meaning and effects** Exam text: • Two unseen prose texts, one of which may be literary non-fiction Exam questions and marks: • One short-answer question (1 x 4 marks) • Two medium-answer questions (1 x 6 marks and 1 x 12 marks) • One extended question (1 x 18 marks)	Reading: A01 A02 A03 A04	2 hours	Reading: 40 marks (25% GCSE) Writing: 40 marks (25% GCSE) Paper 2 total: 80 marks (50% of GCSE)
	Section B: Writing imaginatively and creatively • Original creative writing Exam question and marks: • Choice of two extended writing tasks (24 marks for content, 16 marks for technical accuracy)	Writing: A05 A06		

Paper 1: Communicating information and ideas

This exam paper focuses on reading and writing non-fiction texts and has two sections:

- Section A: Reading information and ideas.

- Second B: Writing for audience, impact and purpose.

You will have two hours to complete this exam paper and it is worth 50% of your GCSE English Language grade.

Section A: Reading information and ideas

In Section A you will read and respond to two unseen non-fiction texts, one of which will be a text from the 19th century. The non-fiction texts included in the exam will be linked by theme and taken from a range of non-fiction genres including for example, essays, journalism, travel writing, speeches and biographical writing. .

You are advised to spend one hour on Section A of the exam paper and should answer all the questions. The reading questions will assess the following assessment objectives:

- **AO1** Identify and interpret explicit and implicit information and ideas.

- **AO1** Select and synthesize evidence from different texts.

- **AO2** Explain, comment on and analyse how writers use language and structure to achieve effects and influence readers, using relevant subject terminology to support your views.

- **AO3** Compare writer's ideas and perspectives, as well as how these are conveyed, across two texts.

- **AO4** Evaluate texts critically and support this with appropriate textual references.

The reading questions are designed to increase in challenge, moving from short- to medium-answer response questions, focused on the writer's meaning and purpose, to a final, more detailed task that asks you to evaluate the two texts you have read. This section of the exam paper is worth 25% of your GCSE English Language grade.

Section B: Writing for audience, purpose and impact

In Section B you will write a piece of original non-fiction writing. You will be given a choice of two extended writing tasks, using an idea related to the reading theme, and have to answer one of these tasks. The writing tasks might ask you to:

- write in a range of non-fiction forms, for example, an article, speech or letter

- write for a specific purpose, for example, to describe, explain, inform, instruct, argue or persuade

- write for a specific audience.

You are advised to spend one hour on Section B of the exam paper and should answer only one of the writing tasks. Each writing task will assess the following assessment objectives:

- **AO5** Communicate clearly, effectively and imaginatively, selecting and adapting tone, style and register for different forms, purposes and audiences

- **AO5** Organize information and ideas, using structural and grammatical features to support coherence and cohesion of texts

- **AO6** Use a range of vocabulary and sentence structures for clarity, purpose and effect, with accurate spelling and punctuation

This section of the exam paper is worth 25% of your GCSE English Language grade.

Paper 2: Exploring effects and impact

This exam paper focuses on reading and writing narrative fiction and literary non-fiction and has two sections:

● Section A: Reading meaning and effects

● Second B: Writing imaginatively and creatively

You will have two hours to complete this exam paper and it is worth 50% of your GCSE English Language grade.

Section A: Reading meaning and effects

In Section A you will read and respond to two unseen prose from the 20th and 21st centuries. The texts included in the exam will be linked by theme and one text may be literary non-fiction.

You are advised to spend one hour on Section A of the exam paper and should answer all the questions. The reading questions will assess the following assessment objectives:

● **AO1** Identify and interpret explicit and implicit information and ideas.

● **AO2** Explain, comment on and analyse how writers use language and structure to achieve effects and influence readers, using relevant subject terminology to support your views.

● **AO3** Compare writer's ideas and perspectives, as well as how these are conveyed, across two texts.

● **AO4** Evaluate texts critically and support this with appropriate textual references.

The reading questions are designed to increase in challenge, moving from short- to medium-answer response questions, focused on the writer's meaning and effects, to a final, more detailed task that asks you to evaluate the two texts you have read. This section of the exam paper is worth 25% of your GCSE English Language grade.

Section B: Writing imaginatively and creatively

In Section B you will write a piece of original creative writing. You will be given a choice of two creative writing tasks, at least one of which will have a clear relation to the reading theme, and have to answer one of these tasks. The writing tasks might ask you to write in a range of forms, for example, short stories and autobiographical writing.

You are advised to spend one hour on Section B of the exam paper and should answer only one of the writing tasks. The following assessment objectives will be assessed in this section:

● **AO5** Communicate clearly, effectively and imaginatively, selecting and adapting tone, style and register for different forms, purposes and audiences

● **AO5** Organize information and ideas, using structural and grammatical features to support coherence and cohesion of texts

● **AO6** Use a range of vocabulary and sentence structures for clarity, purpose and effect, with accurate spelling and punctuation

This section of the exam paper is worth 25% of your GCSE English Language grade.

Grades

Your GCSE English Language grade will be awarded solely on the basis of your performance in these two exams and you will be awarded a grade from 1 to 9, with 9 being the top grade.

Spoken Language

The Spoken Language component is focused on your speaking and listening skills. This component will be assessed by your teacher and you will need to demonstrate your ability to give spoken presentations for different purposes and audiences, including in a formal setting. Your Spoken Language performance will be digitally recorded and following assessment objectives used to assess this:

- **AO7** Demonstrate presentation skills in a formal setting.

- **AO8** Listen and respond appropriately to spoken language, including to questions and feedback to presentations.

- **AO9** Use spoken Standard English effectively in speeches and presentations.

You will be awarded a separate grade for Spoken Language at one of three 'pass' grades which will be recorded on your GCSE English Language certificate. If you do not achieve the minimum standard in Spoken Language or do not attempt the Spoken Language assessment this will be indicated on your GCSE English Language certificate.

The Assessment Objectives

AO1	• identify and interpret explicit and implicit information and ideas • select and synthesize evidence from different texts
AO2	Explain, comment on and analyse how writers use language and structure to achieve effects and influence readers, using relevant subject terminology to support their views
AO3	Compare writers' ideas and perspectives, as well as how these are conveyed, across two or more texts
AO4	Evaluate texts critically and support this with appropriate textual references
AO5	Communicate clearly, effectively and imaginatively, selecting and adapting tone, style and register for different forms, purposes and audiences. Organize information and ideas, using structural and grammatical features to support coherence and cohesion of texts
AO6	Candidates must use a range of vocabulary and sentence structures for clarity, purpose and effect, with accurate spelling and punctuation.
AO7	Demonstrate presentation skills in a formal setting
AO8	Listen and respond appropriately to spoken language, including to questions and feedback on presentations
AO9	Use spoken Standard English effectively in speeches and presentations.

Introduction to this book

How this book will help you

Develop your reading and writing skills

The primary aim of this book is to develop and improve your reading and writing skills. Crucially however, in this book you will be doing this in the context of what the exam papers will be asking of you at the end of your course. So, the skills you will be practising throughout this book are ideal preparation for your two English Language exam papers.

Explore the types of texts that you will face in the exams

In your English Language exams you will have to respond to a number of unseen texts. In order to prepare you fully for the range and types of text that you might face in the exam, this book is structured thematically so you can explore the connections between texts. This is ideal preparation for your exams as the unseen texts in your exam papers will be of different types (fiction and non-fiction), from different historical periods (from the 19th, 20th and 21st centuries) and will in some instances be connected.

Become familiar with the Assessment Objectives and the exam paper requirements

Assessment Objectives are the skills that underpin all qualifications. Your GCSE English Language exam papers are testing seven Assessment Objectives (see page 9). Chapters 1 to 5 of this book take exactly the same approach – each chapter develops your reading and writing skills addressing the same Assessment Objectives. This revisiting of Assessment Objectives and supported practising of tasks, in different thematic contexts and with different texts, will ensure that your skills improve and that you're in the best possible position to start your exam preparation. Chapter 6 pulls all the skills together that you have been practising in order to help prepare you for 'mock' exam papers at the end of the book.

Practise the types of task you will face in the exams

Chapters 1 to 5 in this book include substantial end of chapter assessments that enable you to demonstrate what you have learnt and help your teacher assess your progress. Each of these assessments includes tasks that prepare you for the types of task that you will be facing in your GCSE English Language exams. The sample papers at the end of the book give you the opportunity to bring together all that you have been learning and practising in a 'mock' exam situation.

A note on spelling

Certain words, for example 'synthesize' and 'organize' have been spelt with 'ize' throughout this book. It is equally acceptable to spell these words and others with 'ise'.

How is the book structured?

Chapters 1 to 5

Chapters 1 to 5 develop your reading and writing skills within different themes. Each chapter opens with an introductory page that introduces the theme, explains the skills you will be developing and includes an introductory activity.

Chapters 1 and 2 include a range of non-fiction texts, from the 19th, 20th and 21st centuries, to help you develop the reading skills you will need for Paper 1. Chapters 3 and 4 include a range of fiction and literary non-fiction texts, from the 20th and 21st centuries, to help you develop the reading skills you will need for Paper 2. Chapter 5 includes a range of fiction, non-fiction and literary non-fiction texts, from different historical periods, to help you develop your reading skills of comparing and evaluating texts that you will need for Papers 1 and 2. Each chapter covers all the same reading Assessment Objectives and across the chapters you will encounter all of the text types from all of the historical periods that your exam paper texts will be taken from at the end of your course.

Your writing skills are also developed throughout every chapter including a focus on improving your technical accuracy (or SPAG – Spelling, Punctuation And Grammar). This is done in the context of the chapter to help embed these vital skills into your writing.

Chapter 6

Chapter 6 pulls all of the skills together that you have learnt throughout the course, revisiting key points and providing you with revision practise. The chapter and book concludes with sample exam papers, in the style of the OCR exam papers, to enable you and your teacher to see how much progress you have made.

What are the main features within this book?

Activities, Stretch and Support

To develop your reading responses to the wide range of texts included in this book as well as developing your writing skills, you will find many varied activities. The 'Support' feature provides additional help with the activity whilst the 'Stretch' feature introduces further challenge to help develop a more advanced response.

Tips, Key terms and glossed words

These features help support your understanding of key terms, concepts and more difficult words within a source text. These therefore enable you to concentrate fully on developing your reading and writing skills.

Progress check

In addition to the summative end of chapter assessments, you will also find regular formative assessments in the form of 'Progress checks'. These enable you to establish whether through peer or self-assessment how confident you feel about what you have been learning.

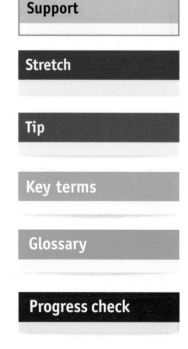

Support

Stretch

Tip

Key terms

Glossary

Progress check

Further OCR GCSE English Language resources

OCR GCSE English Language Student Book 2: Assessment Preparation for Component 01 and Component 02

Student Book 2 provides students with all the exam preparation and practice that they need to succeed. The book is divided into Component 01 and Component 02 sections with each component further divided into reading and writing sections to reflect the format of the two exam papers. Within each section, students are guided through the Assessment Objective and question requirements. The book features:

- an overview of what to expect in the exams
- paper-by-paper and question-by-question practice
- a range of texts and tasks similar to those students will encounter in the exam
- activities to practise and reinforce the key skills with advice on how to improve their responses
- marked sample student responses at different levels
- opportunities for self-assessment and peer assessment
- sample exam papers.

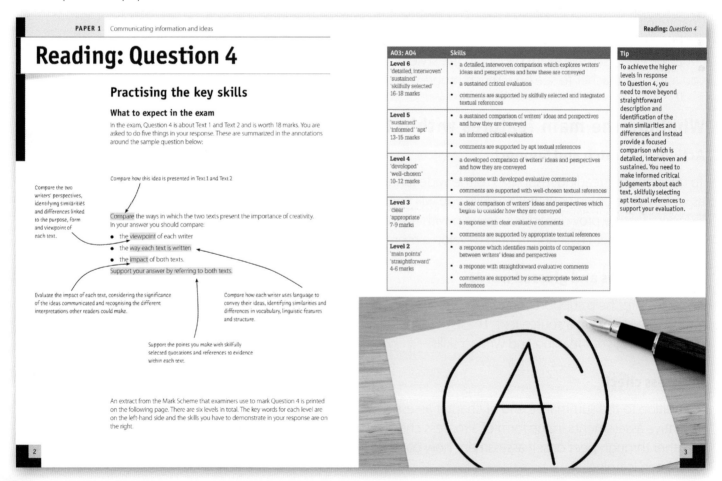

OCR GCSE English Language Teacher Companion

The Teacher Companion provides holistic support for teachers to help them plan and deliver their GCSE programme, including:

- specification insight and planning guidance to aid planning and delivery of the specification

- teaching tips and guidance for effective lesson delivery to all students of the material in Student Book 1, with additional support for differentiation and personalisation

- exam preparation guidance and planning with links to English Language Student Book 2

- guidance and support for delivering Spoken Language assessments

- links to, and guidance on, the additional resources on the accompanying OCR GCSE English Language Teacher Companion CD-ROM.

OCR GCSE English Language Teacher Companion CD-ROM

The Teacher Companion is accompanied by a CD-ROM containing the following resources:

- activity worksheets to support and extend activities in Student Book 1

- differentiated worksheets to support and stretch activities in Student Book 1

- Progress Check self-assessment and peer assessment checklists

- mark schemes for end-of-chapter assessments in Student Book 1

- mark schemes for sample exam papers in Student Book 1

- short, medium and long term editable plans to aid the planning and delivery of the course.

1 ON THE MIND

'Biology gives you a brain. Life turns it into a mind.'

Jeffrey Eugenides, writer

'Non-fiction speaks to the head. Fiction speaks to the heart.'

Ellen Hopkins, writer

'The illiterate of the 21st century will not be those who cannot read and write, but those who cannot learn, unlearn, and relearn.'

Alvin Toffler, writer and futurist

Introduction

Every idea starts in the mind. The brain is the most complex and important organ in the body and scientists are finding out more about it all the time. In this chapter you will read and discuss a range of non-fiction texts about the mind, covering topics such as brain-training, mental health and creative thinking and including extracts from essays, articles, speeches and autobiographies. You will investigate how writers use language, form and structure to present and shape different ideas, and you will draw on the techniques you explore to communicate your own ideas in speech and in writing.

Exam link

The activities in this chapter are designed to help you develop the skills needed for success in one of the two exam papers you will sit at the end of your course: Component 01 Communicating information and ideas. Section A of this exam paper requires you to read two different non-fiction extracts, one of which will be from the 19th century, and answer questions that ask you to demonstrate your critical reading and comprehension skills by:

- identifying and interpreting information and ideas
- drawing inferences and justifying these with evidence
- comparing and evaluating the usefulness and relevance of content
- reflecting critically on the extracts presented.

Section B of the exam paper asks you to write a piece of non-fiction writing for a particular purpose and audience.

Activity 1

1. Read and discuss the quotations on the facing page. Which do you find most interesting and why?

2. Look at the information about the human brain in Source text A. Which ideas are familiar to you and which are new?

3. Research and create your own 'Did you know?' facts about the human brain. Think about how you can convey this information in an interesting way for teenage readers.

Source text A

Did you know?

- The average adult human brain weighs three pounds, has a texture like firm jelly and is made up of 75 percent water.

- There is no evidence that a larger brain is smarter than a smaller brain.

- The brain is the only organ in the body that feels no pain.

- Even when you don't think you are thinking about anything in particular, for example when you are day dreaming, your brain is incredibly active.

Chapter 1 On the mind
Brain power

To learn more about what the brain is like and how it works, it can be helpful to think about some of the ways we think – for example, memorizing and **empathizing** – and consider how these skills can be improved.

Learning objectives

- To identify explicit information and ideas
- To summarize ideas and information

Key term

empathizing
to understand and share in someone else's feelings, to feel empathy

Exam link

In Section A of Component 01 and Component 02, reading questions might ask you to locate specific pieces of information in a text, for example, quotations.

1 Locating information

When you read a text, you need to think about the content: the information and ideas the writer wants to convey. Content can include explicit as well as implicit information and ideas. Explicit information and ideas are stated directly, while implicit ideas are implied or suggested by what the writer has written.

Read the newspaper article in Source text B and complete the activities below.

Activity 1

1. What are your first impressions of this text? Do you find the ideas it presents interesting? Do they chime with your experience?

2. Give one example according to this text of something that is easy to remember and one example of something that is difficult to remember.

3. Explain what a 'mem' is and how it works. Look back at the text to select a quotation to support your explanation.

4. What does the writer suggest is an effective 'mem' for remembering the capital of Saudi Arabia? Why does he suggest this is effective?

Support

Find two quotations from the following section of the text which show why the writer can't remember the capital of Saudi Arabia.

'Let's imagine I'm trying to remember that Riyadh is the capital of Saudi Arabia. This is tricky, because Riyadh and Saudi Arabia have no real detail (in my imagination, at least) – they're basically just sounds, so entirely unmemorable.'

Summarizing involves identifying the key or main ideas in a text and writing them clearly and succinctly in your own words. It is important to present the ideas objectively, as they are conveyed in the text, and not to give your own interpretation.

Activity 2

Write one sentence to summarize what the whole text is about. Discuss your sentence with a partner. How far do you agree with their summary?

Tip

When you are asked to find quotations from a text, it is important to select them precisely. This means choosing a quotation with as few words as possible. Copy them carefully and use quotation marks to show they are quotations.

16

Extract from 'How to Learn Boring Facts' by Ed Cooke

This text is written by Ed Cooke who is one of the founders of Memrise, a website dedicated to imaginative ways of learning.

Understanding memory techniques

The key to understanding memory techniques is to know that some kinds of information are much easier to remember than others.

Nobody forgets being attacked by a kangaroo or kissing Scarlett Johansson, but recalling what we had for lunch last Tuesday is generally much trickier...

There's no surprise here: we remember what is interesting, vivid, unique and amusing. The problem – especially when it comes to exam revision – is that much of what we learn is by no means "interesting, vivid, unique and amusing". Or at least until we've understood it a bit.

...When we're first told that the Spanish word for narrow is estrecho, it probably doesn't make us laugh out loud or fire up Facebook to share the news with our friends.

But one effective way to make these facts more interesting is through the use of mnemonics, or... 'mems' – a kind of visual memory aid.

Mems aim to forge vivid connections in the mind between concepts that we may experience as meaningless. They aim to take connections that are difficult to remember (the link between two names; the connection between a technical term and its meaning; the meaning of a foreign word) and transform that connection into a form which we are good at remembering. They do this often via wordplay, combined with vivid imagery.

How does it work? Let's imagine I'm trying to remember that Riyadh is the capital of Saudi Arabia. This is tricky, because Riyadh and Saudi Arabia have no real detail (in my imagination, at least) – they're basically just sounds, so entirely unmemorable. How to link them together vividly?

One user of online learning platform Memrise suggests we imagine Amy Winehouse singing "They tried to make me go to Riyadh, and I SAUDI no, no, no". Because I know the song, this immediately summons a comic and memorable image into my mind...

An enormous amount of knowledge, both taught in school and elsewhere, is in the form of factual connections. Words connect to definitions, chemicals to their formulae, countries to their capitals... The key is to make these connections – and a huge proportion of them can benefit from the use of mems.

2 Interpreting information

Learning objectives

- To interpret implicit information and ideas

- To select evidence to justify inferences and interpretations

Key terms

inferences something that you infer; a conclusion reached by reasoning

connotation something implied or suggested in addition to the main meaning

Tip

Evidence may be:

- references to the text using your own words

- summarising a point from the text

- quotations from the text.

When you are reading, you have to interpret implicit information and ideas by making **inferences** from what the writer has written. You need to support your interpretation with evidence from the text.

Read Source text C which is an extract from Derren Brown's autobiography, *Confessions of a Conjuror*, and complete the activities below.

Activity 1

1. What explicit information do you learn about the customer Derren Brown is watching? Identify one quotation from the text about his appearance and one quotation about what he is doing.

2a. Which of the following emotions does Derren Brown imagine the man might be experiencing?

   Happiness   Anger   Irritation   Desire   Anticipation   Joy   Surprise

2b. For each emotion you have chosen, find a quotation from the text to justify your choice. The quotation could include explicit or implicit information.

3. Look at the paragraph which begins 'There was something...' . What impression do you get of the barman from this paragraph? Support your ideas with evidence from this paragraph.

Support

Look closely at the words and phrases used to describe the barman's actions and behaviour, for example, 'showy ease'. Discuss the different **connotations** each word or phrase has and what the use of this suggests about the barman.

Writers can use many different techniques to convey information and ideas, for example, through their choice of imagery and descriptive detail.

Stretch

What impression do you get of Derren Brown from this extract? Think about the techniques the author uses and what they might suggest. Support your ideas with evidence from the whole text.

Activity 2

In this extract Derren Brown imagines the physical sensations the man is experiencing as he leans up against the bar and describes what they are like. Look at the picture and write a similar description of what this person is experiencing. Try to convey what the person is feeling through your description without stating it explicitly.

Source text C

Extract from *Confessions of a Conjuror* by Derren Brown

In this extract, Derren describes how he tries to get inside another person's mind and imagine what he is thinking and feeling.

The barman was now busy dealing uninterestedly with a fat man wearing a thin, loose tie who was peering at the whiskies over the counter. The bar was pushing into the man's stomach as he heaved himself high enough to read the labels...

He was pushing up on to the balls of his feet and grasping with both hands a brass rail that ran along the front of the bar perhaps a foot below its edge. I wondered what he was feeling at that moment: the tension in his hamstrings, the cool brass, the push of the counter into his middle section, the straining of his eyes and jutting forward of his slack neck to recognise the labels on the bottles.

I tried to recreate these sensations mentally, and considered, as I tensed and shifted in **microcosm**, that that was what he was feeling right now; that for him the experience of all life revolved in this instant around those sensations, and that I was (with my annoyance and self-hatred and reluctance to work) at most a blur in the corner of his vision.

As he pointed to a bottle and then, a beat later, happy that the barman knew which he required, hauled himself back to standing straight, I tried to lose myself in what I imagined his world to be.

I tried to picture the bar and barman straight-on, to hear the buzz of the restaurant behind me rather than to one side, to imagine the feel of his meal inside me, his weight on my bones, the faint sensation of comfort following the loosening of shoe leather from across the bridge of my toes as he lowered himself back to the floor.

I wondered whether... he was at that moment imagining the walloping peaty taste he knew he was soon to enjoy.

There was something in the showy ease of the barman and the assured way in which he set the glass upon the counter that had about it a hint of performance, a suggestion of the 'flair' that sometimes **flamboyantly** attends the preparation of cocktails; I presumed that the man was noticing this **affectation** too, with mild irritation at its pointlessness, and making quiet judgements accordingly...

A woman passed by, having emerged from the ladies' toilet behind me, and the game ended. The sound of the refilling cistern within was bright and loud, and then abruptly muted as the door bumped closed. The fat man wobbled away from the bar and from me, a little **inebriated**, and my empathy with his thoughts and sensations was lost under the high ceilings of the wide, noisy lounge.

Glossary

microcosm a situation or place capturing in a small way something much larger

flamboyantly to do something in a way to attract attention

affectation behaviour that is intended to impress

inebriated drunk

3 Synthesizing evidence

Learning objectives

- To explore and compare how writers use language to convey ideas

- To select and synthesize evidence from different texts

- To prepare and make a spoken presentation

Key terms

simile where one thing is compared to another thing, using a connective word such as 'like' or 'as'

metaphor describes a person or thing as if they were something else without using a comparison word such as 'like' or 'as'.

Glossary

calibrated set or adjusted in a careful and precise way

Writers can use a range of techniques to convey their ideas. **Similes** and **metaphors** are often used to create comparisons that can help to clarify a writer's ideas or communicate information in a more vivid and interesting way.

Read Source text D and complete the activities on the facing page.

Source text D

Extract from *Sane New World* by Ruby Wax

This is an extract from a non-fiction book about how the mind works.

There's a lot going on in your head

The brain is like a pliable, three-pound piece of play-dough; you can re-sculpt it by breaking old mental habits and creating new, more flexible ways of thinking...

The inside of your head could be compared to Las Vegas, where every experience, sensation, thought and feeling corresponds with billions of electrical lights zapping on and off like a Mexican hand wave on a gigantic electric grid. Your ability to do everything, including your dreams, hopes, fantasies, fears... is created by neuronal connections, chemicals and specialized regions in your brain **calibrated** by your genetic history, your development, the society you're born into and... Mommy and Daddy.

Neurons transmit information to each other via electrical impulses not dissimilar to those used to jolt Frankenstein... and make him kill people...

Learning is about new neurons connecting together; memory is made possible by those changes happening over many times because you're memorizing a new fact and you study it again and again... USE IT OR LOSE IT. If you repeat a mode of thinking or behaving, the pattern of the neurons becomes strengthened. NEURONS THAT FIRE TOGETHER, WIRE TOGETHER. When they don't fire, the connections eventually just shrivel and die...

Your average neuron fires 5 to 50 times a second, meaning there are zillions and zillions of signals travelling inside your head right now carrying... information... All those zillions of emails zapping around in your head are what defines the mind, most of which you will never be aware of...

Whatever you're using or thinking about is reflected in areas lighting up in your brain and you can watch this firework display during brain scanning.

I'm just trying to tell you that there is a lot going on in your head.

Activity 1

1. What is the key idea Ruby Wax is trying to convey in Source text D? Select one sentence from the text which you think best sums it up.

2a. Explain what the simile 'a pliable, three-pound piece of play-dough' suggests about the physical reality of the brain and also what the brain is capable of.

2b. What do the connotations of the word 'play-dough' add to the impression of the brain?

2c. Pick out the other similes and metaphors Ruby Wax uses in this text. Select the one that you think is most effective and explain what idea it helps to convey.

3. Read the following description of the brain by Susannah Calahan:

   'The mind is like a circuit of Christmas tree lights. When the brain works well, all of the lights twinkle brilliantly, and it's adaptable enough that, often, even if one bulb goes out, the rest will still shine on.'

   Here are two students' explanations of her description:

   Zoe: Calahan uses a simile to describe the brain. Christmas tree lights are bright and sparkling and go on and off. She says when the brain works well all the lights twinkle brightly. Then she says if one bulb goes off the rest of the lights will go on shining, which is just like the brain.

   Arbin: Calahan compares the brain with a 'circuit of Christmas tree lights' suggesting that when you are thinking it's like lights flickering on and off – active and dynamic. The link with Christmas makes the brain seem exciting and fun, as though it could do anything. Using the word 'circuit' shows how different parts of the brain are connected. Even if one 'bulb' or part of the brain isn't working, the rest will carry on firing.

3a. Which explanation do you think is better and why?

   Now look at Ruby Wax's description of the brain:

   'The inside of your head could be compared to <u>Las Vegas</u>, where <u>every</u> experience, sensation, thought and feeling corresponds with <u>billions</u> of electrical lights <u>zapping</u> on and off like a <u>Mexican hand wave</u> on a <u>giant</u> electric grid.'

3b. Explain how Ruby Wax's choice of words and phrases in this sentence emphasizes how much is going on in the brain. Comment in particular on how the underlined words help to create and reinforce this idea.

Support

You could start with: 'The comparison with Las Vegas makes the inside of your head sound like a buzzing city, full of people, lights and activity…'

4. The **purpose** of this text is to inform readers about how the mind works. How does Ruby Wax try to make her writing understandable and interesting to people who are not scientists?

Key term

purpose something that you intend to do or achieve, an intended result

Exam link

In Section A of Component 01 and Component 02, look out for reading questions that ask you to find 'similarities' in the two texts you have read. If you are asked to 'draw on evidence from both texts' you will need to select and synthesize relevant ideas and evidence from the two texts you have read to create your own response.

Glossary

elapsed passed

exposure how much light a photograph receives through the lens when taking a picture

underexposures a photograph that receives too little light

Synthesizing is where you bring ideas from more than one text together. It may involve recognizing the similarities or the differences between ideas from different sources or combining them to create a new text.

Now read Source text E. This is an extract from a non-fiction book about how the human brain works, which was first published in 1899.

Source text E

Extract from *The Structure of the Brain* by Dr Albert Wilson

Here, the author describes how memories are made.

If we speak of a familiar person or place, we at once recall the picture or photograph of the subject or person. Think of any relative or friend, or building like St. Paul's Cathedral or the Tower of London, and we see them before us.

But if many years have **elapsed** since seeing a friend, the photograph in our brain may have faded, and it is an effort to recall it. More difficult than to recognise our friend is to remember his or her name, for the simple reason that word memory fades away more easily than visual images.

Those who photograph know too well that a good impression requires correct **exposure. Underexposures** are poor, and do not last. It is the same with our brains. We cannot learn without drilling the subject-matter into our brains. Imagine the case of an assault or two people fighting, and a stranger witnessing it. A few days after, the witness has much difficulty in recognising. the offenders. The reason is that he could not for a sufficient time make observations, and possibly other circumstances are against him. It is an under-exposed photograph. Many people also are not trained to use their eyes. A quick observer might have noted several points which could not fail to commit the offenders. It is a great matter to train one's self to observe.

We see, then, that the brain is like a big album of photographs, and other sensory impressions. We must store the brain with accurate impressions.

Activity 2

1. What is the main point being made in Source text E?

2. What technique does Dr Albert Wilson use to convey his idea about the brain? Is it an effective way to describe the brain?

3. Both Source text D and Source text E directly address the reader. Ruby Wax uses 'you' and Dr Albert Wilson uses 'we'. What effects do these different forms of direct address create in each text?

Stretch

Explain why you think Ruby Wax uses elements of spoken language in Source text D.

4. In Source text D, the phrase 'USE IT' is balanced by 'LOSE IT'. This is an example of a balanced sentence, often used when comparing or contrasting ideas. Find another example of a sentence which is balanced in a similar way in this text.

5. Ruby Wax says: 'Learning is about new neurons connecting together. Memory is made possible by those changes happening many times.' Find a quotation from Source text E that supports this point.

6. What similarities are there between Ruby Wax's and Dr Albert Wilson's views of the brain? Draw on evidence from both texts to support your answer.

7a. In this unit, the brain has been compared to firm jelly, Christmas tree lights, play-dough, and Las Vegas. Brainstorm some other things you could compare a brain to.

7b. Using your own simile or metaphor, write a paragraph of description about the brain and how it works, extending your chosen comparison.

8. Drawing on the information you have read, prepare and deliver a spoken presentation on the power of the human brain. Think about:

- the information and ideas you could include

- how you could organize these in the most effective way

- when you should use Standard English to express your ideas.

Tip

Try to balance the ideas and evidence you select from both texts.

Tip

Reading your writing aloud is a good way to check your work. As you read aloud, check that what you have written makes sense; that you have inserted punctuation to make the meaning clear and that you haven't repeated yourself or gone off at a tangent without meaning to.

A troubled mind

In this section you will read some non-fiction texts which explore what happens when people's minds are overwhelmed by feelings and stop working properly, or work in different and unexpected ways.

Learning objective

- To explore how writers' choices of language and structure can create effects and influence readers

4 Figurative language

It is sometimes said that English has more words than most world languages. Writers certainly have a huge pool of vocabulary to draw on in their writing. They can also choose how they put these words together into sentences and paragraphs to create texts. As you read a text, think about the language a writer has chosen to communicate their ideas and the way sentences have been structured.

The two source texts on these pages describe what it feels like to be overtaken by very strong feelings which you can't control. Read Source text F and complete the activity below.

Source text F

Extract from *Reality Lost and Regained: Autobiography of a Schizophrenic Girl* by Marguerite Sechehaye

Here, Marguerite Sechehaye describes her feelings of fear.

It was New Year's when I first experienced what I called *Fear*. It literally fell on me, how I know not. It was afternoon, the wind was stronger than ever and more mournful. I was in the mood to listen to it, my whole being attuned to it, palpitating, awaiting I know not what. Suddenly Fear, agonizing, boundless Fear, overcame me, not the usual uneasiness of unreality, but real fear, such as one knows at the approach of danger, calamity. And the wind, as if to add to the turmoil, **soughed** its interminable protests, echoing the muffled groans of the forest.

Glossary

soughed a moaning, whistling or rushing sound

Key term

pathetic fallacy giving human feelings to inanimate things or animals

Activity 1

(SPAG)

1. Why do you think Sechehaye writes the word fear with both a lower case f and a capital F? What effect does this create?

2. How does Sechehaye use word order in the first two sentences to create emphasis?

3. Pick out the adjectives used in this extract. What mood do these help to create?

4. Explain how Sechehaye uses an example of **pathetic fallacy** to convey her feelings in this text? How effective do you think this is?

Now read Source text G which is taken from *Why Be Happy When You Could Be Normal?*, an autobiography by the writer Jeanette Winterson.

Source text G

Extract from *Why Be Happy When You Could Be Normal?* by Jeanette Winterson

In this extract, Jeanette Winterson describes a feeling which she doesn't name, but which is linked to a period of depression.

I knew clearly that I could not rebuild my life or put it back together in any way. I had no idea what might lie on the other side of this place. I only knew that the before-world was gone forever.

I had a sense of myself as a haunted house. I never knew when the invisible thing would strike – and it was like a blow, a kind of winding in the chest or stomach. When I felt it I would cry out at the force of it.

Sometimes I lay curled up on the floor. Sometimes I kneeled and gripped a piece of furniture.

This is one moment... know that another...

Hold on, hold on, hold on.

fear unease misery agonizing GLOOM boundless gripped

Activity 2

SPAG

1. How does Winterson's use of verbs help to communicate the strength of her feeling?

2. Winterson uses metaphors of place to convey her feelings in this extract. Explain the metaphors she uses.

3. How do the last two lines of this extract help to convey the extreme nature of her feelings?

4. How do both these writers use **personification** to show the strength of their feelings in these extracts?

Writers use words from the same **lexical field** to create a sense of continuity and cohesion in their writing.

Activity 3

1. Re-read Source text F and identify all the words and phrases that are part of the lexical field that create a feeling of fear and gloom.

2. Add ten words or phrases of your own linked to the same lexical field.

3. Using some of these words, write a description of someone experiencing a moment of extreme fear or misery. Avoid being explicit about what the person is feeling or using **clichés**.

Key terms

personification representing an idea in human form or a thing as having human characteristics

lexical field (or semantic field) words used in a text which have an element of shared meaning

cliché a phrase or idea that is used so often that it has little meaning

5 Language and structure

Learning objectives

- To analyse how language and structure are used to present viewpoints, achieve effects and influence readers

Glossary

fancy a tentative belief or idea

preposterously absurdly

notabilities famous or important people

vexedly with annoyance

delusions a false belief or opinion

Writers of non-fiction have to think about how they are going to use language and construct sentences to achieve specific effects and influence readers to share their viewpoint.

Read Source text H which is taken from an essay by Charles Dickens, and then complete the activities on page 27.

Source text H

Extract from 'Night Walks' by Charles Dickens

Here, Dickens explores his thoughts as he walks past Bethlehem Hospital at night. Bethlehem Hospital was, and still is, a hospital for people with mental illnesses. The word 'bedlam' meaning uproar and confusion is derived from the nickname given to the hospital.

From the dead wall associated on those houseless nights with this too common story, I chose next to wander by Bethlehem Hospital; partly, because it lay on my road round to Westminster; partly, because I had a night **fancy** in my head which could be best pursued within sight of its walls and dome. And the fancy was this: Are not the sane and the insane equal at night as the sane lie a dreaming? Are not all of us outside this hospital, who dream, more or less in the condition of those inside it, every night of our lives? Are we not nightly persuaded, as they daily are, that we associate **preposterously** with kings and queens, emperors and empresses, and **notabilities** of all sorts? Do we not nightly jumble events and personages and times and places, as these do daily? Are we not sometimes troubled by our own sleeping inconsistencies, and do we not **vexedly** try to account for them or excuse them, just as these do sometimes in respect of their waking **delusions**? Said an afflicted man to me, when I was last in a hospital like this, "Sir, I can frequently fly." I was half ashamed to reflect that so could I by night. Said a woman to me on the same occasion, "Queen Victoria frequently comes to dine with me, and her Majesty and I dine off peaches and maccaroni in our night-gowns, and his Royal Highness the Prince Consort does us the honour to make a third on horseback in a Field-Marshal's uniform." Could I refrain from reddening with consciousness when I remembered the amazing royal parties I myself had given (at night), the unaccountable viands I had put on table, and my extraordinary manner of conducting myself on those distinguished occasions? I wonder that the great master who knew everything, when he called Sleep the death of each day's life, did not call Dreams the insanity of each day's sanity.

SPAG

Activity 1

1. Identify the main point Dickens is making in Source text H. Find one sentence which sums up this idea. Do you agree with his view?

2. Dickens uses a lot of questions in this extract. How do they help him explore his ideas in this text?

3. Explain how Dickens presents his ideas about the 'sane' and the 'mad'. You should comment on:

   • his use of different sentence types and structures

   • his choice of language to create a sense of confusion

   • other techniques he uses to convey his ideas.

   Support your ideas with quotations from the text, using terminology where relevant.

Activity 2

1. Dickens' thoughts were prompted by walking past a particular building. Look at the photographs below of different places and discuss what ideas they make you think about, particularly contrasting or conflicting ideas.

2. Write a short essay about a place which creates conflicting thoughts and feelings for you. Follow the steps below to help you plan and draft your essay.

Planning

Note down some of the contrasting thoughts you have about your chosen place. Share your ideas with someone else and try to develop them further, adding questions, explanations and anecdotes to support your ideas.

Drafting

Try to include balanced sentences to show your contrasting feelings. Think about how your choice of language can help to convey your ideas.

Tip

Look at how Dickens uses balanced sentences to contrast the ideas of the sane and the insane. Find an example and explain the effect this creates.

Exam link

In Section B of Component 01, the writing tasks you will be given in the exam will not include any pictures or images. However when developing your writing skills it can be helpful to look at pictures to inspire your writing, for example to think about the descriptive details you could include in a piece of travel writing.

Progress check

Swap the first draft of your essay with someone else. Check that they have tried to use different sentence types, including balanced sentences, in their essay. Share ideas about adding details, developing ideas, adding anecdotes or comments. Refer to the feedback on your own essay as you write your final draft.

6 Form and structure

Learning objectives

- To evaluate how form and structure can be used to achieve effects and influence readers

Key terms

recount to give an account of something

chronologically arranged in the order in which things occurred

cohesive devices words or phrases which link paragraphs together and link points within paragraphs

reference chains different words or phrases used for the same idea, person or thing many times in a piece of writing, like links in a chain

The form of a piece of writing influences the decisions a writer makes about structure. These can include how a text begins and ends, the way ideas are sequenced into paragraphs and the writer's choice of grammatical features. Forms of writing such as biography and journalism which include elements of **recount** are often written **chronologically**.

Read Source text I, taken from an article about the scientist Charles Darwin.

Activity 1

1. How does the first sentence make a good opening for the extract and how does it link with the ending?

2. Explain how the second paragraph links back to the first. Look at the way the ideas and the language are connected.

3. Explore the **cohesive devices** the writer uses to link ideas within and between paragraphs. You could explain how the writer uses:

   - synonyms and pronouns to avoid repetition

   - **reference chains** to link ideas within and between paragraphs

   - any other cohesive devices in the text.

4. Pick out three quotations which link ideas by referring to time or the passing of time.

5. This text is presented chronologically, but it isn't a straightforward biographical account. Explain how the writer has conveyed this chronological account of Darwin's life and how it relates to the form of the text.

Support

An autobiography about Charles Darwin would be written in the first person, while a biography would be written in the third person. Look at which sections of the text are written in the third person and which are written in the first person. How does the writer use these two approaches to structure the article?

Exam link

In Section A of Component 01 and Component 02, a reading question might ask you to explore how a writer uses language and structure. Try to comment equally on both aspects in your answer.

Extract from *Evolution of a genius*

*This article reports how a leading psychiatrist has claimed that Charles Darwin, the Victorian scientist who developed the theory of evolution, was **autistic**.*

As a child, he was an obsessive collector, accumulating hoards of shells, insects and minerals and studying them in minute detail. Spurning the company of his brother and sisters, he spent many hours in solitary pursuits: bird-watching, fishing and taking long walks to explore the natural world. His lack of interest in school led his parents to worry about his future achievements, but Charles Darwin would grow up to become one of the most famous scientists who ever lived.

Now a leading psychiatrist claims that Darwin's intense interest in collecting, his extraordinary attention to detail and the difficulties he faced with social interaction suggest that he had Asperger's syndrome, a form of autism linked to creativity. Professor Michael Fitzgerald of Dublin's Trinity College said: "Asperger's syndrome gave Darwin the capacity to hyperfocus, the extra capacity for persistence, the enormous ability to see detail that other people missed".

Darwin wrote himself of his solitary childhood and how his passion for collecting led him to feel different from his friends and family: "**By the time I went to day-school my taste for natural history, and more especially for collecting, was well developed. I tried to make out the names of plants, and collected all sorts of things, shells, seals, franks, coins, and minerals. The passion for collecting, which leads a man to be a systematic naturalist, a virtuoso or a miser, was very strong in me, and was clearly innate, as none of my sisters or brother ever had this taste ... Looking back, I infer that there must have been something in me a little superior to the common run of youths.**"

Later at university, Darwin's intense interest in collecting would lead him to exhibit some rather unusual behaviour. "**One day, on tearing off some old bark, I saw two rare beetles and seized one in each hand; then I saw a third and new kind, which I could not bear to lose, so that I popped the one which I held in my right hand into my mouth. Alas it ejected some intensely acrid fluid, which burnt my tongue so that I was forced to spit the beetle out, which was lost, as well as the third one.**"

Professor Fitzgerald said: "It is suggested that the same genes that produce autism and Asperger's syndrome are also responsible for great creativity and originality." At the age of 22 in 1831, Darwin set out on a five-year voyage around the coast of South America, studying the plants, wildlife and geology of this continent and its islands. He filled countless notebooks with his observations and collected hundreds of specimens including birds, insects, plants and marine life. From these notebooks and specimens, Darwin would construct his theory of evolution which transformed the way we think about life on Earth.

autistic someone suffering from autism, a lifelong condition that affects how someone communicates and interacts with others

virtuoso a person with outstanding skill

innate natural

acrid bitter

Creative thinking

Some people think that creativity is an innate skill, one that can't be taught, but others argue that creativity has an important role to play in everybody's life.

Learning objective

- To identify and compare writers' perspectives and how these are conveyed

Key terms

viewpoint an opinion or point of view

repetition repeating, or being repeated

rule of three (also called tricolon) linking three points or features, for example adjectives, for impact

rhetorical question a question asked for dramatic effect and not intended to get an answer

inverted sentence where the normal word order of a sentence is changed for emphasis, for example, 'Whatever you want, you can have.'

7 Comparing viewpoints

When you read a text for the first time, it is helpful to try to work out what the purpose and **viewpoint** are. You can then think about how the writer has chosen different techniques to fulfil the purpose and convey a viewpoint in his or her writing. Most texts have more than one purpose, although there may be a main purpose. Identifying the writer's perspective or viewpoint can help you to understand the information and ideas presented. Read Source text J, taken from a speech by the educationalist Ken Robinson.

Activity 1

1. What do you think is the purpose of Ken Robinson's speech? What is his viewpoint on education and creativity?

2. Do you agree with Ken Robinson's views? Debate your own ideas on this issue.

3. How does Ken Robinson use the first paragraph to establish the purpose and viewpoint of his speech?

4. What is the purpose of the second paragraph?

5. Track the key ideas Ken Robinson puts forward to support his argument in paragraphs three, four and five of his speech. Sum them up in three sentences.

6. How does the last paragraph link back to the first?

Stretch

What different rhetorical devices does Ken Robinson use in his speech to convey his ideas and keep the audience interested? You could comment on his use of:

- **repetition**
- **rhetorical questions**
- the **rule of three**
- **inverted sentences.**

Extract from 'How schools kill creativity' by Ken Robinson

So I want to talk about education and I want to talk about creativity. My contention is that creativity now is as important in education as literacy, and we should treat it with the same status...

I heard a great story recently – I love telling it – of a little girl who was in a drawing lesson. She was six and she was at the back, drawing, and the teacher said this little girl hardly ever paid attention, and in this drawing lesson she did. The teacher was fascinated and she went over to her and she said, "What are you drawing?" And the girl said, "I'm drawing a picture of God." And the teacher said, "But nobody knows what God looks like." And the girl said, "They will in a minute."

...Kids will take a chance. If they don't know, they'll have a go. Am I right? They're not frightened of being wrong. Now, I don't mean to say that being wrong is the same thing as being creative. What we do know is, if you're not prepared to be wrong, you'll never come up with anything original... And by the time they get to be adults, most kids have lost that capacity. They have become frightened of being wrong... And we're now running national education systems where mistakes are the worst thing you can make. And the result is that we are educating people out of their creative **capacities**... So why is this?

Now our education system is predicated on the idea of academic ability... The hierarchy is rooted on two ideas. Number one, that the most useful subjects for work are at the top. So you were probably steered away from things at school when you were a kid, things you liked, on the grounds that you would never get a job doing that. Is that right? Don't do music, you're not going to be a musician; don't do art, you won't be an artist.

And the second is academic ability, which has really come to dominate our view of intelligence, because the universities designed the system in their image. And the consequence is that many highly talented, brilliant, creative people think they're not, because the thing they were good at at school wasn't valued... And I think we can't afford to go on that way.

Our education system has mined our minds in the way that we strip-mine the earth: for a particular commodity. And for the future, it won't serve us. We have to rethink the fundamental principles on which we're educating our children.

What TED celebrates is the gift of the human imagination. We have to use this gift wisely... And the only way we'll do it is by seeing our creative capacities for the richness they are and seeing our children for the hope that they are. And our task is to educate their whole being, so they can face this future... We may not see this future, but they will. And our job is to help them make something of it.

capacities the ability or power to do something

31

Source text K is an extract from a feature article about creativity and inspiration from *The Guardian* newspaper.

Activity 2

1. Note down the words and ideas you associate with the words 'creativity' and 'inspiration'. Discuss what creativity and inspiration mean to you and then create a mind map drawing on the words and ideas suggested by others too.

2. Discuss how you find creative inspiration. This could be inspiration for art, writing, or any other creative activity.

3. Write your own definitions for the words 'creativity' and 'inspiration'. Compare these with others and discuss any similarities and differences you find.

Source text K

Extract from *The Guardian* newspaper article by Fyfe Dangerfield

Here, the musician Fyfe Dangerfield explains how he finds inspiration for writing music.

'Top artists reveal how to find creative inspiration'

I used to think that being inspired was about sitting around waiting for ideas to come to you. That can happen occasionally: sometimes, I'm walking down the street and suddenly hear a fragment of music that I can later work into a song. But generally, it's not like that at all. I liken the process to seeing ghosts: the ideas are always there, half-formed. It's about being in the right state of mind to take them and turn them into something that works.

One of the most difficult things about writing music is the sheer number of distractions: mobiles, email, Twitter, YouTube. When you're writing, you have to be very disciplined, to the point of being awkward: turn off your phone and find a space to work without any of these distractions.

For me, the image of the tortured artist is a myth – you don't need to be miserable to write songs. In fact, if I am feeling down, the last thing I want to do is write; though it's important sometimes just to sit down and get on with it, however you're feeling. Your creativity is like a tap: if you don't use it, it gets clogged up.

We all have that small voice that tells us we're rubbish, and we need to learn when to silence it. Early in the songwriting process, comparisons do nothing but harm: sometimes I put on a David Bowie record and think, "Why do I bother?" But when it comes to recording or mixing, you do need to be your own critic and editor. It's a bit like having children: you don't interfere with the birth, but as your child grows up, you don't let it run wild.

Activity 3

1. Identify one thing that helps Fyfe Dangerfield to write music and one thing which makes it difficult.

2. What is Fyfe Dangerfield's view of creativity?

3. Identify the three comparisons Fyfe Dangerfield uses to describe creativity. Explain the impact of each one.

Making comparisons involves explaining the ways in which texts are similar and the ways in which they are different, focusing on different aspects of the texts. One way to approach this is to imagine you are filming: start from a distance and make generalized comments about the texts, for example, identifying the form, purpose and main ideas and then you zoom in to explore in close up how these are presented and explored in similar ways and in different ways in each one.

Activity 4

1. Re-read Source texts J and K and identify Robinson's and Dangerfield's attitudes and views about creativity. You could copy and complete a diagram like the one below to identify similarities and differences in viewpoint and attitude.

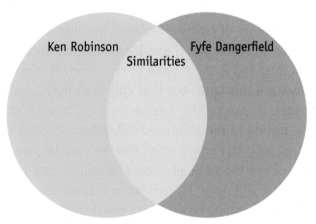

2. Compare Fyfe Dangerfield's view of creativity with that of Ken Robinson. Think about the standpoint of each writer – Ken Robinson is an education expert and Fyfe Dangerfield is a musician – and the purpose of each text. Explain how these aspects inform the viewpoint presented in each text. In your comparison you should:

   • provide an overview of both texts – form, purpose and viewpoint

   • explore the different ways these are conveyed

   • explain which you found more successful and why.

   Support your ideas by referring to both texts, using terminology where relevant.

Exam link

In Section A of Component 01 a question might ask you to compare how ideas about a specific subject or theme are presented.

Tip

When you are comparing, remember to line the two texts up against each other in each point you make. It is easy to fall into the trap of writing about one text and then the other separately, which is not comparing. Some of the following words and phrases will help you to do this.

Identifying similarities:

• Both texts/writers

• also

• in the same way

• similarly

Identifying differences:

• The first text... while the second text...

• Ken Robinson... whereas Fyfe Dangerfield...

• Unlike Ken Robinson... Fyfe Dangerfield...

• however

• in contrast

• instead

• on the other hand

8 Critical evaluation

Learning objective

- To evaluate a text critically

Exam link

In Section A of Component 01: Communicating information and ideas at least one question could ask you to critically evaluate the two unseen non-fiction texts you have read, comparing writers' ideas and perspectives as well as how these are conveyed. This question might present a statement about the texts you have read and ask you how far you agree with this.

As a reader, being able to critically evaluate the non-fiction texts that you encounter is an important skill. Critical evaluation involves analysing how a writer has conveyed specific ideas and explaining how effectively they have done this. This involves:

- providing an overview of the text's purpose, content and viewpoint
- analysing how the writer has conveyed their viewpoint and ideas
- giving your own critical response to the text and considering different interpretations
- supporting your analysis with references to the text and the correct use of subject terminology.

Read Source text L, taken from *An Autobiography* written by the 19th-century author, Anthony Trollope.

Source text L

Extract from *An Autobiography* by Anthony Trollope

Here, he writes about the process of writing and the dangers writers need to avoid.

And then let him beware of creating tedium! Who has not felt the charm of a spoken story up to a certain point, and then suddenly become aware that it has become too long and is the reverse of charming. It is not only that the entire book may have this fault, but that this fault may occur in chapters, in passages, in pages, in paragraphs. I know no guard against this so likely to be effective as the feeling of the writer himself. When once the sense that the thing is becoming long has grown upon him, he may be sure that it will grow upon his readers. I see the smile of some who will declare to themselves that the words of a writer will never be tedious to himself. Of the writer of whom this may be truly said, it may be said with equal truth that he will always be tedious to his readers.

Activity 1

1. What do you think the purpose of this text is?

2. What dangers that writers need to avoid in their writing does Trollope identify?

3. Do you agree with Trollope's views? How convincing do you find his ideas and the way he conveys them?

Progress check

1. Read the following critical evaluation of this extract by a student and discuss how effective you think this is.

> In this text, Trollope as a writer seems to be giving advice on writing, based on his experience as a writer. The main point he makes is that the greatest crime a writer can commit is boring his or her readers – and that the best way of guarding against this weakness is being aware, as a writer, of when you are boring yourself.

Overview of purpose, content and viewpoint

> The text seems to start in mid flow, with 'and' and suggests Trollope has already made other points. It is written in a conversational style in the first person as though he is talking to a group of people in front of him. The first sentence is an exclamation to emphasize the point he wants to make – and it's followed by a question addressed to the readers, suggesting that this experience is one everyone has had – and he goes on to say it could happen anywhere – in a whole book or at any part of it. The sentence beginning 'When...' is balanced to show that once a writer is bored with what he has written, his readers most certainly will be too. 'I see the smile...' again suggests he is talking directly to his audience and anticipating their reactions and the final sentence again is balanced, this time to contrast between the writer who is never aware of boring people, will always be boring.

Reference to the text

Terminology

Analysing how the writer has conveyed his ideas and viewpoint

> Trollope seems to be speaking about more than just writers and writing. This is also true of people in general – everyone can be boring sometimes and often isn't aware of it. As you read, you can imagine sitting there listening to him, speaking with a twinkle in his eye wondering whether he is thinking of you. I think his comments are about the importance of people being self aware – and self critical – in all aspects of life, not just in evaluating what they write.

Informed personal and critical response

2. Identify any additional points that you would add to your own critical evaluation of this text. Remember to refer to the text and use relevant subject terminology when expressing the points you want to make.

Now read Source text M where the journalist, Lucy Mangan describes the experience of writing a column in a weekly magazine.

Activity 2

1. What is the main point Mangan is making about writing a column? Summarize this in a single sentence.

2. List the key advice Mangan gives about writing a column.

3. Identify the techniques Lucy Mangan uses to make her writing interesting for the reader. Think about her vocabulary choices and use of different grammatical features.

Tip

When you are asked 'How far do you agree with this statement?', you should interpret this as an invitation to explain why you agree, although you may wish to express some reservations.

Activity 3

'This text presents the challenges of writing a magazine column.'

How far do you agree with this statement?

In your critical evaluation, you should:

• discuss what you learn about the challenges of writing a magazine column

• explain the impact of these ideas on you as a reader.

Support your ideas by referring to the text, using terminology where relevant.

Progress check

1. Look back at the annotated critical evaluation on page 35. You are now going to annotate the critical evaluation you produced in Activity 3 in the same way. Your annotation should identify where you have:

   • provided an overview of the text's purpose, content and viewpoint

   • analysed how the writer has conveyed their viewpoint and ideas

   • given your own critical response to the text and considered different interpretations

   • supported your analysis with references to the text and use of subject terminology.

2. Compare and discuss the annotations you have made. What do you think you have done well and what improvements could you make?

Source text M

Glossary

sociopathic someone whose behaviour is antisocial or who lacks moral responsibility

Extract from 'How to be a columnist' by Lucy Mangan

Sometimes, just sometimes, columns are easy. An idea or story captures your imagination, an arresting opening line presents itself, and the piece flows from your fingers as they skip joyfully and unstoppably across the keyboard. It makes perfect sense, it has the right pace and rhythm, it's funny, it hits a nerve and everyone writes in to say they laughed and/or agreed with you. This happens about once every five years. For the remaining 209 weeks, you must fake it. You must fake it like a ballerina fakes smiling, up on her bleeding, battered toes, by writing and re-writing, striking out dud phrases and bringing in new ones that turn out to be even worse and abandoning them without a backward glance too. It's awful.

That is why, to write a good column one of the most vital skills you have to acquire is the ability to turn off that second voice in your head that tells you that whatever you are doing is always going to be crap. All writers (with a few, essentially **sociopathic**, exceptions) and all women (ditto) have this voice. Women writers, therefore, have a double dose and can easily be crippled by it. Things are even harder these days, because the internet now allows everyone to comment on your work. The inner voice gets backed up by a hundred outer ones and until your skin thickens (I'm still waiting) you will want to kill yourself every time.

You have to learn to ignore other people's comments (I'm operating on the 'do as I say, not as I do' principle here, as the husband who comes in to find me ashen-faced and weeping at the comment threads every Saturday and takes the laptop away from me will tell you) turn the inner critic off and just listen to yourself. Accept that you won't get it right first time – no-one does. Read your favourite columnists to remind yourself that it can and will be done. Remember your brief, remember your audience, remember your word count, decide on your argument or forge your jokes and go for it. All you have to do, as the American journalist Gene Fowler once said, is sit down and stare at a blank sheet of paper until drops of blood form on your forehead. Enjoy!

Assessment

In this section you will have the chance to apply what you have learned in this chapter about reading information and ideas and writing for audience, impact and purpose as you complete the reading and writing activities. The activities are organized by assessment objective, so think carefully about the specific skills required by each assessment objective and demonstrate these skills in your response to the activities.

Reading

Exam link

You will have two hours to complete Component 01: Communicating information and ideas. The exam paper will advise you to spend one hour on Section A: Reading information and ideas, where you will read two unseen non-fiction texts and answer questions about the texts. However, this is just a guide and you might wish to spend more time on this section and less time on Section B: Writing for audience, impact and purpose.

Read Source text N and then complete the activities below. The extract is taken from an article in *The Guardian* newspaper about a girl called Megan.

AO1

- Identify and interpret explicit and implicit information and ideas
- Select and synthesize evidence

Activity 1

1. Re-read the first paragraph. Summarize in a single sentence the explicit information you learn about Megan's name, age, family and where she lives.

2. Identify three different ways Megan gets ideas for inventions, according to the explicit information in the article.

3. How can you tell that Megan's inventions are good? Identify two quotations which show you this.

4. What impression do you get of the Ward household? Support your ideas with quotations from the text.

5. Paula says that Megan 'thinks differently'. In what ways is she like many other children, and in what ways is she different? Support your ideas with quotations from the text.

6. Write a brief biographical summary of who Megan is and what she has achieved so far in her life. You should include only the important points and use your own words as far as possible.

Extract from *The Gaurdian* newspaper article by Patrick Barkham

'Child geniuses: What happens when they grow up?'

When Paula and Rory Ward are not running a plumbing and drainage company in Kent, they are busy marshalling the lives of their children, Alfie, 6, Joe, 8, Charlie, 13, Steph, 19, and, squeezed in the middle, Megan, 10. While her home reverberates with footballing kids, sulky teens, three bounding dogs, a rabbit and a hamster called Spotty, Megan is quietly inventing. A year ago, she had to design an anti-smoking poster for a school project. Rather than a poster, she came up with the idea of creating a translucent, squidgy pair of lungs containing brown food colouring that shows the average amount of tar a smoker collects from just four packs of cigarettes.

"I like people to play with things more than read and write," she says. So she researched her idea on the internet, found a company in China that could make the device, saved up her pocket money and, with a bit of financial assistance from her mum, got her idea made. Paula helped her daughter get a patent and since then, anti-smoking consultancy Gasp has placed an order worth £12,000 for 25,000 of Megan's keyrings.

Megan is dyslexic. Paula says her daughter "thinks differently": she "prefers drawings and is obviously quite creative". Ideas pop into her mind when she watches TV. After she got sunburnt on holiday, Megan devised a small plastic bracelet that changes colour in the sun, telling you when to put on sunscreen, and a T-shirt that does the same thing. Several sunscreen companies have expressed an interest in the idea. "We were walking the dogs once and what did you come out with?" asks Paula. "A ball that could be filled with water and you called it Quetch – like fetch! – because it quenches a dog's thirst. But we didn't do anything with it. There's a lot we haven't done, but I backed her on the anti-smoking one because I thought, actually, Meg, it's good."

There is also Megan's idea for a dog collar containing a speaker so that owners can call their dog on the collar. Then she pulls out a picture of a special fishing rod she has designed. "There is a camera at the end of the rod, on the hook," she explains, "and it's waterproof, and the screen is on the handle, and it shows you if you've caught a fish or not."

Megan goes to Girl Guides, doesn't want to go to university, and likes the inventor Trevor Baylis, trampolining, the film *Marley & Me*, Miley Cyrus and *The BFG*. She keeps her pink-and-cream bedroom immaculately tidy. Paula is amazed and a bit confused by her daughter, who is a quiet, yet also slightly demanding presence in their hectic household. "Everything has to be routine," Paula says. "Her brothers and sisters go with the flow, but with Meg it's, 'What time will that be happening?' or, 'Where am I being picked up from today?' That's why, when she does enjoy something, I encourage her. She needs a lot of encouragement."

Now read Source text O, taken from Bill Bryson's autobiography *The Life and Times of the Thunderbolt Kid*. Here, he describes his experiences growing up in Des Moines in the USA in the 1950s.

Source text O

Extract from *The Life and Times of the Thunderbolt Kid* by Bill Bryson

The **illimitable** nature of the weekends was both a good and a necessary thing because you always had such a lot to do in those days. A whole morning could be spent just getting the laces on your sneakers right since all sneakers in the 1950s had over seven dozen lace holes and the laces were fourteen feet long. Each morning you would jump out of bed to find that the laces had somehow become four feet longer on one side of the shoe than the other...

Hours more of weekend time needed to be devoted to picking burrs off socks, taking corks out of bottle caps, peeling frozen wrappers off Popsicles, prising apart Oreo cookies without breaking either chocolate disc half or disturbing the integrity of the filling, and carefully picking labels off jars and bottles for absolutely no reason.

In such a world, injuries and other physical setbacks were actually welcomed. If you got a splinter you could pass an afternoon, and attract a small devoted audience, seeing how far you could insert a needle under your skin – how close you could get to actual surgery. If you got sunburned you looked forward to the moment when you could peel off a sheet of translucent **epidermis** that was essentially the size of your body. Scabs in Kid World were cultivated the way older people cultivate orchids. I had knee scabs that I kept for up to four years, that were an inch and three quarters thick and into which you could press drawing pins without rousing my attention. Nosebleeds were much admired, needless to say, and anyone with a nosebleed was treated like a celebrity for as long as it ran.

Because days were so long and so little occurred, you were prepared to invest extended periods in just sitting and watching things on the off chance that something diverting might take place. For years, whenever my father announced that he was off to the lumberyard I dropped everything to accompany him in order to sit quietly on a stool in the wood-cutting room in the hope that Moe, the man who trimmed wood to order on a big buzzsaw, would send one of his few remaining digits flying. He had already lost most of six or seven fingers, so the chances of a lively accident seemed good...

Other long periods of the day were devoted to just seeing what would happen – what would happen if you pinched a matchhead while it was still hot or made a vile drink and took a sip of it or focused a white-hot beam of sunlight with a magnifying glass on your Uncle Dick's bald spot while he was napping. (What happened was that you burned an amazingly swift, deep hole that would leave Dick and a team of specialists at Iowa Lutheran Hospital puzzled for weeks.)

Glossary

illimitable endless

epidermis outermost layer of skin

AO2

- Explain, comment on and analyse how writers use language and structure to achieve effects and influence readers, using relevant subject terminology to support your views

---

Activity 2

1. How does the opening paragraph introduce the ideas in this section?

2. Explain two ways Bryson links ideas between paragraphs in this text.

3. Identify an example of each of the following stylistic or language features and, in each case, explain the effect it has in the text:

   - exaggeration

   - repetition

   - metaphor.

4. Re-read the third paragraph and explain how Bryson creates humour in this section of the text.

Exam link

In Section A of Component 01: Communicating information and ideas, at least one question could ask you to critically evaluate the two unseen non-fiction texts you have read, comparing writers' ideas and perspectives as well as how these are conveyed.

AO3

- Compare writers' ideas and perspectives, as well as how these are conveyed, across two texts

AO4

- Evaluate texts critically and support this with appropriate textual references

---

Activity 3

'Source texts N and O present a view of children and their creativity.'

How far do you agree with this statement? In your answer you should:

- list what you learn about children and their creativity

- explain the impact of these ideas on you as a reader

- compare the ways ideas about children and their creativity are presented.

Support your response with quotations from both texts.

Writing

In Section B of Component 01: Communicating information and ideas, you will have one hour to complete a writing task, selecting this from a choice of two. You will need to be able to write original non-fiction for a specific audience and purpose and will be assessed on the quality of your extended response.

AO5

- Communicate clearly, effectively and imaginatively, selecting and adapting tone, style and register for different forms, purposes and audiences
- Organize information and ideas, using structural and grammatical features to support coherence and cohesion of texts

AO6

- Use a range of vocabulary and sentence structures for clarity, purpose and effect, with accurate spelling and punctuation

Activity 4

Do you agree that children see the world in a completely different way from adults?

Write an article for a magazine aimed at parents of teenagers about this topic.

In your article, you could:

- explain your views on the topic
- include **anecdotes** from your own experience or observations
- use a range of language features to influence readers and reflect the purpose of your article.

Remember to plan your work carefully, thinking about how you are going to develop and structure your ideas. In particular, you need to think about:

- providing an opening which engages the reader's interest
- linking your paragraphs or sections
- using a range of sentence structures for clarity, purpose and effect.

Key term

anecdote a short entertaining story about a real person or event

Spoken Language

Exam link

Spoken Language is assessed as part of your GCSE English Language course but does not form part of the exam papers you will sit at the end of your course. Instead, you will receive a separately reported grade for Spoken Language alongside your overall GCSE English Language grade. However, you might be asked to write the text for a speech or presentation in Section B of Component 01: Communicating information and ideas, so this is an important form of writing to practise.

Activity 5

You have been asked to give a speech on the following topic at a national conference for young people aged 15 to 20, which will be attended by government ministers.

How do you think schools could help students to develop their creative skills for life in the 21st century?

In your speech you should:

- identify the main ideas or arguments you want to put forward

- include supporting evidence

- use a range of techniques and stylistic features to convey your ideas and keep the audience interested.

Plan and draft your speech by selecting and organizing the information and ideas you want to include in your speech.

As you write your speech, consider the different ways you can make your writing persuasive and present information in a way that supports the argument you are making. You could include:

- statistics that reinforce specific points, for example, *According to one study, 75% of people think they are not living up to their creative potential*

- comments or quotations to add authenticity or interest, for example, *As Albert Einstein said, 'Creativity is about knowing how to hide your sources.'*

- anecdotes to illustrate your ideas, for example, *The pressure of studying for my GCSEs has led me to drop many creative activities, such as attending drama club, as I no longer have time for this.*

Progress check

When you have finished, check that what you have written is clear and accurate, in Standard English, with correct punctuation and spelling. Check particularly for errors that you know you tend to make in your writing.

2 THIS LIFE

'The true story of a person's life can never be written. It is beyond the power of literature.'

Isaac Bashevis Singer, writer

'Non-fiction... is often as much about character and story and emotion as fiction is.'

Chimamanda Ngozi Adichie, writer

'Life is not a problem to be solved, but a reality to be experienced.'

Soren Kierkegaard, philosopher

Introduction

Reading non-fiction can give you insights into different lives and lifestyles. In this chapter you will explore issues which affect people's lives in different ways, such as hardship, housing and happiness. You will read a range of forms of non-fiction writing, including journalism, letters and blogs, and use these to explore how writers use language and form to express their views and try to influence readers' thinking. You will use the knowledge and skills you gain from your reading to develop your own writing of non-fiction texts in different forms and for different purposes and audiences.

Exam link

The activities in this chapter are designed to help you develop the skills needed for success in one of the two exam papers you will sit at the end of your course, Component 01: Communicating information and ideas. The first section of this exam requires you to read two different non-fiction extracts, one of which will be from the 19th century, and answer questions focused on the writers' meaning and purpose. You will have to answer questions about both extracts separately and then together. The second section of the exam asks you to write a piece of non-fiction writing for a particular purpose and audience.

Activity 1

1. Read and discuss the quotations on the facing page. Which do you agree with and why?

2. How effective do you think non-fiction is in helping you to understand different lives and lifestyles? Think about the following forms of non-fiction writing:

   - essays
   - reviews
   - speeches
   - journalism
   - travel writing
   - biographical writing
   - multi-modal texts, for example, websites and blogs.

A hard life

The divide between rich and poor is a subject which writers often focus on, encouraging us to think about the impact of poverty and the struggles faced on a daily basis by groups and individuals in our communities.

Learning objectives

- To analyse how vocabulary is used to influence readers' opinions

- To compare how writers' viewpoints are conveyed

Key terms

viewpoint an opinion or point of view

stereotype an over-simplified image or idea of a type of person or thing that has become fixed through being widely held

pejorative language words and phrases that express contempt or disapproval

1 Vocabulary and viewpoint

A writer's choice of vocabulary can influence the way a reader responds to the information and ideas presented in a text. Being able to identify specific words, phrases and techniques that a writer has used to influence readers and explain the effects these create, can help you to develop an understanding of the writer's **viewpoint** on the subject they are writing about.

> ### Activity 1
>
> The following headlines are taken from two newspaper reports of the same story.
>
>
>
> Three-quarters of incapacity benefit claimants are fit to work, says Department of Work and Pensions
>
> 75% ON SICK LEAVE ARE SKIVING
>
> How do these headlines present the same story in different ways? How might the vocabulary used influence your reading of each headline?

Read Source text A, taken from a newspaper column written by the journalist Caitlin Moran about people living on state benefits. This was first published in *The Times Magazine* in 2013.

> ### Activity 2
>
> 1. How does Caitlin Moran suggest people who receive state benefits are often **stereotyped**?
>
> 2. Find examples of **pejorative language** used to describe this stereotype. What effect do these create?
>
> 3. Discuss how this stereotype could influence your views about people on benefits.
>
> 4. How does Caitlin Moran challenge this stereotype? Identify the words and phrases she uses to present her ideas and explain the effects these create.

Extract from 'Cutting to the heart of the welfare state' by Caitlin Moran

A council estate on benefits isn't what you think – if you must imagine it, rather than remember, or just look out of the window. Popular imagination has it that it's full of obese, tracksuit-wearing peasants smoking Rothmans on the front doorstep, rehearsing for their spot on *Jeremy Kyle* while spending their **fraudulent** benefits on a plasma TV.

Benefits spent on plasma TVs is the **totemic** fury-provoker of the professionally angry social commentator – "They're spending YOUR taxes on A FORTY-TWO INCH SONY!!! You couldn't MAKE IT UP!" – ignoring the fact that if you live somewhere with broken-glass parks and looming teen-clusters on each street corner, and gave up on the idea of having a car or a holiday long, long ago, then staying at home, safe, together as a family, and watching 15 hours of TV a day is a **peerlessly** cost-effective, gentle and harmless way of trying to buy happiness.

Besides, they almost certainly won't have spent "your" taxes on it. They'll have got a massive overdraft, like everyone else in the Western world. They'll have got their telly the way you got your telly. People on benefits are just people – on benefits. Some of them are dodgy, most of them are doing their best, and a few need more help than we could ever imagine. The mix is about the same as on your street. If you are having to imagine it – rather than remember it, or look out of the window.

What's it like, being on benefits? Being on disability benefits – "I've had a hard day's limping, to put that tea on the table!" my dad would say, as we sat down to eat something based around a lot of potatoes and ketchup. Well, mainly, you're scared. You're scared that the benefits will be frozen, or cut, or done away with completely. I don't remember an age where I wasn't scared our benefits would be taken away. It was an anxiety that felt like a physical presence in my chest – a small, black, eyeless insect that hung off my ribs. Every Tory budget that announced a freezing of benefits – new means-testing, new grading – made the insect drill its face into the bone. They froze benefits for four years in a row, as I recall: "freezing" being the news's way of telling you that you – already poor – will be at the checkout, apologising as you take jam and squash out of your bag, put them back on the shelves and ask them to add it up again. Every week you fear that this is the week the pennies won't stretch any further and something will disappear: gas, food. Your home.

fraudulent
dishonestly obtained

totemic symbolic

peerlessly without equal

Now read Source text B, taken from *The Road to Wigan Pier* by George Orwell. This non-fiction book, first published in 1937, describes the lives of poor people living in the north of England before the Second World War.

Glossary

slag-heaps mounds of waste material

drudgery dull, tiring work

Source text B

Extract from *The Road to Wigan Pier* by George Orwell

The train bore me away, through the monstrous scenery of **slag-heaps**, chimneys, piled scrap-iron, foul canals, paths of cindery mud criss-crossed by the prints of clogs. This was March, but the weather had been horribly cold and everywhere there were mounds of blackened snow. As we moved slowly through the outskirts of the town we passed row after row of little grey slum houses running at right angles to the embankment. At the back of one of the houses a young woman was kneeling on the stones, poking a stick up the leaden waste-pipe which ran from the sink inside and which I suppose was blocked. I had time to see everything about her – her sacking apron, her clumsy clogs, her arms reddened by the cold. She looked up as the train passed, and I was almost near enough to catch her eye. She had a round pale face, the usual exhausted face of the slum girl who is twenty-five and looks forty, thanks to miscarriages and **drudgery**; and it wore, for the second in which I saw it, the most desolate, hopeless expression I have ever seen. It struck me then that we are mistaken when we say that 'It isn't the same for them as it would be for us,' and that people bred in the slums can imagine nothing but the slums. For what I saw in her face was not the ignorant suffering of an animal. She knew well enough what was happening to her – understood as well as I did how dreadful a destiny it was to be kneeling there in the bitter cold, on the slimy stones of a slum backyard, poking a stick up a foul drain-pipe.

Activity 3

1. How does Orwell's choice of vocabulary describing the **setting** contribute to the mood of the piece? Select three specific details and discuss what mood you think they help create.

Stretch

Try to link the different details and explain how they build a specific mood.

2. What impression do you get of the young woman from the way she is described?

3. Rewrite the description of the young woman, experimenting with different vocabulary choices to make the reader feel less sympathetic towards her.

Perspective is the viewpoint from which a text is written and the experience brought to it by the **narrator** or writer. The way a writer conveys their perspective can influence the opinions and attitudes that the reader forms.

Activity 4

1. What perspective is the extract from *The Road to Wigan Pier* written from?

2. Caitlin Moran draws on her own personal experience to describe what life on benefits is like. Explain how this could influence a reader's opinion.

Support

Think about:

- the use of the **personal pronouns** 'I' and 'you'
- references to her own family's story
- the **simile** she uses to describe her feelings.

3. Look at the following two statements from Source texts A and B:

    Source text A: 'People on benefits are just people – on benefits.'

    Source text B: 'It struck me then that we are mistaken when we say that "It isn't the same for them as it would be for us," and that people bred in the slums can imagine nothing but the slums.'

    What are both writers saying about poverty in these statements? Write a statement of your own which conveys the same idea.

4. Compare the ways in which Caitlin Moran and George Orwell present the lives of people in poverty. Think about:

    - the viewpoint of each writer
    - the style of writing in each text
    - the impact of both texts on the reader.

Key terms

setting the way or place in which something is set

narrator the person or character who recounts the events of a story

personal pronoun each of the pronouns (I, me, we, us, you, he, him, she, her, it, they, them) that indicate person, gender, number, and case

SPAG

- **first-person pronouns** such as 'I' and 'we' refer to the speaker or to the speaker and others

- **second-person pronouns** such as 'you' refer to the person or people being addressed

- **third-person pronouns** such as 'she', 'it' and 'they' refer to third parties other than the speaker or the person being addressed.

simile where one thing is compared to another thing, using a connective word such as 'like' or 'as'

Tip

Look for similarities and differences between Source texts A and B. Remember to explore how the writers present their ideas and viewpoints, linking the points you make to carefully selected quotations.

2 Interpreting implicit ideas

Learning objectives

- To interpret implicit information and ideas
- To understand the techniques writers use to convey these ideas

Key terms

inference something that you infer; a conclusion reached by reasoning

personification representing an idea in human form or a thing as having human characteristics

hyperbole a deliberately exaggerated statement that is not meant to be taken literally

purpose something that you intend to do or achieve, an intended result

Tip

Think about the **purpose** of the text and how useful and relevant to this the information and ideas presented are.

The information and ideas in a text can be implied rather than stated explicitly. By reading closely you can make **inferences** about a writer's thoughts and feelings on the subject they are writing about. Sometimes a writer will use specific techniques in order to convey their ideas. In the article in Source text C, which was published in 1881, George Sims uses **personification** and **hyperbole** to describe the living conditions of London's poor.

Activity 1

1. Summarize what you have learned about the living conditions for poor people in London at the time Sims was writing.

2. What do you think Sims wants his readers to feel about this situation? Explain how effectively the article achieves this aim.

3. How is personification used in this extract? Think about which objects are personified and what it makes you feel about them.

4. Identify an example of hyperbole and explain the effect this creates.

5. Which sentences in the extract do you think a reader might find amusing? Choose one and explain why it is humorous.

Activity 2

Using the title 'How the Poor Live', write the opening of an article describing the living conditions of people living in poverty today. Think about the key information and ideas you want to convey and how you can use personification and hyperbole to emphasize these.

Planning

Select information and ideas that will capture the reader's attention. You could choose one of the following ways of opening an article:

- Statement: present a statement about the topic that will shock or surprise the reader.

- Fact: present an interesting and relevant fact or statistic.

- Question: pose an interesting or intriguing question related to the topic.

Drafting

Think about the techniques you could use to convey your ideas, such as personification and hyperbole.

Reviewing

Re-read the opening of your article to check that it makes sense and is creating an appropriate emotional impact.

Extract from 'How the Poor Live' by George Sims

One room in this district is very like the other. The family likeness of the chairs and tables is truly remarkable, especially in the matter of legs. Most chairs are born with four legs, but the chairs one meets with here are a two-legged race – a four-legged chair is a **rara avis**, and when found should be made a note of. The tables, too, are of a type **indigenous** to the spot. The survival of the fittest does not obtain in these districts in the matter of tables. The most positively unfit are common, very common objects. What has become of the fittest I hesitate to **conjecture**. Possibly they have run away. I am quite sure that a table with legs would make use of them to escape from such surroundings.

As to the bedsteads, they are wretched, broken-down old things of wood and iron that look as though they had been rescued a little late from a fire, then used for a barricade, afterwards buried in volcanic eruption, and finally dug out of a dust-heap that had concealed them for a century. The bedding, a respectable coal-sack would blush to acknowledge even as a poor relation.

I have **enumerated** chairs, tables, and beds, not because they are found in every poor home – there are several rented rooms which can boast of nothing but four walls, a ceiling, and a floor – but because these articles placed in one of these dens constitute what are **euphemistically** called 'furnished apartments', a species of accommodation with which all very poor neighbourhoods abound.

The 'furnished apartments' fetch as much as tenpence a day, and are sometimes occupied by three or four different tenants during a week.

The 'deputy' comes for the money every day, and it is pay or go with the occupants. If the man who has taken one of these furnished rooms for his 'home, sweet home' does not get enough during the day to pay his rent, out he goes into the street with his wife and children, and enter another family **forthwith**.

The tenants have not, as a rule, much to be flung after them in the shape of goods and **chattels**. The clothes they stand upright in, a battered kettle, and, perhaps, a bundle, make up the catalogue of their worldly possessions.

rara avis a rare person or thing

indigenous particular to a certain area

conjecture guess

enumerated counted

euphemistically using a more polite word or phrase for something unpleasant

forthwith immediately

chattels belongings

3 A consistent viewpoint

Learning objectives

- To explore how rhetorical devices can be used to maintain a consistent viewpoint

- To establish and maintain a consistent viewpoint in non-fiction writing

When writing non-fiction you need to establish and maintain a consistent viewpoint in order to clearly communicate your ideas about the subject you are writing about. To do this, you need to consider the usefulness and relevance of the information you include and think carefully about the language you use to present this. Sometimes a document such as a letter of protest may be written on behalf of a group of people yet present a single viewpoint. Read the following letter which was sent to the editor of *The Times* in 1849.

Source text D

Letter to *The Times* newspaper, published 5th July 1849

This letter was written by fifty-four people living in London slums.

THE EDITUR OF THE TIMES PAPER

Sur, — May we beg and beseech your proteckshion and power. We are Sur, as it may be, livin in a Wilderniss, so far as the rest of London knows anything of us, or as the rich and great people care about. We live in muck and filth. We aint got no priviz, no dust bins, no drains, no water-splies, and no drain or suer in the hole place. The Suer Company, in Greek St., Soho Square, all great, rich and powerfool men, take no notice watsomdever of our complaints. The Stenche of a Gully-hole is disgustin. We all of us suffer, and numbers are ill, and if the Colera comes Lord help us.

Some gentlemans comed yesterday, and we thought they was comishioners from the Suer Company, but they was complaining of the noosance and stenche our lanes and corts was to them in New Oxforde Strect. They was much surprized to see the seller in No. 12, Carrier St., in our lane, where a child was dyin from fever, and would not believe that Sixty persons sleep in it every night. This here seller you couldent swing a cat in, and the rent is five shillings a week; but theare are greate many sich deare sellars. Sur, we hope you will let us have our complaints put into your hinfluenshall paper, and make these landlords of our houses and these comishioners (the friends we spose of the landlords) make our houses decent for Christions to live in. Preaye Sir com and see us, for we are living like piggs, and it aint faire we shoulde be so ill treted.

We are your respeckfull servents in Church Lane, Carrier St., and the other corts. Teusday, Juley 3, 1849.

Activity 1

SPAG

1. How does the information provided about the authors help you to understand their viewpoint?

2. Discuss the purpose of this letter. What do the authors want to happen as a result of their letter being published?

3. The writers of this letter feel strongly about the conditions they are living in. Explain how each of the following rhetorical devices is used to convey the strength of their feelings:

   - **Emotive language**
   - **Imagery**
   - **Repetition**
   - **Rule of three**
   - **Anecdote**

4. What do you notice about the way the word 'powerful' is spelt? Discuss why this could be described as **ironic**.

5. Proofread the letter to identify any other spelling, punctuation and grammatical errors and discuss the changes you would make.

Activity 2

SPAG

Write a letter to *The Times* newspaper in which you argue that more action needs to be taken to solve the problems of poverty today. Use the following guidelines to help you:

- Poverty is an extensive topic. Focus on a particular aspect of it which interests you, for example, should free breakfast and tea clubs be provided at schools?

- Select the information you want to use with care. Avoid lists of complaints and focus instead on developing your main ideas in sufficient detail.

- Provide anecdotal evidence using relevant, real examples to illustrate your viewpoint. You can invent these anecdotes if you need to.

- Use rhetorical devices such as repetition, emotive language and the rule of three to emphasize your viewpoint.

- Think about the structure of your letter. The opening should establish your viewpoint and gain the reader's interest, while the ending should reinforce this viewpoint. You could use sentence openers such as 'Moreover', 'Indeed', 'In addition to' and 'Without doubt' to organize your points clearly and coherently.

Key terms

emotive language words and phrases used to arouse a reader's emotions

imagery the use of figurative or other special language to convey an idea to readers or hearers

repetition repeating, or being repeated

rule of three (also called tricolon) linking three points or features, for example, adjectives, for impact

anecdote a short entertaining story about a real person or event

ironic where the intended meaning differs from the expected one

Exam link

In Section B of Component 01: Communicating information and ideas, you may be asked to write for a specific audience and purpose.

The high life

Our lives can be changed by the places in which we live. As populations increase and space becomes more precious, especially in large cities, many architects and planners have explored high-rise options such as skyscrapers and tower blocks. From the building of the very first skyscrapers in the 19th century, these high-rise buildings have generated intense debate and still provoke strong opinions today.

Learning objective

- To identify how bias is displayed through vocabulary choices

Key term

bias an opinion or feeling that strongly favours one side in preference to another

Tip

You can use alternative terms such as 'spin', 'slant' and 'angle' when talking about bias, for example: 'The inclusion of the phrase "great transport links" puts a positive spin on how close the property is to the motorway.'

4 Identifying bias

In certain types of non-fiction, such as advertisements, **bias** is used intentionally. Marketing a product or selling an idea requires writers and speakers to persuade the reader or listener that something is the best. However, bias can also be misleading as a text may present opinion as fact or favour a particular point of view. As a reader, you need to consider the purpose of a text and look closely at the vocabulary a writer uses to identify evidence of bias.

Writers and speakers can also misuse the evidence they include to give the reader or listener a false or misleading impression. As a reader, you need to evaluate the evidence presented and decide whether it has been used appropriately.

Activity 1

1. Estate agents carefully select the vocabulary they use to describe the properties they are selling. Read the following quotations in the table below. For each one, discuss what meaning the estate agent wants to imply and what the actual meaning might be. The first one has been done for you.

Quotation	Implied meaning	Actual meaning
'A bijou apartment.'	The apartment is elegant.	The apartment is very small.
'An up-and-coming area.'		
'A characterful cottage.'		
'A mature garden.'		
'A cosy living room.'		

2. In the following sentences, select one word that makes the statement biased.

   a. The house was too close to the main road.

   b. The garden was stunning but small.

   c. Ideally located in a central location.

Read Source text E, taken from a blog called 'Completely London' posted by an estate agency based in the capital.

Source text E

Extract from Kinleigh Folkard & Hayward's 'Completely London' blog

LIVING THE HIGH LIFE

Stylish, secure and modern high rise apartments in and around zone one are finally putting one in the eye of the negative perceptions associated with their '60s predecessors. The shiny new London towers offer unbeatable panoramic views across the capital making them some of the most desirable properties on the market at the moment.

For anyone who wants to live in the heart of the city, minutes from a tube station, opting for an apartment in a high rise can mean a serious bargain as they don't command the multi-million pound prices of central town houses.

The advantages go further than just the price and location though. Doormen, on-site fitness centres, controlled entry, security systems, on-site maintenance and underground parking all separate these new blocks from your average London property. Utility bills are often lower too, as construction standards and practices ensure maximum energy efficiency and savings, and some buildings bulk-negotiate lower rates – even when residents pay their bills individually. Many have courtyards, communal gardens, roof terraces or balconies meaning that you don't need to sacrifice outside space.

Key terms

connotation something implied or suggested in addition to the main meaning
tone a manner of expression in speaking or writing

Activity 2

1. Identify the words and phrases the writer of the blog uses to make high-rise apartments sound appealing. Analyse the **connotations** of the words and phrases you have identified.

2. Identify two sentences that clearly convey a biased point of view about high-rise living. Rewrite each sentence in a more neutral **tone**.

Tip

When rewriting the sentences, consider using less emotive vocabulary and include qualifying phrases such as 'sometimes', 'in certain cases' and 'at times'.

The writer of this blog sometimes presents opinion as if it were fact. This is one way of making ideas seem indisputable. To identify whether a statement is a fact or an opinion, you need to determine whether the statement can be proven to be true.

Activity 3

Look at the following heading from an estate agent's listing:

Flat for sale, One St George Wharf, London SW8 – 2 bedrooms £4,800,000

1. Which statement from the blog does this heading directly contradict?

2. Rewrite the statement from the blog to make it clear that this is a statement of opinion rather than fact.

5 Statements and evidence

Learning objective

- To distinguish between statements that are supported by evidence and those that are not

When reading non-fiction, it is important to be able to identify when ideas and opinions are supported by reliable evidence and when they are not. **Direct** and **reported speech** can be used in non-fiction texts to convey a sense of realism and truth. By reading what people have actually said, we feel as though the writer's point is supported by evidence in the form of direct experience and so this must be the truth.

Keep this in mind as you read Source text F, which is taken from an article in the *Wall Street Journal* about living in the kinds of skyscrapers that are becoming increasingly popular in big cities across the globe.

Key terms

direct speech when the words a person has spoken are relayed to the reader exactly, using speech marks, for example, *She said, 'It's cold.'*

reported speech a speaker's words as reported by another person and put into the tense of the reporting verb (such as 'said' or 'replied')

contrast a difference clearly seen when things are compared or seen together

Activity 1

1. What drawbacks to living in high-rise buildings does Jackson identify? Rank these in order of the most to the least serious.

2. Do Michael Berman and Thomas Guss seem like reliable sources? Use evidence from the text to support your response.

3. Why do you think Jackson chooses to combine reported speech with direct speech in the article? How does this influence your opinions as a reader?

4. Jackson aims to give a relatively balanced view of living in tall buildings. Explain the techniques she uses to do this and the effects these create.

Think about:

- use of **contrasting** statements

- impact of the closing two paragraphs.

Activity 2

Imagine you have recently moved into a luxury apartment in a tower building. Write an email to the estate agent you rent the apartment from, expressing your satisfaction at certain aspects of the apartment but complaining about others. In your email you should:

- aim to develop one or two significant details; for example, you could explain how frustrating it is not to be able to use the balcony because it is too windy

- include some indirect speech; for example, something the estate agent told you about the apartment before you moved in

- include some direct speech; for example, you could quote a neighbour who has similar views to you.

Remember to include evidence to support the points you make.

Extract from 'Living the High Life' by Candace Jackson

Developers are erecting super-skyscrapers for the very wealthy, selling apartments with helicopter views for massive price tags. Why everyone's looking up; plus, the realities of life on the 90th floor.

Living at 1,000 feet does have drawbacks. Outdoor terraces are generally impossible above 40 or 50 stories, because of the wind. Though many of the new buildings have walls of mostly glass to capture the views, the windows only partially open at the highest floors. Experts say that while asking prices go up with every floor, views improve only marginally above a certain height, depending on how tall the surrounding buildings are...

Michael Berman, who owns car dealerships in Chicago, moved from the suburbs to a four-bedroom condominium on the 57th floor of Chicago's 92-story Trump International Hotel and Tower in 2009. Though he was one of the building's first buyers, he wasn't interested in living on one of the very top floors, noting that 30 years ago he and his wife lived in a different high rise and often lost the views on a cloudy day.

The one downside Mr. Berman noticed about living in Trump Towers, which houses the highest residences in the U.S., is that opening the windows means letting in a swift breeze, and on the windiest days, the usually ultrafast elevators slow down somewhat. "But everything else more than makes up for it," he says, noting the building's five-star restaurant below and optional hotel maid service.

Thomas Guss, a New York real-estate broker who currently has a $39 million penthouse listed in a 19-story building, the Centurion, says he typically warns buyers that the taller the building, the more it naturally sways toward the top. "Not many people think about that until the first storm comes." Mr. Guss says a 45th-story rental unit he owns in the Financial District has views of the Statue of Liberty— but waves appear in the bathtub during thunderstorms. "A lot of people are very uncomfortable with that," he adds...

In the end, views remain the big selling point. Kenneth Allen lives above the 70th floor in Chicago's Trump Towers. He and his wife moved there from the suburbs after their kids left for college to be closer to the theater, Chicago Symphony and top restaurants.

"I can see Michigan, Indiana and Wisconsin," he says. He watches storms roll in over Lake Michigan. "It's like National Geographic."

6 Comparing perspectives

Learning objectives

- To select and synthesize evidence from different texts
- To compare how writers use language and structure to convey their ideas and perspectives

Exam link

In your exam you might be asked to summarize information and ideas from two different texts in a single response. To do this you will need to bring evidence together to demonstrate your understanding of both texts.

Tip

Think about the content of the sentence as well as its structure. For example, in the sentence beginning 'In the modern mail-chute.', dashes are used to separate the explanation of what a mail-chute is.

Different writers can provide different perspectives on the same subject with the ideas and information they choose to present depending on the purpose they are writing for. Over time, ideas about subjects such as skyscrapers and high-rise buildings can also change and, by selecting and comparing evidence from texts written at different times, you can develop your understanding of these changes.

Source text G is taken from a non-fiction book called *The Boy's Book of Inventions*, written by Ray Stannard Baker in 1899.

Activity 1

1. What predictions does Baker make about the future of the skyscraper? Discuss which of Baker's predictions have come to pass.

2. Identify three details that suggest a positive view of skyscrapers.

3. Identify three details that suggest possible concerns about skyscrapers.

4. What do you think the purpose of this text is? How balanced a view of skyscrapers do you think the text provides? Discuss your ideas.

The opening paragraph clearly indicates the subject in focus, with grammatical features helping to clarify the information presented.

Semi-colon separates the two main clauses in the sentence which contrast the prevalence of skyscrapers at two different points in time.

'Ten years ago, in 1889, there was not a "skyscraper" in the world; today there are scores of them in American cities; the heights ranging from seven storeys up to thirty, making them by all odds the greatest structures reared by the hand of man.'

Commas used to demarcate a phrase which provides clarifying information about which year the writer is referring to.

Use of quotation marks suggests the newness of this term at this time.

Commas used to introduce two subordinate clauses providing additional information about the size of skyscrapers.

Activity 2

Select another sentence and explain how its grammatical features help to communicate the information and ideas presented.

SPAG

Extract from *The Boy's Book of Inventions* by Ray Stannard Baker

This extract explores the then recent 'invention' of high-rise buildings which, at the time, were used to house offices and not residential units.

The Modern Skyscraper

Ten years ago, in 1889, there was not a "skyscraper" in the world; today there are scores of them in American cities, the heights varying from seven storeys up to thirty, making them by all odds the greatest structures reared by the hand of man.

The time may come and come soon, when buildings higher than even this one [the thirty-storey Park Row Building in New York City completed in 1899] may be built. There is nothing in the engineering problem to prevent the construction of a fifty-storey building, but such a sight will probably never **vex** the eye of man. Already various American cities are passing laws limiting the height of buildings. Moreover, many property owners feel that time should be given to ascertain how the skyscraper will endure – whether the steel will weaken with rust, whether the foundations will hold true, whether the fire-proofing is efficient.

In the modern mail-chute – a long glass and iron tube through which a tenant may drop a letter to the big box in the basement – the skyscraper has its own mail system.

And of late some of the great buildings have actually been provided with a bedroom and bachelor apartments, so that a tenant may sleep near his offices if he is busy. Indeed, a man might live in a modern skyscraper, year in and year out, luxuriously, too, with every want richly supplied, and never pass beyond the revolving storm doors at the street entrance.

As to the future of the skyscraper no-one knows definitely, but all architects prophesy greater beauty. They are learning how to treat these great slim towers so that the effect is pleasing to the eye. In times past the necessity of a **façade** from 250 to 350 feet high has often resulted in the bold, staring resemblance to a chimney, which is both ugly and painful to the sight. But the architect is learning to relieve this tendency by treating the storeys in groups of four or five. This lessens the effect of extreme height. At the same time the width is made to seem greater than it really is by the addition of heavy **cornices** and projecting balconies.

While it is perhaps too much to expect that a skyscraper shall become an object of beauty, these various devices do much to give the building personality and **distinction**, and perhaps this is as far as the architect can ever go.

Glossary

vex to upset or irritate

façade frontage of a building

cornices decorative ledges

distinction merit

Now read Source text H, taken from an article by Harry Mount which appeared in *The Telegraph* newspaper in 2013.

Activity 3

1. What do you think the purpose of this text is? How balanced a view of high-rise buildings do you think the text provides? Discuss your ideas.

2. What are Mount's main complaints about tower blocks?

3. Select three words or phrases that you think convey his feelings most strongly. Discuss why you have chosen these specific words and phrases.

4. Pick out any grammatical features which you think are effective in helping to convey Mount's opinion.

In order to compare two texts effectively, you need to identify similarities and contrasts between them.

Activity 4

1. Discuss how effective you find the following comparison. Think about how you could develop the explanation of the effects created and relate these to the purpose of each text.

    > In his text written in 1899, Baker predicts that in the future people will live 'luxuriously' in modern skyscrapers, 'with every want richly supplied' and no need for residents to 'pass beyond' their doors. Similarly, Mount refers to 'optimistic' visions of tower blocks as 'magical, amenity-crammed… streets-in-the-sky', reinforcing this utopian ideal that was held in the past.

2. Identify other similarities and contrasts between Source texts G and H. Make notes about the:

    *   information and ideas included in each text

    *   grammatical features used and the effects these create

    *   form and structure of each text.

3. Write two paragraphs comparing Source texts G and H. The first paragraph should analyse a similarity and the second paragraph a contrast between the two texts.

Activity 5

Create a presentation exploring how views about high-rise buildings have changed over time. Select and synthesize information and ideas from both of the texts you have read in your presentation.

Tip

Use connectives such as 'similarly', 'equally', and 'likewise' to compare features that are similar or linked in some way, and connectives such as 'whereas', 'alternatively' and 'on the other hand' to contrast ideas and techniques.

Exam link

Spoken language is assessed as part of your GCSE English Language course but does not form part of the exam papers you will sit at the end of your course. Instead, you will receive a separately reported grade for Spoken language alongside your overall GCSE English Language grade. However, you might be asked to write the text for a speech or presentation in Section B of Component 01: Communicating information and ideas, so this is an important form of writing to practise.

Source text H

Extract from *The Telegraph* newspaper article by Harry Mount

'The tower block was a disastrous low point in British urban life'

Good for Policy Exchange, the **think tank** that has just suggested knocking down the tower blocks and replacing them with terraced houses. Of all the misguided government programmes that have wrecked our cities over the last 60 years, the tower block was the worst by far.

The first ones arrived in 1954 – the government's replacement housing for people made homeless by slum clearances. These were the optimistic days when tower blocks were envisaged as streets-in-the-sky; magical, amenity-crammed, modern alternatives to the old, run-down terraced houses.

The 1957 Park Hill estate in Sheffield set the pattern for the next decade of council-house tower blocks across the country. Lifts took the blocks higher and higher; the taller the tower blocks got, the bigger the government **subsidies**. As well as being plain ugly, the concrete, steel and glass of post-War tower blocks and office buildings don't vary much – relentlessly right-angled, relentlessly straight-lined...

Slowly the tide changed. In 1967, government subsidies were removed from the tower-block council estates. The peak year for tower blocks was 1968, when 160 residential towers over 150 foot were built. Then, in the same year, Ronan Point tower block in Newham, east London, collapsed, only two months after it was built.

The golden days of the tower block had come to an end. In April 2011, demolition began on the Heygate Estate, the 1974 block for 3,000 residents in the Elephant and Castle, in south London. Hailed as a **neo-brutalist** masterpiece when it was built, it soon became crime-ridden and **dilapidated**. In its final days, it became a popular film set, used for the Michael Caine vigilante film, *Harry Brown*, and for episodes of *The Bill*.

The tower block had turned into an outdated yet iconic image of hellish urban living. Here's hoping the rest of them will be torn down and replaced with good, decent, terraced housing – Britain's greatest contribution to domestic architecture.

think tank a group of experts providing advice and ideas

subsidies money granted by the government

neo-brutalist plain, functional style of architecture

dilapidated in a state of disrepair and ruin

The Bill a long-running TV police series set in London

A happy life

For thousands of years writers and philosophers have tried to define happiness and explain how to achieve it. A Greek philosopher named Solon believed that happiness could only be achieved once you were dead, because only then would you know for sure if you had lived a good life and died an honourable death.

Learning objectives

- To explore how a text's structure can reflect its purpose

- To analyse how a writer's choice of grammatical features can contribute to the effectiveness of a text

7 Audience and purpose

When writing for a specific purpose you need to consider the most effective way to structure your text. In an advice text, for example, a writer may choose to organize information and ideas in a way that helps a reader to follow the advice they provide. Often, a writer will aim to establish trust in their knowledge so that readers want to take their advice on board, for example, by illustrating their ideas with examples from their own experience or that of well-known people.

Read Source text I. This is taken from *The 10 Minute Life Coach* by Fiona Harrold, a non-fiction book which provides advice and guidance about improving your life.

Activity 1

1. Re-read the opening paragraph of Source text I and discuss how effectively this introduces the subject of happiness.

   ### Support

   How useful and relevant are the information and ideas included in the text about improving your own happiness? How might the way these ideas are presented interest a reader?

2. Harrold uses the example of the Dalai Lama to illustrate her ideas. Why do you think she has chosen this figure? What effect might this example have on a reader?

3. Identify any other examples Harrold uses and explain how these help to support her points.

Writers need to set their advice out in a way readers can understand and use effectively. The second half of Source text I is organized into a list of numbered points.

Activity 2

1. How does the way the text is structured help to present the advice clearly?

2. How does the writer emphasize the importance of being happy?

Extract from *The 10 Minute Life Coach* by Fiona Harrold

The very people you'd assume would be ecstatically happy are frequently unhappy. Rock stars, who must surely 'have it all' have been identified as suffering from something called Paradise Syndrome, a listless boredom and dissatisfaction which seems to come on when everything you could possibly want is available to you on tap.

Spiritual masters and great statesmen are often the most cheerful of all, even when their own circumstances are anything but. Nearly every time you see the Dalai Lama he's laughing or smiling. And he makes everyone else around him feel like smiling. The Dalai Lama is probably one of the few people in the world who if asked if he's happy, even though he's suffered the loss of his country, will give you an unconditional yes. What's more, he'll tell you that happiness is the very purpose of life... Western thinkers from Aristotle to William James have agreed with this idea. But isn't a life based on seeking personal happiness self-centred, even self-indulgent? Not necessarily. Many surveys have shown that it is unhappy people who tend to be the most self-focused. Happy people... are shown to be more sociable, creative and flexible, and able to tolerate life's daily frustrations more easily. More importantly, they are found to be more loving and forgiving than unhappy people. Scientific evidence as well as our own experience tells us that there is an intimate connection between personal happiness and kindness to others.

BE HAPPY

1. *Choose happiness.*

It begins with a decision. Don't put it off until you've got the perfect job, man, woman, body. Start right now to smile, to adopt happiness as your natural state, whatever your circumstances. Instead of looking for happiness, look for reasons to be happy. Cherish the smaller moments that give you joy, pleasure and contentment. Don't take them for granted. Make them count. Build them into each day. They all add up.

2. *Be responsible for cultivating personal happiness.*

Eliminate the conditions that make happiness difficult. If you're locked into a job or relationship that you loathe, it's tough to feel happy. Resentment and bitterness make it difficult for happiness to flourish. Don't let yourself be a moaner or a martyr. Do something about it.

3. *Curb envy.*

Feeling that you never measure up, that you fall short by comparison, is bad for the spirit. Remind yourself how much you've got in your life, how much is great, compared to so many others. You're absolutely fine. There'll always be someone you could envy. Choose not to. Manage your aspirations and ambitions. Don't let them leave you feeling deprived, diminished or inferior right now. Keep a perspective.

4. *Broaden your horizons.*

Look for companionship and community. Make sure you have a gang of at least four great people to laugh and share with. Get connected to people with a common goal. Find something important, other than your career, to care about. Don't look for payment. Kindness and generosity of spirit cost nothing. The payback will be greater depth, meaning, purpose and joy for you. You'll be the real beneficiary.

5. *Cultivate compassion.*

Show it to yourself first before you try to share it with others. Personal happiness is your right and your responsibility. Respect yourself, care for yourself, be committed to yourself and take responsibility for helping yourself to become all that you can be.

Do what you have to do. But whatever you do,

Be happy.

Key terms

imperative expressing a command

rhetorical question a question asked for dramatic effect and not intended to get an answer

A writer's choice of grammatical features is informed by the purpose of their writing. For example, when writing to advise, it is important to offer direction to a reader. To do this, writers often use the **imperative** form of the verb. An imperative tells the reader what to do or demands some form of action or response. For example, 'You should make happiness your goal' becomes 'Make happiness your goal'.

Activity 3

SPAG

1. Re-read Source text I on page 63 and identify three imperatives. Rewrite these as suggestions rather than commands.

2. Why do you think Fiona Harrold has decided to use the imperative form? Discuss how this might contribute to the effectiveness of the text.

Advice texts also commonly make use of the personal pronoun 'you' to address the reader directly. This can help make readers feel that what they are reading is relevant and aimed directly at them personally.

Tip

Think about the idea each sentence is trying to convey and how this relates to the overall purpose of the text.

Activity 4

SPAG

Explain what effects are created by the use of personal pronouns in the following quotations:

- 'Don't put it off until you've got the perfect job, man, woman, body.'

- 'If you're locked into a job or relationship that you loathe, it's tough to feel happy.'

- 'Don't let yourself be a moaner or a martyr.'

Stretch

Can you identify the **rhetorical question** used in the second paragraph of Source text I? Why do you think the writer has included this?

Activity 5

Summarize what you have learned about happiness from Source text I on page 63 in 200 words or fewer. Use the following steps to help you to summarize:

- Make a list of bullet points about what you can remember from the text.

- Skim the text again to see if there are any really important points you have missed.

- Write your bullet points up into a paragraph using your own words.

- Exchange your writing with a partner and see if they agree that you have captured the essence of the text.

SPAG

Activity 6

You have been asked to find information and advice to include in a guidebook for stressed-out students called 'How to Live a Happy School Life'. Re-read Source text I from *The 10 Minute Life Coach* on page 63 and write a brief report evaluating the usefulness of its content for this new guidebook. You should:

- identify the advice you think is most relevant for students

- evaluate the usefulness of the advice given

- propose any changes that need to be made to the advice to make it more relevant for a student audience.

Remember to consider both the information and ideas included and the way these are expressed. Support your evaluation by including quotations and evidence from the text.

Support

You could use the following prompts to help you to structure your report:

- 'Be happy' is the kind of text which will appeal to many students as...

- The advice given in 'Be happy' is relevant and useful because...

- Vocabulary and grammar changes I would recommend include...

SPAG

Activity 7

You are now going to write a section of the 'How to Live a Happy School Life' guidebook for stressed-out students. Follow the steps below to help you to plan, draft and review your writing.

Planning

Select the information and ideas you are going to include. Think about how you can adapt these to make them particularly useful and relevant to school students. You will need to organize your ideas into a clear and logical structure.

Drafting

As you write, think about how you can most effectively express the advice you want to give. You need to consider the vocabulary you choose and the grammatical features you use in order to influence readers and reflect the purpose of your writing.

Reviewing

Re-read each sentence to check that it makes sense and is creating the effects you want to achieve. Look at the overall structure of your text and check that you have used signposts to guide the reader through the advice you have presented.

8 Form and impact

Learning objective

- To evaluate how form contributes to the impact of a text

When reading a non-fiction text, you need to consider how its form contributes to the impact it creates. Source text J is a personal letter which was written in 2006 by the actor Stephen Fry to a young woman Crystal Nunn, who during a bout of depression had written to him for advice.

Key terms

informal language language used in everyday speech

extended metaphor a metaphor which is continued through a series of lines or sentences in a text

Activity 1

SPAG

1. What is your initial reaction to this letter? Think about:
   - what kinds of words you would use to describe it
   - the identity of the author and whether this affects your reaction
   - how helpful you think the advice provided is
   - which parts of it stick in your mind and why.

2. Discuss what you can infer about Stephen Fry from this letter. Refer to the text to support the inferences you make.

3. How formal is the language used in this personal letter? Identify examples of formal and **informal language** and explain the different effects these might have on the recipient.

4. The indefinite pronoun 'one' can be used to replace personal pronouns such as 'you' and 'we'. What does Fry achieve by using 'one' in some parts of his letter?

5. What is the **extended metaphor** that Stephen Fry uses to convey his thoughts about our moods? How effective do you think this is?

6. How would you describe the tone of this letter? Find examples of words and phrases that you think are particularly effective in helping to create this tone and explain why.

Exam link

As part of your learning for GCSE, you will be expected to use relevant subject terminology when reading and responding to texts to show your understanding of the language features used and the effects they create.

Activity 2

Think of a person you would like to ask for advice. This could be a famous person or somebody you know. Write a personal letter to this person explaining why you would like their advice.

In your letter you should:

- think about the tone you want to create
- consider the formality of the language you use
- try to elicit an emotional response from your reader.

Source text J

A letter from Stephen Fry to Crystal Nunn

April 10, 2006

Dear Crystal,

I'm so sorry to hear that life is getting you down at the moment. Goodness knows, it can be so tough when nothing seems to fit and little seems to be fulfilling. I'm not sure there's any specific advice I can give that will help bring life back its savour. Although they mean well, it's sometimes quite galling to be reminded how much people love you when you don't love yourself that much.

I've found that it's of some help to think of one's moods and feelings about the world as being similar to weather:

Here are some obvious things about the weather:

It's real.
You can't change it by wishing it away.
If it's dark and rainy it really is dark and rainy and you can't alter it.
It might be dark and rainy for two weeks in a row.

BUT

It will be sunny one day.
It isn't under one's control as to when the sun comes out, but come out it will.
One day.

It really is the same with one's moods, I think. The wrong approach is to believe that they are illusions. They are real. Depression, anxiety, listlessness – these are as real as the weather – AND EQUALLY NOT UNDER ONE'S CONTROL. Not one's fault.

BUT

They will pass: they really will.

In the same way that one has to accept the weather, so one has to accept how one feels about life sometimes. "Today's a crap day," is a perfectly realistic approach. It's all about finding a kind of mental umbrella. "Hey-ho, it's raining inside: it isn't my fault and there's nothing I can do about it, but sit it out. But the sun may well come out tomorrow and when it does, I shall take full advantage."

I don't know if any of that is of any use: it may not seem it, and if so, I'm sorry. I just thought I'd drop you a line to wish you well in your search to find a little more pleasure and purpose in life.

Very best wishes

Stephen Fry

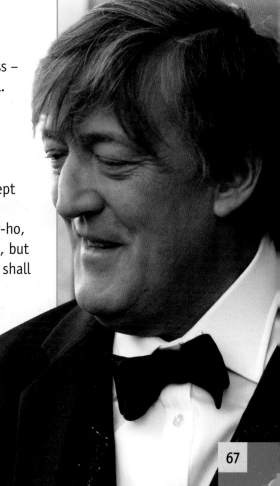

Now read Source text K, a personal letter written in 1820 by a famous writer and clergyman Sydney Smith to his friend Lady Georgiana Morpeth, who was suffering from depression.

Activity 3

SPAG

1. What is your initial reaction to Sydney Smith's letter? Think about:
   - what kinds of words you would use to describe it
   - the identity of the author and whether this affects your reaction
   - how helpful you think the advice provided is
   - which parts of it stick in your mind and why.

2. Discuss what you can infer about Sydney Smith from this letter. Refer to the text to support the inferences you make.

3. How formal is the language used in this letter? Identify examples of formal and informal language and explain the different effects these might have on the recipient.

4. Pick out examples of the personal pronouns that Sydney Smith uses in his letter. What effects do these help to create?

5. What is unusual about the form of Sydney Smith's letter? Discuss why you think he might have chosen to structure the letter in this way.

Activity 4

"These letters present helpful advice in a sympathetic and encouraging way."

How far do you agree with this statement?

In your answer you should:

- discuss the helpfulness of the advice provided
- explain the impact of this advice on you as a reader
- compare the ways the advice is presented.

Progress check

1. Re-read your answer to Activity 4. Using differently coloured highlighter pens:
   - highlight the similarities between the two texts you have identified
   - highlight the differences between the two texts you have identified
   - underline where you have referred to relevant subject terminology
   - circle the quotations you have included to support the points you have made.

2. Compare your annotated answer with a partner. Discuss what you feel you did well and which parts of the answer you could improve.

Source text K

A letter from Sydney Smith to Lady Georgiana Morpeth, 1820

Foston, Feb. 16th, 1820

Dear Lady Georgiana,

Nobody has suffered more from low spirits than I have done—so I feel for you.

1st. Live as well as you dare.

2nd. Go into the shower-bath with a small quantity of water at a temperature low enough to give you a slight sensation of cold, 75° or 80°.

3rd. Amusing books.

4th. Short views of human life—not further than dinner or tea.

5th. Be as busy as you can.

6th. See as much as you can of those friends who respect and like you.

7th. And of those acquaintances who amuse you.

8th. Make no secret of low spirits to your friends, but talk of them freely—they are always worse for **dignified concealment**.

9th. Attend to the effects tea and coffee produce upon you.

10th. Compare your lot with that of other people.

11th. Don't expect too much from human life—a sorry business at the best.

12th. Avoid poetry, dramatic representations (except comedy), music, serious novels, melancholy sentimental people, and every thing likely to excite feeling or emotion not ending in active **benevolence**.

13th. Do good, and endeavour to please everybody of every degree.

14th. Be as much as you can in the open air without fatigue.

15th. Make the room where you commonly sit, **gay** and pleasant.

16th. Struggle by little and little against idleness.

17th. Don't be too severe upon yourself, or underrate yourself, but do yourself justice.

18th. Keep good blazing fires.

19th. Be firm and constant in the exercise of rational religion.

20th. Believe me, dear Georgiana, your devoted servant, Sydney Smith

SYDNEY SMITH

Glossary

dignified noble, worthy

concealment hiding

benevolence kindness

gay joyous, happy

Assessment

In this section you will have the chance to apply what you have learned in this chapter about reading information and ideas and writing for audience, impact and purpose as you complete the reading and writing activities.

Reading

Read Source text L and then complete the activities below. The extract is taken from the opening of an essay entitled 'On Being in the Blues' by Jerome K. Jerome which was written in 1886.

Exam link

In Section A of Component 01: Communicating information and ideas, you will have one hour to read two unseen non-fiction texts and answer questions about the texts. One of the non-fiction texts will be from the 19th century.

AO1

- Identify and interpret explicit and implicit information and ideas
- Select and synthesize evidence from different texts

Activity 1

1. Re-read the first paragraph. The effects of which physical conditions are compared to the effects of the blues?

2. Now re-read the second paragraph. What does the behaviour the writer describes here imply about the effects of the blues?

AO2

- Explain, comment on and analyse how writers use language and structure to achieve effects and influence readers, using relevant subject terminology to support your views

Activity 2

1. The writer has used the words 'crushed' and 'bury' in the third paragraph. Explain what this choice of language suggests about his emotions and analyse the effects these words might have on the reader.

2. How does the writer use exaggeration to add humour to the text? Select quotations to support your analysis.

3. Select three sentences and explain how the grammatical features they use help the writer to communicate his ideas.

blues a term for sadness or depression

Extract from 'On Being in the Blues' by Jerome K. Jerome

I can enjoy feeling melancholy, and there is a good deal of satisfaction about being thoroughly miserable; but nobody likes a fit of the **blues**. Nevertheless, everybody has them; notwithstanding which, nobody can tell why. There is no accounting for them. You are just as likely to have one on the day after you have come into a large fortune as on the day after you have left your new silk umbrella in the train. Its effect upon you is somewhat similar to what would probably be produced by a combined attack of toothache, indigestion, and cold in the head. You become stupid, restless, and irritable; rude to strangers and dangerous toward your friends; clumsy, maudlin, and quarrelsome; a nuisance to yourself and everybody about you.

While it is on you can do nothing and think of nothing, though feeling at the time bound to do something. You can't sit still so put on your hat and go for a walk; but before you get to the corner of the street you wish you hadn't come out and you turn back. You open a book and try to read, but you find Shakespeare trite and commonplace, Dickens is dull and prosy, Thackeray a bore, and Carlyle too sentimental. You throw the book aside and call the author names. Then you "shoo" the cat out of the room and kick the door to after her. You think you will write your letters, but after sticking at "Dearest Auntie: I find I have five minutes to spare, and so hasten to write to you," for a quarter of an hour, without being able to think of another sentence, you tumble the paper into the desk, fling the wet pen down upon the table-cloth, and start up with the resolution of going to see the Thompsons. While pulling on your gloves, however, it occurs to you that the Thompsons are idiots; that they never have supper; and that you will be expected to jump the baby. You curse the Thompsons and decide not to go.

By this time you feel completely crushed. You bury your face in your hands and think you would like to die and go to heaven. You picture to yourself your own sick-bed, with all your friends and relations standing round you weeping. You bless them all, especially the young and pretty ones. They will value you when you are gone, so you say to yourself, and learn too late what they have lost; and you bitterly contrast their presumed regard for you then with their decided want of veneration now.

These reflections make you feel a little more cheerful, but only for a brief period; for the next moment you think what a fool you must be to imagine for an instant that anybody would be sorry at anything that might happen to you. Who would care two straws (whatever precise amount of care two straws may represent) whether you are blown up, or hung up, or married, or drowned? Nobody cares for you. You never have been properly appreciated, never met with your due deserts in any one particular. You review the whole of your past life, and it is painfully apparent that you have been ill-used from your cradle.

Now read Source text M. This is the opening section of an essay entitled 'Joy' by the writer Zadie Smith, which was published in *The New York Review of Books* in 2013.

Extract from 'Joy' by Zadie Smith

It might be useful to distinguish between pleasure and joy. But maybe everybody does this very easily, all the time, and only I am confused. A lot of people seem to feel that joy is only the most intense version of pleasure, arrived at by the same road—you simply have to go a little further down the track. That has not been my experience. And if you asked me if I wanted more joyful experiences in my life, I wouldn't be at all sure I did, exactly because it proves such a difficult emotion to manage. It's not at all obvious to me how we should make an accommodation between joy and the rest of our everyday lives.

Perhaps the first thing to say is that I experience at least a little pleasure every day. I wonder if this is more than the usual amount? It was the same even in childhood when most people are miserable. I don't think this is because so many wonderful things happen to me but rather that the small things go a long way. I seem to get more than the ordinary satisfaction out of food, for example—any old food.

An egg sandwich from one of these grimy food vans on Washington Square has the genuine power to turn my day around. Whatever is put in front of me, foodwise, will usually get a five-star review.

You'd think that people would like to cook for, or eat with, me—in fact I'm told it's boring. Where there is no discernment there can be no awareness of expertise or gratitude for special effort. "Don't say that was delicious," my husband warns, "you say everything's delicious." "But it was delicious." It drives him crazy. All day long I can look forward to a popsicle. The persistent anxiety that fills the rest of my life is calmed for as long as I have the flavour of something good in my mouth. And though it's true that when the flavor is finished the anxiety returns, we do not have so many reliable sources of pleasure in this life as to turn our nose up at one that is so readily available, especially here in America. A pineapple popsicle. Even the great anxiety of writing can be stilled for the eight minutes it takes to eat a pineapple popsicle.

AO3

- Compare writer's ideas and perspectives, as well as how these are conveyed, across two texts

AO4

- Evaluate texts critically and support this with appropriate textual references

---

Activity 3

'Source texts M and N show how we can be controlled by our emotions.'

How far do you agree with this statement?

In your answer you should:

- discuss what you learn about the power of emotions and their effect on our everyday lives

- explain the impact these ideas have on you as a reader

- compare the ways in which each writer presents their ideas.

   Support your response with quotations from **both** texts.

Writing

A05

- Communicate clearly, effectively and imaginatively, selecting and adapting tone, style and register for different forms, purposes and audiences

- Organize information and ideas, using structural and grammatical features to support coherence and cohesion of texts

A06

- Use a range of vocabulary and sentence structures for clarity, purpose and effect, with accurate spelling and punctuation

Exam link

In Section B of Component 01: Communicating information and ideas, you will have one hour to complete a writing task, selecting this from a choice of two. You will need to be able to write original non-fiction for a specific audience and purpose and will be assessed on the quality of your extended response.

Activity 4

You have been asked to write an article entitled 'An Uphill Struggle?' which will appear on a new website for young adults called Flying the Nest. This website aims to provide young adults with information, ideas and opinions about topics such as living away from home and starting a career. You can write about any of the following topics:

- the importance of an adequate income

- the pros or cons of high-rise living

- the elements of a happy lifestyle.

In your article, you should:

- decide on the purpose of your writing and maintain a consistent viewpoint throughout

- make vocabulary choices which express your ideas and opinions effectively

- include a range of linguistic devices which will add impact to your writing

- structure your writing carefully, using some of the grammatical features you have explored in this chapter.

3 FRIENDSHIP AND FAMILY

'A mother's love for her child is like nothing else in the world ... it dares all things and crushes down remorselessly all that stands in its path.'

Agatha Christie, writer

'All happy families are alike; each unhappy family is unhappy in its own way.'

Leo Tolstoy, writer

'What do we live for, if it is not to make life less difficult for each other?'

George Eliot, writer

'True friends stab you in the front.'

Oscar Wilde, writer

Introduction

Relationships are central to our lives. From family to friends, the bonds we make and break influence and shape who we are. In this chapter, you will read a range of prose fiction and literary non-fiction texts and use these to explore how writers use language, structure and grammatical features to create meaning and impact in their writing. You will use the knowledge and skills you gain from your reading to develop your own creative writing skills, producing imaginative and original texts in a range of forms.

Exam link

The activities in this chapter are designed to help you develop the skills needed for success in Component 02: Exploring effects and impact. The first section of this exam requires you to read two different extracts for meaning and effects and answer questions about both extracts. The second section asks you to write imaginatively to produce a piece of original creative writing.

Activity 1

1. Read and discuss the quotations on the facing page. Which do you agree with and why?

2. Think about the novel you are currently reading or one which you have recently read. Can you identify any important friendships or family relationships in this novel? Discuss your ideas.

3. Think about an important friendship or family relationship in your life, past or present. Draft a piece of personal writing that:

    *   describes who the person is and your relationship with them

    *   relates an anecdote about a special event or memory connected with this person

    *   explains the positive impact this person has had on your life.

Friends and enemies

The divide between rich Friends can have an important impact in our lives, influencing the way we act and how we think. However, friendships can often be complex relationships and, for writers of fiction, a source of inspiration for the narratives they create.

Learning objectives

- To draw inferences from textual details
- To interpret writers' meanings and effects
- To justify your points with carefully selected evidence

Key term

inference something that you infer; a conclusion reached by reasoning

1 Inferences and interpretations

When you read a novel or a short story, you need to be able to draw **inferences** about characters, events and themes to develop your understanding of the story. Reading closely to explore details from the text can help you to interpret a writer's meanings, drawing out inferences which are not immediately obvious. Different people can respond to the same text in different ways, justifying their views with the evidence they find. Read Source text A, taken from the novel *Anita and Me* by Meera Syal, and complete the activities below.

Activity 1

1. What feelings do you have as a reader towards Anita? Discuss your impressions of this character.

2. Identify details from the extract that helped to give you this impression of Anita. You could consider:
   - Anita's actions and the way these are described
   - what Anita says and how she says it
   - how Meena responds to Anita
   - the way Anita is described.

3. Select three specific details and for each one explain the inferences you can draw from this.

Stretch

Think about the effects of these details and the overall impact they create together.

4. What impression do you get of Meena? Discuss your ideas and explore any different responses to this character.

5a. Identify one quotation which suggests Meena admires Anita.

5b. Discuss what this shows about Meena and Anita's relationship.

Exam link

In Component 02: Exploring effects and impact, reading questions that ask you to identify phrases or give examples are asking you to identify details from the text. You might also be asked to make inferences from the details you identify.

Extract from *Anita and Me* by Meera Syal

In this novel, Meena Kumar is a nine-year-old girl growing up in the only Punjabi family in the village of Tollington, near Birmingham. Here, Meena describes an encounter with Anita Rutter, another girl from her school.

A shadow fell over my T-bar sandals and I looked up to see Anita Rutter staring at me through squinted eyes ringed in bright blue eyeshadow. She broke off a twig from our privet hedge and thrust it under my nose, pointing at a part of the branch where the leaves were not their usual straight darts but were rolled up in on themselves, neat and packaged as school dinner sandwiches. "See them leaves?" She carefully unrolled one of them: it came away slowly like sticky tape, to reveal a sprinkling of tiny black eggs. "Butterflies' eggs, them is. They roll up the leaf to hide them, see."

She stripped all the leaves off the twig in one movement and smelled her fingers, before flicking the naked branch at my ankles. It stung but I did not pull my legs back. I knew this was a test.

"What you got?"

I held out my crumpled bag of swollen sweets. She peered inside disdainfully, then snatched the bag off me and began walking away as she ate. I watched her go, confused. I could still hear my parents talking inside, their voices now calmer, conciliatory. Anita stopped momentarily, shouting over her shoulder, "**Yow** coming then?"

It was the first week of the long summer holidays and I had six whole weeks which I could waste or taste. So I got up and followed her without a word.

I was happy to follow her a respectable few paces behind, knowing that I was privileged to be in her company. Anita was the undisputed **'cock' of our yard**, maybe that should have been hen, but her foghorn voice, foul mouth, and proficiency at lassoing victims with her frayed skipping rope indicated she was carrying enough testosterone around to earn the title. She ruled over all the kids in the yard with a mixture of pre-pubescent feminine **wiles**, pouting, sulking, clumsy cack-handed flirting and unsettling mood swings which would often end in minor violence.

yow you

'cock' of our yard best fighter in school

wiles cunning, persuasive strategies

Anita and Me by Meera Syal is a set text for Component 01/Section A: Exploring modern and literary heritage texts in the OCR GCSE English Literature specification.

Key terms

irony the use of words that mean the opposite of what you really intend, done either for emphasis or for humour

narrative viewpoint the perspective a story is narrated from

Tip

Refer closely to evidence from the text to support your point of view. You should weigh up different interpretations of meaning and decide which is best supported by the evidence. Use words such as 'suggests', 'implies', and 'conveys' to show how you are offering your own interpretation of the meanings and effects created.

Progress check

Swap what you have written with a partner. Read it carefully and discuss your impressions of the characters and setting depicted. Write down one thing you like about the story opening and one thing they could do to improve it further.

Exploring a writer's language choices can help you to interpret the meanings they want to convey. Sometimes writers can use techniques such as **irony**, where the meaning expressed is opposite to the meaning intended. Read Source text B, taken from the opening of the novel *The Interestings* by Meg Worlitzer, and complete the activities below.

Activity 2

1a. Re-read the first two sentences. Why do you think the group decide to call themselves 'the Interestings'?

1b. Would you want to be one of the Interestings?

1c. Discuss the reasons why someone might want to be a member of this group of friends.

2a. How does Julia react to being invited to join the Interestings?

2b. Identify three phrases which suggest Julia feels as though she doesn't belong in the group?

2c. What do these details suggest about Julia's character?

2d. Share your impressions of Julia. Are there any differences in the ways you have interpreted details from the text? Which interpretation do you think the evidence supports best?

3. Think about Source texts A and B. Both Meena and Julia want to make new friends. What other similarities do these two narrators share? Refer to evidence from both texts to support your answer.

Activity 3

Write the opening of a story where somebody tries to make a new friend. This could be based on something that has actually happened to you or an invented experience. Follow the steps below to help you to plan and draft the opening of your story.

Planning

Decide on the characters and setting for your story. Think about the characteristics your characters will have and how you could convey these. Choose a **narrative viewpoint** to tell the story from. You could choose to follow the model of Source text A and use a first-person narrator, or follow the model of Source text B which has a third-person, subjective narrator, focused on Julie Jacobson's viewpoint.

Drafting

As you write, think about the language you use to help readers draw inferences about the characters and situation.

Source text B

Extract from *The Interestings* by Meg Worlitzer

In this novel, an American girl called Julie Jacobson meets a new group of friends during a summer camp in 1974. This group of friends decide to call themselves 'the Interestings'.

On a warm night in early July of that long-evaporated year, the Interestings gathered for the very first time. They were only fifteen, sixteen, and they began to call themselves the name with **tentative** irony. Julie Jacobson, an outsider and possibly even a freak, had been invited in for obscure reasons, and now she sat in a corner on the unswept floor and attempted to position herself so she would appear **unobtrusive** yet not pathetic, which was a difficult balance. The teepee, designed ingeniously though built cheaply, was airless on nights like this one, when there was no wind to push in through the screens. Julie Jacobson longed to unfold a leg or do the side-to-side motion with her jaw that sometimes set off a gratifying series of tiny **percussive** sounds inside her skull. But if she called attention to herself in any way now, someone might start to wonder why she was here; and really, she knew, she had no reason to be here at all. It had been miraculous when Ash Wolf had nodded to her earlier in the night at the row of sinks and asked if she wanted to come join her and some of the others later. *Some of the others*. Even that wording was thrilling.

Julie had looked at her with a dumb, dripping face, which she then quickly dried with a thin towel from home. *Jacobson*, her mother had written along the puckered edge in red laundry marker in a tentative hand that now seemed a little tragic. "Sure," she had said, out of instinct. What if she'd said *no*? she liked to wonder afterward in a kind of strangely pleasurable, **baroque** horror. What if she'd turned down the lightly flung invitation and went about her life, thudding obliviously along like a drunk person, a blind person, a moron, someone who thinks that the small packet of happiness she carries is enough. Yet having said "sure" at the sinks in the girls' bathroom, here she was now, planted in the corner of this unfamiliar, ironic world. Irony was new to her and tasted oddly good, like a previously unavailable summer fruit. Soon, she and the rest of them would be ironic much of the time, unable to answer an innocent question without giving their words a **snide** little adjustment. Fairly soon after that, the snideness would soften, the irony would be mixed in with seriousness, and the years would shorten and fly. Then it wouldn't be long before they all found themselves shocked and sad to be fully grown into their thicker, finalized adult selves, with almost no chance for reinvention.

2 Narrative voice

Learning objective

- To understand how writers create a narrative voice

The opening of a story introduces the point of view the story is being told from. The two main points of view are:

- first-person narration – this is where the narrator is a participant in the story and can be identified by the use of first-person pronouns such as 'I'

- third-person narration – this is where the narrator is outside of the story and can describe or comment on the events of the story.

The language and style a writer chooses to create a **narrative voice** can influence the impression the reader gets of a narrator and influence their experience of the story. Read Source text C, taken from Neil Gaiman's novel *The Ocean at the End of the Lane*, where the narrator is a middle-aged man looking back on events from his childhood.

Key terms

narrative voice the personality or character of the narrator as it is revealed through dialogue or descriptive and narrative commentary

narrative hook a literary technique used in the opening of a story to engage readers so that they will keep reading

Activity 1

SPAG

1. Look again at the opening sentence. How effective do you think this sentence is as a **narrative hook**?

2a. What impression do you get of the narrator in Source text C? Is he someone you feel sympathy for?

2b. Identify three techniques used by the writer that gave you this impression. Discuss the effects created by each of these techniques.

3. Look at the final paragraph of Source text C. Discuss how you think the writer wants the reader to feel towards the narrator here.

4a. The narrator of this story is a middle-aged man looking back on his childhood. How does the language and style used help to create a convincing narrative voice? Think about:

- the formality of the language

- vocabulary choices and the effects these create

- sentence lengths and structures and how these contribute to the narrative voice.

4b. Write a paragraph analysing how the writer uses language to create a convincing narrative voice.

Support

Does the narrator use simple, straightforward vocabulary or more complex, unusual words? Are mostly short or long sentences used? Are any other stylistic devices or grammatical features used? Consider the reasons for these choices and the effects specific examples create.

For example, *The repetition of 'nobody' emphasizes the narrator's loneliness and sense of isolation as a young boy, evoking sympathy on the part of the reader...*

Extract from *The Ocean at the End of the Lane* by Neil Gaiman

In this extract, the narrator remembers his seventh birthday party.

Nobody came to my seventh birthday party.

There was a table laid with jellies and trifles, with a party hat beside each place and a birthday cake with seven candles on it in the centre of the table. The cake had a book drawn on it, in icing. My mother, who had organised the party, told me that the lady at the bakery said that they had never put a book on a birthday cake before, and that mostly for boys it was footballs or spaceships. I was their first book.

When it became obvious that nobody was coming, my mother lit the seven candles on the cake, and I blew them out. I ate a slice of the cake, as did my little sister and one of her friends (both of them attending the party as observers, not participants), before they fled, giggling, to the garden.

Party games had been prepared by my mother, but nobody was there, not even my sister, none of the party games were played, and I unwrapped the newspaper around the pass-the-parcel gift myself, revealing a blue plastic Batman figure. I was sad that nobody had come to my party, but happy that I had a Batman figure, and there was a birthday present waiting to be read, a boxed set of the Narnia books, which I took upstairs. I lay on the bed and lost myself in the stories.

I liked that. Books were safer than other people anyway.

My parents had also given me a *Best of Gilbert and Sullivan* LP, to add to the two I already had. I had loved Gilbert and Sullivan since I was three, when my father's youngest sister, my aunt, took me to see *Iolanthe*, a play filled with lords and fairies. I found the existence and nature of the fairies easier to understand than that of the lords. My aunt died soon after, of pneumonia, in the hospital.

That evening, when my father arrived home from work, he brought a cardboard box with him. In the cardboard box was a soft-haired kitten of uncertain gender, which I immediately named Fluffy, and which I loved utterly and wholeheartedly.

Fluffy slept on my bed at night. I talked to it, sometimes, when my little sister was not around, half expecting it to answer in a human tongue. It never did. I did not mind. The kitten was affectionate and interested and a good companion for someone whose seventh birthday party had consisted of a table with iced biscuits and a blancmange and cake and fifteen empty folding chairs.

I do not remember ever asking any of the other children in my class at school why they had not come to my party. I did not need to ask them. They were not my friends after all. They were just the people I went to school with.

3 Character and dialogue

Learning objective

- To explore how dialogue and structure can be used to reveal character

There are many techniques that writers of fiction use to create the characters that populate their stories. From description detailing a character's actions and appearance to **dialogue** that reveals their personality, as a reader you need to look carefully at the language authors use to convey character.

Source text D is taken from Mark Haddon's novel *The Curious Incident of the Dog in the Night-Time*. This novel is narrated by a 15-year-old boy called Christopher who has emotional and behavioural difficulties and finds it difficult to make friends.

Key terms

dialogue the words spoken by characters in a play, film, or story

metaphor the use of a word or phrase in a special meaning that provides an image

simile where one thing is compared to another thing, using a connective word such as 'like' or 'as'

Activity 1

1. Before you read the extract, discuss what expectations you have about the character of Christopher. How do you think the writer might want readers to feel towards a character who has emotional and behavioural difficulties?

2. Now read the extract. Discuss whether your expectations about the character of Christopher have been met.

3a. What does Christopher's answer, 'I am 15 years, 3 months and 2 days' suggest about him?

3b. Look at his other responses to the policeman's questions. What do you find interesting about them?

3c. What do these following lines reveal about Christopher? 'This was a difficult question. It was something I wanted to do. I like dogs. It made me sad to see that the dog was dead.'

4a. Discuss how effective the writer's use of **metaphor** and **simile** is in helping to understand how Christopher's mind works.

4b. How does the writer organize the dialogue in a way which helps the reader to understand how Christopher thinks?

Support

Discuss why you think Christopher's answers are in short sentences. What effect does this create?

5. How do you think the policeman is feeling during this conversation? Explain your ideas with reference to his dialogue.

6. Discuss the impact of the final sentence. Were you surprised by how the extract ended?

Source text D

Extract from *The Curious Incident of the Dog in the Night-time* by Mark Haddon

Here, Christopher has just found a dead dog and is talking to a policeman who has arrived at the scene.

The policeman squatted down beside me and said, 'Would you like to tell me what's going on here, young man?'

I sat up and said, 'The dog is dead.'

'I'd got that far,' he said.

I said, 'I think someone killed the dog.'

'How old are you?' he asked.

I replied, 'I am 15 years and 3 months and 2 days.'

'And what, precisely, were you doing in the garden?' he asked.

'I was holding the dog,' I replied.

'And why were you holding the dog?' he asked.

This was a difficult question. It was something I wanted to do. I like dogs. It made me sad to see that the dog was dead.

I liked the policeman, too, and I wanted to answer the question properly, but the policeman did not give me enough time to work out the correct answer.

'Why were you holding the dog?' he asked again.

'I like dogs,' I said.

'Did you kill the dog?' he asked.

I said, 'I did not kill the dog.'

'Is this your fork?' he asked.

I said, 'No.'

'You seem very upset about this,' he said.

He was asking too many questions and he was asking them too quickly. They were stacking up in my head like loaves in the factory where Uncle Terry works. The factory is a bakery and he operates the slicing machines. And sometimes a slicer is not working fast enough but the bread keeps coming and there is a blockage. I sometimes think of my mind as a machine, but not always as a bread-slicing machine. It makes it easier to explain to other people what is going on inside it.

The policeman said, 'I am going to ask you once again…'

I rolled back onto the lawn and pressed my forehead to the ground again and made the noise that Father calls groaning. I make this noise when there is too much information coming into my head from the outside world. It is like when you are upset and you hold the radio against your ear and you tune it halfway between two stations so that all you get is white noise and then you turn the volume right up so that this is all you can hear and then you know you are safe because you cannot hear anything else.

The policeman took hold of my arm and lifted me onto my feet.

I didn't like him touching me like this.

And this is when I hit him.

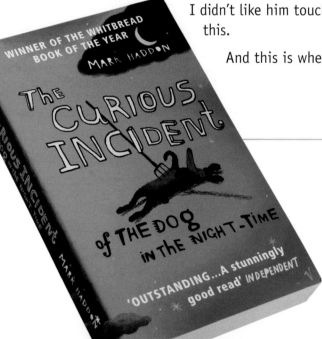

Key term

stream of consciousness a narrative mode that attempts to reflect the narrator's thought processes

In first-person narratives, writers sometimes use a literary technique called **stream of consciousness** to convey a character's thoughts and point of view. This technique is characterized by a lack of punctuation and disregard for grammatical conventions as it seeks to convey the narrator's thought process. Read Source text E which is taken from the novel *The Butcher Boy* by Patrick McCabe.

Activity 2

1. What are your first impressions of Francie? Identify any specific details from the text that contribute to this impression.

2a. What do you find interesting about the way the writer presents the conversation between Mrs Nugent and Francie's mother?

2b. How does the way the writer presents this conversation make you feel about Francie?

3. What does the use of the stream of consciousness technique suggest about Francie's state of mind? Discuss your ideas.

Activity 3

Imagine and write the dialogue between Mrs Nugent and Francie's mother. Draw on details from the text and think about how the dialogue you write can reveal the characters' attitudes towards each other.

Support

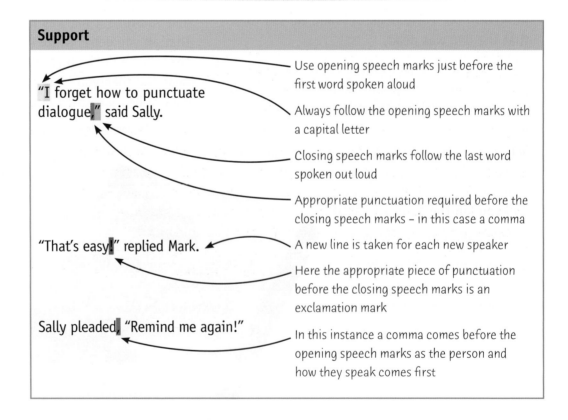

"I forget how to punctuate dialogue," said Sally.

— Use opening speech marks just before the first word spoken aloud

— Always follow the opening speech marks with a capital letter

— Closing speech marks follow the last word spoken out loud

— Appropriate punctuation required before the closing speech marks – in this case a comma

"That's easy!" replied Mark.

— A new line is taken for each new speaker

— Here the appropriate piece of punctuation before the closing speech marks is an exclamation mark

Sally pleaded, "Remind me again!"

— In this instance a comma comes before the opening speech marks as the person and how they speak comes first

ma colloquial term for 'mother'

Extract from *The Butcher Boy* by Patrick McCabe

Set in a small town in Ireland in the 1960s, this novel is narrated by Francie, a twelve-year-old boy. Here, Francie describes the consequences after he and his friend Joe decide to trick Philip Nugent, a new boy at their school, into giving them his collection of comics.

We cleaned him out. I admit it. It was only a laugh. We'd have given them back if he asked for them. All he had to say was: Look chaps, I think I want my comics back and we'd have said: OK Phil.

But of course Nugent couldn't wait for that. Anyway we left Philip with his pile of junk and off we went to the hide going on about it all until the tears ran down our faces. Wait till you hear this one Joe would say one flea says to the other what do you say will we walk or take a dog. He was reading out all these jokes I couldn't stop the laughing, I was choking. We got so bad I was hitting the grass with my fists crying stop Joe stop. But we weren't laughing the next day when Nugent got on the job.

I met Joe coming across the Diamond and he says to me watch out Francie we're in the wars with Nugent. She called at our house and she'll be round to you. Sure enough I was lying on the bed upstairs and the knock comes to the front door. I could hear **ma** humming and the shuffle of her slippers on the lino. Ah hello Mrs Nugent come in but Nugent was in no humour for ah hello come in or any of that. She lay into ma about the comics and the whole lot and I could hear ma saying *yes yes I know I will of course!* and I was waiting for her to come flying up the stairs, get me by the ear and throw me on the step in front of Nugent and that's what she would have done if Nugent hadn't started on about the pigs. She said she knew the kind of us long before she went to England and she might have known not to let her son anywhere near the likes of me what else would you expect from a house where the father's never in, lying about the pubs from morning to night, he's no better than a pig. You needn't think we don't know what goes on in this house oh we know all right! Small wonder the boy is the way he is what chance has he got running about the town at all hours and the clothes hanging off him it doesn't take money to dress a child God love him it's not his fault but if he's seen near our Philip again there'll be trouble. There'll be trouble now mark my words!

Family life

Relationships with family are arguably the most important an individual will have during their lifetime. Fiction often explores these complex and sometimes emotionally charged relationships, allowing readers to see reflections of their own lives as well as understanding other people's relationships

Learning objective

- To understand how writers successfully create characters through description

Tip

Selecting the right quotation to back up your point is very important. Embedding this skilfully into what you write will help to create an effective analysis. Look at the example below and use it as a model for your own analysis:

The adjectives, 'dirty and inflamed' describe the father's face negatively and suggest a lack of respect for himself and damage due to too much alcohol...

4 Description and character

In narrative fiction, description can be used in several ways in order to create realistic and memorable characters. Writers can describe what a character looks like, what they are wearing, their actions and how other characters react to them. Read Source text F which is taken from D. H. Lawrence's novel *Sons and Lovers*, where the character of the father of the family is described.

Activity 1

1. What impression do you get of the father from this extract? Discuss your ideas.

2. Write an analysis of how the writer uses description to create the character of the father. In your answer you should comment on:
   - how he is physically described
   - how he speaks
   - how he behaves
   - how others react to him

   Select quotations to support your ideas, using appropriate terminology to identify any specific language choices.

Stretch

What impression do get of the character of Paul? Refer to evidence from the text to justify your analysis.

Activity 2

Write a description of a person, real or imagined. Think carefully about how you describe their physical appearance, their actions and how they talk to maximize the effect you want these to have on the reader.

Stretch

Rewrite Source text F from the father's point of view. Think about how you can use language to create a sympathetic narrative voice for the father and how he might describe the character of Paul.

Source text F

Extract from *Sons and Lovers* by D.H. Lawrence

And everybody in the house was still, because he was dangerous. He ate his food in the most brutal manner possible and, when he had done, pushed all the pots in a heap away from him, to lay his arms on the table. Then he went to sleep.

Paul hated his father so. The collier's small, mean head, with its black hair slightly soiled with grey, lay on the bare arms, and the face, dirty and inflamed, with a fleshy nose and thin, paltry brows, was turned sideways, asleep with beer and wearisomeness and nasty temper. If anyone entered suddenly, or a noise were made, the man looked up and shouted:

'I'll lay my fist about thy y'ead, I'm tellin' thee, if tha doesna stop that clatter! Dost hear?'

And the last two words, shouted in a bullying fashion, usually at Annie, made the family writhe with hate of the man.

He was shut out from all family affairs. No one told him anything. The children, alone with their mother, told her all about the day's happenings, everything. Nothing had really taken place in them until it was told to their mother. But as soon as the father came in, everything stopped. He was like the **scotch** in the smooth, happy machinery of the home. And he was always aware of this fall of silence on his entry, the shutting off of life, the unwelcome. But now it was gone too far to alter.

He would dearly have liked the children to talk to him, but they would not. Sometimes Mrs Morel would say:

'You ought to tell your father.'

Paul won a prize in a competition in a child's paper. Everybody was highly jubilant.

'Now you'd better tell your father when he comes in,' said Mrs Morel. 'You know how he carries on and says he's never told anything.'

'All right,' said Paul. But he would almost rather have forfeited the prize than have to tell his father.

scotch an old-fashioned word for a wedge used to prevent a wheel from moving

The narrative viewpoint chosen by a writer can influence readers' responses to the characters in the story. There are two main types of third-person narration:

- third-person omniscient where the narrative voice has access to the thoughts of all the characters within the story

- third-person limited where the narrative voice is restricted to one character's perspective.

Read Source text G, taken from Kate Atkinson's short story 'Dissonance' and then complete the activities below.

Activity 3

1. Discuss your feelings towards Simon and his mother? Which character do you feel most sympathy for and why?

2. How does the writer present Simon's attitude towards his mother? Think about:

   - the vocabulary he uses to describe his feelings towards her

   - the way her dialogue is incorporated into the narrative

   - how the description of Simon's actions suggests his attitude

   - the structure of the extract, especially the opening and ending.

   ### Support

   Explore how the writer uses **repetition** to emphasize Simon's attitude.

Activity 4

1. What similarities and differences can you identify in Source texts F and G? Think about:

   - the **settings** and situations described

   - the ideas and attitudes presented

   - how the characters are portrayed.

2. Write two paragraphs comparing the two texts. The first paragraph should explore a point of similarity and the second should explore a difference.

Activity 5

Think about a particular moment when you experienced an intense emotion towards someone, such as love or sympathy. Write a description of this experience. In your writing:

- carefully consider the vocabulary you choose in order to convey your emotions to the reader

- think about how you can use grammatical features such as repetition to create deliberate effects.

Key terms

repetition repeating, or being repeated

setting the way or place in which something is set

Progress check

Swap what you have written in Activity 5 with a partner. Read their description carefully, identifying the language features they have used to convey emotions and create deliberate effects. Write down one thing you thought was particularly effective and one thing they could do to improve it further.

Source text G

Glossary

Extract from 'Dissonance' by Kate Atkinson

The opening of this short story describes a teenage boy called Simon playing on his PlayStation. Here he expresses some strong emotions as he reflects on a conversation he had with his mother after she discovered he has been shoplifting.

Simon wished his mother would die. Right that minute. Right where she was sitting, which was almost undoubtedly down in the kitchen, at the bloody kitchen table, doing her bloody marking. *I'm at my wits' end with you, Simon. I worry about what's going to happen to you, I really do.* Well, if she was dead she wouldn't have to worry, would she? And he wouldn't have to listen to her bloody nagging. *Shoes don't live in the kitchen, Simon. If you spill something, do you think you could wipe it up, Simon?* He knew what would go on her bloody headstone as well. *I've just cleaned that, Simon.*

Korn's *Life is Peachy* pounded on the stereo, helping keep his thoughts in rhythm with Tekken 3 on the PlayStation. Hwoarang hammered machine-gun punches into Lei Wulong's stomach. *Simon, if you're going to finish all the milk, could you buy more?* Paul Phoenix pulled a three-hit combo with a God Hammer punch on Yoshimitsu. *If you use something, could you put it back when you've finished with it, Simon?* Simon snorted with adolescent **schadenfreude** as he imagined his mother in the King of the Iron Fists tournament, Forest Law thwacking junkyard kicks into her virtual body parts, Jin Kazama chopping her into submission. *Do you remember when you used to kiss and cuddle me and call me 'Mummy'?*

She was going to tell his father. *Shoplifting, Simon. That's theft, pure and simple.* Like the shops weren't ripping him off in the first place. *And how do you work that one out, Simon?* She knew he couldn't argue like Rebecca. She was always trying to get him to explain things. *Why did you do that, Simon? What were you thinking?* Stupid cow. *Just because your father doesn't live with us any more doesn't mean he can **abdicate** his responsibilities.* 'Tell Dad if you want, I haven't even seen him in weeks.' Dad wasn't interested in them any more anyway. He had Jenny now. *It'll never last.* Jenny who was pregnant, except their mother didn't know it. *What do you think will happen to you if you keep on this path, Simon? Hm?* King punched Ling Xiaoyu and then jumped on her body. KO. Ling Xiaoyu gave a girly little scream. Game Over. You Win.

schadenfreude taking pleasure from another person's misfortune

abdicate give up a responsibility or duty

5 Themes and ideas

A good starting point when reading a novel or short story is to think about its **themes**. A theme is never explicitly stated, but can be woven into a narrative text in different ways. Exploring the language a writer uses can help you to think about the themes in a text and how these are conveyed.

Read Source text H on the facing page. This is taken from Frank McCourt's memoir *Angela's Ashes* and recounts an incident from his childhood, growing up in a poor immigrant family in America in the 1920s.

Activity 1

1. Discuss the impact of this text on you as a reader. Identify any specific details that you found particularly powerful and explain why you have selected these.

2. Reread the text to explore how language is used to present the theme of grief and loss.

Support

Look at how the following student analyses the effect of the word 'wails' to present the theme of grief:

The mother is becoming increasingly panic stricken about the situation. The writer uses the verb 'wails' to emphasize this. This makes clear that her voice is high pitched and sounds desperate. It suggests an intense, prolonged sound that would be difficult to listen to as it is full of pain, worry and grief.

— The point is clearly made here

— The student accurately identifies the part of speech used

— A well selected supporting quotation is used

— More than just one point is made, analysing the effect of the word on the reader

— A link is made back to the focus of the question

3. Another theme presented in this text is the idea of 'family'. Discuss what the different family relationships shown suggest about this theme. Think about:

   - Frankie's relationship with his mother
   - his mother and father's relationship
   - his mother's relationship with Margaret.

leanv the Gaelic word
for baby

Extract from *Angela's Ashes* by Frank McCourt

Here, Frank McCourt describes an incident from his childhood where the family awoke to discover that something is wrong with Margaret, his young baby sister.

My mother's whisper wakes me. What's up with the child? It's still early and there isn't much morning in the room but you can see Dad over by the window with Margaret in his arms. He's rocking her and sighing, Och.

Mam says, Is she, is she sick?

Och, she's very quiet and she's a wee bit cold.

My mother is out of bed, taking the child. Go for the doctor. Go for God's sake, and my father is pulling on his trousers over his shirt, no jacket, shoes, no socks on this bitter day.

We wait in the room, the twins asleep at the bottom of the bed, Malachy stirring beside me. Frankie, I want a drink of water. Mam rocks in her bed with the baby in her arms. Oh, Margaret, Margaret, my own little love. Open your lovely blue eyes, my little **leanv**.

I fill a cup of water for Malachy and me and my mother wails, Water for you and your brother. Oh indeed, Water, is it? And nothing for your sister. Your poor little sister. Did you ask if she had a mouth in her head? Did you ask if she'd like a drop of water? Oh, no. Go on and drink your water, you and your brother, as if nothing happened. A regular day for the two of you, isn't it? And the twins sleeping away as if they didn't have a care and their poor little sister sick here in my arms. Sick in my arms. Oh, sweet Jesus in heaven.

Why is she talking like this? She's not talking like my mother today? I want my father. Where is my father?

I get back into bed and start to cry. Malachy says, Why you cry? Why you cry? till Mam is at me again. Your sister is sick in my arms and you're there whining and whinging. If I go over to that bed I'll give you something to whinge about.

Dad is back with the doctor. Dad has the whiskey smell. The doctor examines the baby, prods her, raises her eyelids, feels her neck, arms, legs. He straightens up and shakes his head. She's gone. Mam reaches for the baby, hugs her, turns to the wall. The doctor wants to know, Was there any kind of accident? Did anyone drop the baby? Did the boys play too hard with her? Anything?

My father shakes his head. Doctor says he'll have to take her to examine her and Dad signs the paper. My mother begs for another few minutes with the baby but the doctor says he doesn't have all day. When Dad reaches for Margaret my mother pulls away against the wall. She has the wild look, her black curly hair is damp on her forehead and there is sweat all over her face, her eyes are wide open and her face is shiny with tears, she keeps shaking her head and moaning, Ah, no, ah, no, till Dad eases the baby from her arms. The doctor wraps Margaret completely in a blanket and my mother cries, Oh, Jesus, you'll smother her.

Key terms

motif a distinctive theme in a literary work or piece of music

juxtaposition putting things side by side or close together

One of the things which makes reading fiction so interesting is how different writers will present similar themes in different ways. Source text I is the opening of short story by Victoria Hislop about a single mother taking her teenage son to the airport to begin his gap-year travels.

Activity 2

1. What impression do you get of Valerie in Source text I? Pick out three quotations from the extract and explain how they help to create this impression.

2. What is the writer's attitude to Valerie? Discuss how you think she wants the reader to feel towards the character.

3. What themes can you identify in this text? Justify your ideas with reference to the text.

4. Copy and complete a grid like the one below to identify the **motifs** used by the writer to suggest specific themes and explore their meanings. The first one has been done for you.

Motif	Theme	Meaning
Luggage tag	Growing up	The reference to the 'luggage tag' echoes the name tag given to newborn babies, and the way the mother fastens this with 'a double-knot' emphasizes her desire to hold on to her son as a child.

Stretch

Explain how the writer **juxtaposes** images of Valerie's son James as a boy and a man in the text and the effect this creates.

Tip

Rather than answering each bullet point in turn, you could combine your response to the bullet points. Remember to relate the comparisons you make to the statement presented and your response to this.

Activity 3

'Both Source texts H and I explore the theme of loss.'

How far do you agree with this statement?

In your answer you should:

- discuss your impressions of the situations depicted in each text
- explain the impact of each text on you as a reader
- compare the ways the writers present the theme of loss in both texts.

Support your response with quotations from both texts.

Extract from 'Red Pins on a Map' by Victoria Hislop

The opening of this short story describes a single mother called Valerie Smith taking her teenage son, James, to Heathrow Terminal 5 to begin his gap-year travels.

Heathrow Terminal 5. "Terminal" suggested an ending rather than a beginning, a place from which people left but never returned. This is how it seemed to Valerie Smith that morning. A venue for farewells.

In the centre of this vast and gleaming space, her teenaged son bent double beneath a rucksack, fiddled with his mobile phone. Valerie looked at her watch and then glanced up at the board. From counting the weeks, days and hours until her boy's departure, she realised that it was now only a matter of minutes away. She cast a brief glance at him and then stooped to pick something up from the polished floor. His luggage tag already lay at his feet and she re-attached it, fastening it with a double-knot.

"James Smith." His handwriting still seemed so childlike, the simple, rounded letters almost unchanged since primary school days. She fought back her tears, busying herself with one of the backpack's zips that gaped open to reveal the contents: T-shirts, socks and an impractical, near-empty tube of toothpaste.`

James was deep in conversation.

"Here? Where? Right. Right ... OK. Yep. Yep ..."

Valerie looked around at the other passengers in the terminal. Most people checking in were men with suits, some of them leaving small cases at the Bag Drop, but most of them breezing through with their executive brief cases.

They filed across the empty space like robots, calm, purposeful, focused, knowing to the last split second how many minutes they required for passport control, security and boarding.

Valerie knew that James's life in the next few months would be anything but micro-managed. This was his chance to amble freely round the world and visit places on a whim. Perhaps these self-assured men in suits had once travelled in jeans and a fleece, but she found it impossible to imagine James ever turning into one of them.

Oblivious to his mother's fiddling with tags and zips, James began to wander off. She saw where he was heading and then recognised a boy she had once met at school, another snail-like figure, carrying his worldly goods upon his back.

James reached out and took his friend's hand in a manly handshake.

Two adults stood behind the other boy. The woman was whimpering. In one hand she held what looked like a table tennis ball, but was actually a tightly screwed up handkerchief. A few feet away, a tall, greying man stood looking distractedly in the other direction, away from his son and away from his wife.

6 Figurative language

Learning objective

- To explore how figurative language is used to convey plot, setting and character

Writers can use figurative language, such as simile, metaphor and **personification**, to describe powerful moments or experiences. Read Source text J, taken from the opening of 'Superman and Paula Brown's New Snowsuit', a short story by Sylvia Plath.

Key terms

personification representing an idea in human form or a thing as having human characteristics

symbol a thing thought of as representing or standing for something else

context the circumstances or background in which something happens

foreshadow to be a sign of something that is likely to happen

Activity 1

1. What do you learn about the narrator from the opening paragraph?

2a. Identify three examples of figurative language from the second paragraph.

2b. Discuss the sentence lengths and structures in this paragraph and the effects these create.

2c. Explain how the writer's use of language and structure help to build a picture of the setting?

Stretch

Draw connections between the quotations you select to develop your explanation.

3. What impression do you get of the narrator from the way she describes her dreams? Identify examples of the figurative language she uses and explain the effects these create.

Stretch

Flying is a very significant **symbol** in this extract. What does it suggest about the narrator?

4. Summarize what you know about the **context** of this text.

5. Discuss your ideas about how you think the story might develop. Consider how the following quotation might **foreshadow** later events:

   'That was also the winter of Paula Brown's new snowsuit...'

Exam link

In Component 02: Exploring effects and impact, reading questions that ask about the writer's use of language and structure require you to analyse these features equally. You need to integrate relevant terminology into your answer in order to demonstrate your understanding of specific features of language and structure and the effects they create.

Extract 1 from 'Superman and Paula Brown's New Snowsuit' by Sylvia Plath

Set in the United States of America in 1941, this short story is narrated by an unnamed girl.

The year the war began I was in the fifth grade at the Annie F. Warren Grammar School in Winthrop, and that was the winter I won the prize for drawing the best Civil Defence signs. That was also the winter of Paula Brown's new snowsuit, and even now, thirteen years later, I can recall the changing colours of those days, clear and definite patterns seen through a kaleidoscope.

I lived on the bay side of town, on Johnson Avenue, opposite the Logan Airport, and before I went to bed each night, I used to kneel by the west window of my room and look over to the lights of Boston that blazed and blinked far off across the darkening water. The sunset flaunted its pink flag above the airport, and the sound of waves was lost in the perpetual droning of the planes. I marvelled at the moving beacons on the runway and watched, until it grew completely dark, the flashing red and green lights that rose and set in the sky like shooting stars. The airport was my Mecca, my Jerusalem. All night I dreamed of flying.

Those were the days of my technicolour dreams. Mother believed that I should have an enormous amount of sleep, and so I was never really tired when I went to bed. This was the best time of the day, when I could lie in the vague twilight, drifting off to sleep, making up dreams inside my head the way they should go. My flying dreams were believable as a landscape by **Dalí**, so real that I would awake with a sudden shock, a breathless sense of having tumbled like **Icarus** from the sky and caught myself on the soft bed just in time.

These nightly adventures in space began when Superman started invading my dreams and teaching me how to fly. He used to come roaring by in his shining blue suit with his cape whistling in the wind, looking remarkably like my Uncle Frank, who was living with Mother and me. In the magic whirring of his cape I could hear the wings of a hundred seagulls, the motors of a thousand planes.

Dalí a surrealist artist whose paintings mix dreams with reality

Icarus a figure from Greek myth whose wings melted when he flew too close to the sun

Now read Source text K, taken from the same story.

Activity 2

1. What does the figurative language in this extract reveal about the narrator? Copy and complete a table like the one below to analyse the effects of the examples identified.

Quotation	Language feature	Analysis of its effect
'the words came out like hard, dry little seeds'	Simile	This suggests that the narrator feels it is pointless even trying to claim her innocence. Her words will not be believed, just as 'hard, dry little seeds' will not bear fruit.
'the blood beat in my ears like a slack drum'		
'the black shadow creeping up the underside of the world like a flood tide'		
'The silver airplanes and the blue capes all dissolved and vanished'		
'the colossal blackboard of the dark'		

Key term

contrasts
a difference clearly seen when things are compared or seen together

Activity 3

How does the writer use language and structure to show how the narrator's attitude changes between Source texts J and K? Think about:

- the use of **contrasts** such as light and dark
- the narrator's relationship with her uncle
- the ending of the story and how this relates to the opening.

Stretch

Identify any connections between the two extracts and explain what these reveal about the theme of the story.

Extract 2 from 'Superman and Paula Brown's New Snowsuit' by Sylvia Plath

Here, the narrator has been blamed for pushing over another girl, Paula Brown, and ruining her new snowsuit, even though she did not do it.

All at once the doorbell rang, and Mother went to answer it. I could hear David Sterling's high, clear voice in the hall. There was a cold draught from the open doorway, but he and Mother kept on talking, and he did not come in. When Mother came back to the table, her face was sad, 'Why didn't you tell me?' she said, 'why didn't you tell me that you pushed Paula in the mud and spoiled her new snowsuit?'

A mouthful of chocolate pudding blocked my throat, thick and bitter. I had to wash it down with milk. Finally, I said, 'I didn't do it.'

But the words came out like hard, dry little seeds, hollow and insincere. I tried again. 'I didn't do it. Jimmy Lane did it.'

'Of course, we'll believe you, ' Mother said slowly, 'but the whole neighbourhood is talking about you. Mrs Sterling heard the story from Mrs Fein and sent David over to say we should buy Paula a new snowsuit. I can't understand it.'

'I didn't do it,' I repeated, and the blood beat in my ears like a slack drum. I pushed my chair away from the table, not looking at Uncle Frank or Mother sitting there, solemn and sorrowful in the candlelight.

The staircase to the second floor was dark, but I went down to the long hall to my room without turning on the light switch and shut the door. A small unripe moon was shafting squares of greenish light along the floor and the window-panes were fringed with frost.

I threw myself fiercely down on my bed and lay there, dry-eyed and burning. After a while I heard Uncle Frank coming up the stairs and knocking on my door. When I didn't answer, he walked in and sat down on my bed. I could see his strong shoulders bulk against the moonlight, but in the shadows his face was featureless.

'Tell me, Honey,' he said very softly, 'tell me. You don't have to be afraid. We'll understand. Only tell me how it really happened.'

'I told you,' I said. 'I told you what happened, and I can't make it any different. Not even for you I can't make it any different.'

He sighed then and got up to go away. 'OK, Honey,' he said at the door. 'OK, but we'll pay for another snowsuit anyway just to make everybody happy, and ten years from now no one will ever know the difference.'

The door shut behind him and I could hear his footsteps growing fainter as he walked off down the hall. I lay there alone in bed, feeling the black shadow creeping up the underside of the world like a flood tide. Nothing held, nothing was left. The silver airplanes and the blue capes all dissolved and vanished, wiped away like the crude drawings of a child in coloured chalk from the colossal blackboard of the dark. That was the year the war began, and the real world, and the difference.

Assessment

In this section you will have the chance to apply what you have learned in this chapter about reading for meaning and effects as well as writing imaginatively and creatively as you complete the reading and writing activities. The activities are organized by assessment objective, so think carefully about the specific skills required by each assessment objective and demonstrate these skills in your response to the activities.

Reading

Read Source text L and then complete the activities below. The extract is taken from Roddy Doyle's novel *The Woman Who Walked Into Doors*.

Exam link

In Section A of Component 02: Exploring effects and impact, you will have one hour to read two unseen prose texts and answer questions about the texts. One text may be literary non-fiction.

A01

- Identify and interpret explicit and implicit information and ideas

Activity 1

1. Write down three pieces of explicit and implicit information about Paula from the extract and select a supporting quotation to back up each point.

2. Paula says, 'I wanted the power.' What do you think she means by this?

3. What would you say is the theme of this extract? Choose a supporting quotation which you think best supports this.

A02

- Explain, comment on and analyse how writers use language and structure to achieve effects and influence readers, using relevant subject terminology to support your views

Activity 2

1. Look closely at the language Paula uses. What does it suggest about her?

2. Paula's experience is revealed as a memory, in the form of a dialogue. What is the advantage to the writer of structuring the extract in this way?

3. Look closely at the nature of the conversation between Paula and the boy. What does the sentence length and use of repetition imply about them both?

Source text L

Extract from *The Woman Who Walked into Doors* by Roddy Doyle

Here, the narrator, Paula, a middle-aged woman, reflects on how she got her first boyfriend.

Dee was my best friend. She was going to be my messenger. I could trust her and I'd done it for her, gone up to one of her fellas and told him that she wanted to go with him. We were sitting on the back step of our house, just me and Dee. I was nervous. I might have made the wrong choice; I'd see it in Dee's face.

– Yeah, she said. – He's nice.

God, I was happy sitting there. It must have been a sunny day. It couldn't have been cold.

– I'd love to go with him, I said.

– Yeah, she said.

She didn't mean that she wanted to go with him too; she was being nice.

– Will yeh tell him for me? I asked.

– Okay, she said.

I waited at the corner. She went up and told him. She came back.

– He says yeah.

I waited for him. Dee went up to the shops to wait for me. He came over to me.

– Will you go with me?

– Yeah.

– Thanks.

Isn't that lovely? He said Thanks. I remember it. And that was it. I was going with him.

I went after Dee.

– What did he say?

– He said yeah.

– That's brilliant.

I went with him for eleven days, then I broke it off. We never kissed but that was alright; I was happy with that. We only met twice, but that was alright too. The thing was to be going with a fella, not to be with him all the time. You could go with a fella and not ever see him at all, it didn't matter. If you were going with him you were going with him. I broke it off because I wanted to. I just wanted to. I wanted to be able to say it. I wanted the word to go around; she broke it off with him. I wanted the power.

– Why are you breaking it off with him?

– I just am, right.

You had to get a friend to let the fella know that you wanted to go with him but you had to break it off yourself.

– I don't want to go with you anymore; okay?

– Okay.

– We can still be friends.

– Okay.

– Seeyeh.

– Seeyeh.

It was easy.

I never spoke to him again. I had a little cry to myself that night but I really felt great. I could take a few risks now. It didn't matter as much if a fella said no; I'd already had one and blown him out, a nice one too. I could get a few notches on my belt.

Now read Source text M, taken from Nick Hornby's novel *High Fidelity*, and then complete the activities below.

A02

- Explain, comment on and analyse how writers use language and structure to achieve effects and influence readers, using relevant subject terminology to support their views.

Activity 3

How does the writer use language and structure to make this extract entertaining for the reader? You should use relevant subject terminology to support your answer.

A03

- Compare writers' ideas and perspectives, as well as how these are conveyed, across two or more texts.

A04

- Evaluate texts critically and support this with appropriate textual references

Activity 4

'Both Source texts L and M present dating as an exciting and confusing experience for young people.'

How far do you agree with this statement?

In your answer you should:

- discuss your impressions of the narrators' experiences of dating
- explain what you find entertaining or unusual about their experiences
- compare the ways the writers present the narrators' experiences.

Support your response with quotations from both texts.

Extract from *High Fidelity* by Nick Hornby

Here, the narrator reflects on his growing awareness of girls and his first kiss when he was twelve.

We had no irony when it came to girls, though. There was just no time to develop it. One moment they weren't there, not in any form that interested us, anyway, and the next you couldn't miss them; they were everywhere, all over the place. One moment you wanted to clonk them on the head for being your sister, or someone else's sister, and the next you wanted to ... actually, we didn't know what we wanted next, but it was something, something. Almost overnight, all these sisters (there was no other kind of girl, not yet) had become interesting, disturbing even.

See, what did we have that was any different from what we had before? Squeaky voices, but a squeaky voice doesn't do much for you, really – it makes you preposterous, not desirable. And the sprouting pubic hairs were our secret, strictly between us and our Y-fronts, and it would be years before a member of the opposite sex could verify that they were where they should be. Girls, on the other hand, quite clearly had breasts, and, to accompany them, a new way of walking: arms folded over the chest, a posture which simultaneously disguised and drew attention to what has just happened. And then there was make-up and perfume, invariably cheap, and inexpertly, sometimes even comically, applied, but still a quite terrifying sign that things had progressed without us, beyond us, behind our backs.

I started going out with one of them ... no, that's not right, because I had absolutely no input into the decision-making process. And I can't say that she started going out with me, either: it's that phrase 'going out with' that's the problem, because it suggests some sort of **parity** and equality. What happened was that David Ashworth's sister Alison peeled off from the female pack that gathered every night by the bench and adopted me, tucked me under her arm and led me away from the swingboat.

I can't remember how she did this. I don't think I was even aware of it at the time, because halfway through our first kiss, my first kiss, I can recall feeling utterly bewildered, totally unable to explain how Alison Ashworth and I had become so intimate. I wasn't even sure how I'd ended up on her side of the park away from her brother and Mark Godfrey and the rest, nor how we had separated from her crowd, nor why she tipped her face towards me so that I knew I was supposed to put my mouth on hers. The whole episode defies any **rational** explanation. But all of these things happened again, most of them the following evening, and the evening after that.

parity fairness

rational something logical and sensible

Writing

Exam link

In Section B of Component 02: Exploring effects and impact, you will have one hour to complete a creative writing task, selecting from a choice of two. You will be assessed on the quality of your extended response.

AO5

- Communicate clearly, effectively and imaginatively, selecting and adapting tone, style and register for different forms, purposes and audiences

- Organize information and ideas, using structural and grammatical features to support coherence and cohesion of texts

AO6

- Use a range of vocabulary and sentence structures for clarity, purpose and effect, with accurate spelling and punctuation

Exam link

In Component 01 and Component 02 of your GCSE English Language exams, the writing tasks will not include any pictures or images. However when developing your writing skills it can be helpful to look at pictures to inspire your writing, for example, when exploring imagery you could use in a story or piece of personal writing.

Activity 5

SPAG

Look at the photographs on the facing page. Choose one of these as the inspiration for a short story or a piece of personal writing about a meeting with a long-lost relative. This could be a real event or you could base your writing on one of the following ideas:

- meeting a grandparent who lives far away from you
- the return of a brother or sister who had run away from home
- your own idea.

In your writing, you should:

- create and maintain a consistent narrative point of view
- make thoughtful choices of vocabulary and grammar to create deliberate effects
- include a range of linguistic devices which will add impact to your writing
- structure your writing carefully, using some of the grammatical features you have explored in this chapter.

4 NEW HORIZONS

'Fiction was invented the day Jonah arrived home and told his wife that he was three days late because he had been swallowed by a whale.'
Gabriel Garcia Marquez, writer

'When you're writing a book, it's rather like going on a very long walk, across valleys and mountains and things.'
Roald Dahl, writer

'The land of literature is a fairy land to those who view it at a distance, but, like all other landscapes, the charm fades on a nearer approach, and the thorns and briars become visible.'
Washington Irving, writer

Introduction

It is human nature to be curious and to want to travel to new places, meet new people and have new experiences. Some people love the excitement of new horizons, whilst others find leaving people and places behind difficult and even painful. Most of us have mixed feelings about venturing out into the wider world but very few of us expect to stay in one place forever.

In this chapter you will read a range of prose fiction and literary non-fiction texts in which writers aim to convey the emotions and experiences of travel and visiting different places. You will explore how writers use language and structure to create meaning and impact in their writing. You will use the knowledge and skills you gain from your reading to develop your own creative writing skills, producing imaginative and original texts in a range of forms.

Exam link

The activities in this chapter are designed to help you develop the skills needed for success in Component 02: Exploring effects and impact. The first section of this exam requires you to read two different extracts for meaning and effects and answer questions about both extracts. The second section asks you to write imaginatively to produce a piece of original creative writing.

Activity 1

1. Discuss different reasons people might have for travelling or moving to new places. In your discussion, consider:

   • which of these reasons are about choice and which are about necessity

   • why people choose to stay in one place and the factors that enable them to do so

   • which of these situations you can relate to.

2. You have been asked to take part in a school assembly on the theme of 'home' for Year 7 students. Plan and prepare a five-minute presentation in which you:

   • explain how you came to live where you do

   • describe any moves you and your family have made

   • describe a move you might like to make in the future.

Arrivals and departures

Arriving in new places and leaving familiar places behind can stir strong emotions.

Learning objectives

- To draw inferences from textual details
- To justify your interpretations with carefully selected evidence

Key terms

inference something that you infer; a conclusion reached by reasoning

dialogue the words spoken by characters in a play, film or story

Tip

Use some of the following terms to help you to talk and write about the interpretations you make of different details from the text:

'this could mean...'

'this suggests...'

'this indicates...'

'seems as if...'

'hints at...'

'insinuates...'

1 Inference and interpretation

Authors often use the expression 'show, don't tell'. This means not telling readers information directly, but allowing them to interpret details from the text to draw their own conclusions, for example, using the skills of **inference** to draw conclusions about a character from their **dialogue** and the way this is presented.

Read Source text A from E. M. Forster's novel *A Room With A View* and then complete the activities below.

Activity 1

1a. Copy and complete the table below to explore what Forster implies about the different characters. Think about the details you identify and how these can be interpreted. The first one is done for you.

Character	Textual detail	Inference
Miss Bartlett	'She assumed a dazed expression when he spoke to her'	She does not approve of the older man and is trying to dissuade him from talking to her.
The older man		
Lucy		
George		

1b. Compare the inferences you have made about the different characters with those made by other students. Discuss any differences in the ways you have interpreted details from the text.

2. Look at the following statements and decide whether you agree or disagree with them, selecting evidence to support your decision:

- Miss Bartlett is an easy-going and relaxed tourist.
- The older man is kind and considerate.
- Lucy likes to assert herself.
- George is self-assured.

3. Which characters do you think the author wants the reader to like more? Select evidence from the text to support your inference.

Extract from *A Room With A View* by E. M. Forster

In the following extract, set at the turn of the 20th century, Lucy and her chaperone Miss Bartlett have just arrived in Italy to find that they have not been allocated rooms with a view at the small hotel they have booked. They are deeply disappointed about this and begin to argue about who should have the first room with a view which might become available.

pension a small hotel

got into the swim got into the flow of things

repressed prevented the expression of ideas or feelings

Some of their neighbours interchanged glances, and one of them—one of the ill-bred people whom one does meet abroad—leant forward over the table and actually intruded into their argument. He said:

"I have a view, I have a view."

Miss Bartlett was startled. Generally at a **pension** people looked them over for a day or two before speaking, and often did not find out that they would "do" till they had gone. She knew that the intruder was ill-bred, even before she glanced at him. He was an old man, of heavy build, with a fair, shaven face and large eyes. There was something childish in those eyes, though it was not the childishness of senility. What exactly it was Miss Bartlett did not stop to consider, for her glance passed on to his clothes. These did not attract her. He was probably trying to become acquainted with them before they **got into the swim**. So she assumed a dazed expression when he spoke to her, and then said: "A view? Oh, a view! How delightful a view is!"

"This is my son," said the old man; "his name's George. He has a view too."

"Ah," said Miss Bartlett, repressing Lucy, who was about to speak.

"What I mean," he continued, "is that you can have our rooms, and we'll have yours. We'll change."

The better class of tourist was shocked at this, and sympathized with the newcomers. Miss Bartlett, in reply, opened her mouth as little as possible, and said "Thank you very much indeed; that is out of the question."

"Why?" said the old man, with both fists on the table.

"Because it is quite out of the question, thank you."

"You see, we don't like to take—" began Lucy. Her cousin again **repressed** her.

"But why?" he persisted. "Women like looking at a view; men don't." And he thumped with his fists like a naughty child, and turned to his son, saying, "George, persuade them!"

"It's so obvious they should have the rooms," said the son. "There's nothing else to say."

2 Viewpoint and voice

Learning objective

- To understand how writers create a narrative voice

Key terms

viewpoint an opinion or point of view

first-person narration when the story is told from the point of view of the narrator - 'I' / 'We'

narrative voice the personality or character of the narrator as it is revealed through dialogue or descriptive and narrative commentary

interior monologue a piece of writing that represents the thoughts of a character

colloquial language informal language used in everyday situations

Writers of fiction have to choose a narrative point of view to convey the plot of their story. Sometimes writers create a narrator who tells the story from the **viewpoint** of their character. This is known as **first-person narration**. In a first-person narrative a writer has to:

- create a convincing **narrative voice** for their narrator
- maintain the narrator's voice to convey the whole story from one perspective.

Read Source text B from the novel *How I Live Now* by Meg Rosoff and then complete the activities below.

Activity 1

1a. Note down your immediate reactions to the character of Daisy. Use adjectives as precisely as you can to describe what you think she is like.

1b. Compare your reactions to Daisy with others. How do they differ? Which details from the text led to your feelings and reactions?

Interior monologue is a technique used by writers to share a narrator's thoughts with the reader. Rosoff aims to give Daisy a distinctive narrative voice by carefully choosing the vocabulary and grammar used to present her thoughts.

Activity 2

1. Identify examples of **colloquial language**. How might these make readers feel about Daisy?

2. The word 'and' is used repeatedly to join lots of clauses together. Discuss which of the following interpretations for this you agree with and explain why:

   - It suggests Daisy is unsettled.
   - It reflects Daisy's train of thought.
   - It implies a very chatty personality.
   - It conveys a childlike quality.

3. Rosoff uses capital letters in phrases such as 'Big Fat Zero' and 'Being Nice to Daisy'. What effect does this create?

4a. In Source text B, Rosoff doesn't follow the usual rules of speech punctuation. Explain how this helps readers to feel as though they are experiencing Daisy's own thoughts.

4b. Rewrite part of the extract, punctuating the dialogue according to the usual rules.

Source text B

Extract from *How I Live Now* by Meg Rosoff

Fifteen-year-old Daisy has been sent by her father from her home in the United States to live with her cousins in England for the summer.

According to my best friend Leah, **D. the D.** would have liked to poison me slowly till I turned black and swelled up like a pig and died in agony but I guess that plan flopped when I refused to eat anything and in the end she got me sent off to live with a bunch of cousins I'd never met a few thousand miles away while she and Dad and the **devil's spawn** went on their merry way. If she was making even the slightest attempt to address centuries of bad press for stepmothers, she scored a Big Fat Zero.

Before I could work myself up into a full-blown attack of hyperventilating, I heard a tiny noise at the door and there was Piper again, looking in, and when she saw I was awake she gave a little happy squeak like a mouse-cheer and asked Did I want a cup of tea?

OK, I said, and then Thank you, remembering to be polite, and I smiled at her because I still liked her from yesterday. And off she drifted just like the fog on little cat feet.

I went to the window again and looked out and saw the mist had cleared and everything was so green and then I put some clothes on and managed to find the kitchen after discovering some pretty amazing rooms by mistake, and Isaac and Edmond were there eating marmalade on toast and Piper was making my tea and seeming worried that I'd had to get out of bed to get it. In New York, nine-year-olds usually don't do this kind of thing, but wait for some grown-up to do it for them, so I was impressed by her **intrepid** attitude but also kind of wondering if good old Aunt Penn had died and no one could figure out a good way to tell me.

Mum was working all night, said Edmond, so she's gone to bed but she'll be up for lunch and then you'll see her.

Well that answered that, thank you Edmond.

While I drank my tea I could see Piper squirming around wanting to tell me something and she kept looking at Edmond and Isaac who just looked back and at last she said Please come to the barn Daisy. And the Please was more like a command than a request, and then she gave her brothers a look like I couldn't help it! And when I got up to go with her she did the nicest thing, which was to hold my hand and it made me want to hug her, especially since Being Nice to Daisy hadn't been anyone's favourite hobby lately.

Glossary

D. the D. Daisy's name for her stepmother, short for Davina the Diabolical

devil's spawn Daisy's name for her father and stepmother's baby

intrepid fearless

3 Imagery and setting

Learning objectives

- To understand how writers create a narrative voice

Key terms

setting the way or place in which something is set

atmosphere a feeling or tone conveyed by something

imagery the use of figurative or other special language to convey an idea to readers or hearers

simile where one thing is compared to another thing, using a connective word such as 'like' or 'as'

metaphor the use of a word or phrase in a special meaning that provides an image

personification representing an idea in human form or a thing as having human characteristics

As readers, we can be encouraged, through a range of literary techniques, to feel as if we are seeing and experiencing a journey along with the narrator. One technique commonly used to convey **setting** and **atmosphere** is **imagery**. Imagery can include **similes**, **metaphors** and **personification**, which bring texts to life by helping readers to picture the scene.

Read Source text C from Joseph Conrad's novel *Heart of Darkness*, and then complete the activities below.

Activity 1

1. Select three of the following quotations used to describe the setting. Identify the form of imagery used and explain the effects created by each quotation.
   - 'vegetation rioted'
   - 'the big trees were kings'
   - 'silvery sandbanks'
   - 'a mob of wooded islands'
   - 'like a sluggish beetle'
   - 'the heart of darkness'
   - 'the curtain of trees'

   #### Support

   Look at the example below to help you to structure your explanation:

   The writer describes the steamboat as 'hugging the bank' which makes it sound like it is clinging to the land. The use of personification, 'hugging', suggests the boat can't bear to be separated from the safety of the shoreline.

2. Identify another example of imagery that you think is effective in helping to create a sense of the setting. Explain the effect it creates and why you think this is effective.

Source text C

Extract from *Heart of Darkness* by Joseph Conrad

In the following extract, Joseph Conrad describes one man's journey into the Congo in Africa at the turn of the 20th century. At the time, this part of Africa was still relatively unexplored and Conrad aims to convey the kind of unnerving effect arriving in such a strange place could have on someone.

Going up that river was like traveling back to the earliest beginnings of the world, when vegetation rioted on the earth and the big trees were kings. An empty stream, a great silence, an **impenetrable** forest. The air was warm, thick, heavy, sluggish. There was no joy in the brilliance of sunshine. The long stretches of the waterway ran on, deserted, into the gloom of overshadowed distances. On silvery sandbanks hippos and alligators sunned themselves side by side. The broadening waters flowed through a mob of wooded islands; you lost your way on that river as you would in a desert, and butted all day long against **shoals**, trying to find the channel, till you thought yourself bewitched and cut off for ever from everything you had known once—somewhere—far away—in another existence perhaps. There were moments when one's past came back to one, as it will sometimes when you have not a moment to spare to yourself; but it came in the shape of an unrestful and noisy dream, remembered with wonder amongst the overwhelming realities of this strange world of plants, and water, and silence. And this stillness of life did not in the least resemble a peace. It was the stillness of an **implacable** force brooding over an **inscrutable** intention. It looked at you with a **vengeful** aspect...

...Trees, trees, millions of trees, massive, immense, running up high; and at their foot, hugging the bank against the stream, crept the little begrimed steamboat, like a sluggish beetle crawling on the floor of a lofty **portico**. It made you feel very small, very lost, and yet it was not altogether depressing, that feeling... We penetrated deeper and deeper into the heart of darkness. It was very quiet there. At night sometimes the roll of drums behind the curtain of trees would run up the river and remain sustained faintly, as if hovering in the air high over our heads, till the first break of day. Whether it meant war, peace, or prayer we could not tell. The dawns were heralded by the descent of a chill stillness; the woodcutters slept, their fires burned low; the snapping of a twig would make you start. We were wanderers on a prehistoric earth, on an earth that wore the aspect of an unknown planet.

Glossary

impenetrable impossible to access

shoals shallows or sandbanks

implacable impossible to appease

inscrutable hard to understand

vengeful wanting revenge

portico porch or covered walkway

111

Key terms

sibilance a literary device where strongly stressed consonants create a hissing sound

repetition repeating, or being repeated

Atmosphere can also be conveyed though a writer's choice of vocabulary and sentence structures.

Activity 2

1a. Look at the following vocabulary from the first paragraph of Source text C:

empty   deserted   bewitched   brooding

1b. Discuss what atmosphere these words help to create.

1c. Find two other words which help to create a similar atmosphere. Explain the ideas, feelings or sensations associated with each word.

2a. Look at the following example of **sibilance** from the extract: 'On silvery sandbanks hippos and alligators sunned themselves side by side.'

2b. Discuss which of the following analyses of the effect this creates you agree with:

- The 's' sound is repeated to create a sinister hissing effect.

- The 's' sound is repeated to slow the reader and evoke a sense of relaxation at this point.

- The **repetition** of the 's' sound draws our attention to the dangers lurking in the jungle.

2c. Write a sentence explaining how the use of this technique adds to the mood of the text.

3. Look at the sentence structures used in the second paragraph. Discuss how these help to create a sense of the setting and atmosphere.

Activity 3

Write your own description of a threatening or unfamiliar place. Think about how you can use vocabulary, imagery and sentence structures to create a strong atmosphere.

Now read Source text D from *The Worst Journey in the World*, a memoir by the explorer Apsley Cherry-Garrard who travelled with Sir Robert Falcon Scott to the Antarctic in the early 20th century.

Source text D

Extract from *The Worst Journey in the World* by Apsley Cherry-Garrard

Here, he describes Midwinter Night and the Northern Lights at Cape Evans in the Antarctic.

A hard night: clear, with a blue sky so deep that it looks black: the stars are steel points: the glaciers burnished silver. The snow rings and thuds to your footfall. The ice is cracking to the falling temperature and the **tide crack** groans as the water rises. And over all, wave upon wave, fold upon fold, there hangs the curtain of the aurora. As you watch, it fades away, and then quite suddenly a great beam flashes up and rushes to the **zenith**, an arch of palest green and orange, a tail of flaming gold. Again it falls, fading away into great searchlight beams which rise behind the smoking crater of Mount Erebus.

Activity 4

1. How would you describe the atmosphere created in Source text D? Refer to details from the text that you think are particularly effective in helping to create this atmosphere.

2. What similarities can you find between the extracts from *Heart of Darkness* and *The Worst Journey in the World*? Think about:

   • the ideas and attitudes presented

   • the writers' use of language including imagery and the effects created

   • the writers' use of structure including repetition and the effects created.

3. Write a one-page essay comparing the ways in which Source texts C and D convey a sense of setting and atmosphere.

Support

Use the following model to help you to develop your analysis:

• Make a *point*.

• Select *evidence* to support this point.

• Use *terminology* to refer to specific techniques or features.

• Develop your *explanation* of the effects created.

• *Relate* your point back to the subject of the essay.

4 Structure and repetition

Learning objectives

- To explore how repetition can be used to emphasize ideas and convey emotions

Key terms

motif a distinctive theme in a literary work or piece of music

anaphora the use of a short word (e.g. a pronoun such as 'it' or a verb such as 'do') to refer back to a word or phrase used earlier

Glossary

cob natural building material made from clay, sand, straw and earth

Writers often use deliberate repetition to emphasize important ideas or convey particular emotions in a text. Repetition can take different forms including:

- repetition of a word, a phrase or even a full sentence
- repetition of an image or **motif**
- techniques such as **anaphora**.

Read Source text E, which is taken from *The Colour* by Rose Tremain, and then complete the activities below.

Source text E

Extract from *The Colour* by Rose Tremain

Harriet and her husband, Joseph, have emigrated from England to New Zealand in the 1860s. Here, Harriet is desperate to go with her husband when he leaves for the wilds where they plan to build a house and farm for themselves.

Harriet had asked her new husband to take her with him. She clung to him and pleaded – she who never whined or complained, who carried herself so well. But she was a woman who longed for the unfamiliar and the strange. As a child, she'd seen it waiting for her, in dreams or in the colossal darkness of the sky: some wild world which lay outside the realm of everything she knew. And the idea that she could build a house out of stones and earth and put windows and doors in it and a chimney and a roof to keep out the weather and then live in it thrilled her. She wanted to see it take shape like that, out of nothing. She wanted to learn how to mash mud and chop the yellow tussock to make the **cob**. She wanted to see her own hand in everything. No matter if it took a long time. No matter if her skin was burned in the summer heat. No matter if she had to learn each new task like a child. She had been a governess for twelve years. Now, she had travelled an ocean and stood in a new place, but she wanted to go still further, into a wilderness.

Activity 1

1. Identify three different examples of repetition in the text and decide which of these is anaphoric.

2. Explain how repetition is used to convey Harriet's emotions. Select examples and explain the effects these create.

Now read Source text F, which is taken from an essay entitled 'The Aspect of London', written by Arthur Symons and published in 1909. Here, the writer has used two specific forms of repetition – **diacope** and **polyptoton**.

Source text F

Extract from 'The Aspect of London' by Arthur Symons

English air, working upon London smoke, creates the real London. The real London is not a city of uniform brightness, like Paris, nor of savage gloom, like Prague; it is a picture continually changing, a continual sequence of pictures, and there is no knowing what mean street corner may not suddenly take on a glory not its own. The English mist is always at work like a subtle painter, and London is a vast canvas prepared for the mist to work on. The especial beauty of London is the Thames, and the Thames is so wonderful because the mist is always changing its shapes and colours, always making its lights mysterious, and building palaces of cloud out of mere Parliament Houses with their jags and turrets. When the mist collaborates with night and rain, the masterpiece is created.

Activity 2

1. Select quotations to identify examples of diacope and polyptoton from Source text F. For each example, explain why you think the writer has used this technique and what effect this creates.

2. Identify the **extended metaphor** used in Source text F. Discuss how effective you think this is in conveying the writer's feelings about London.

Activity 3

Describe a time when you really wanted to go somewhere or do something but obstacles got in the way or stopped you. Use different forms of repetition to convey your emotions and to help a reader **empathize** with your situation.

Key terms

diacope repetition of a word or phrase broken up by one or more intervening words

polyptoton repetition of words of the same root with different endings, for example, 'strong', 'strength, etc.

extended metaphor a metaphor which is continued through a series of lines or sentences in a text

empathizing to understand and share in someone else's feelings, to feel empathy

5 Emotive language

Learning objectives

- To analyse how writers use emotive language and contrasts to create specific effects

In fiction and other forms of narrative writing, writers often want to provoke a reaction from their readers and to make them *feel* something. To do this, they may use **emotive language**. Read Source text G from the novel *Brixton Beach* by Roma Tearne which is set in the late 1960s, and then complete the activities below.

Activity 1

1. What emotions do you feel after reading Source text G? Discuss your ideas.

2a. Copy and complete the table below to explore how vocabulary is used to evoke the sadness and the difficulty of Alice and Sita's departure.

	Verbs	Adverbs	Nouns	Adjectives
Sadness				haunting
Difficulty / discomfort	throbbed			
Danger		unsteadily		

2b. Discuss the words you have selected. Which do you think are particularly effective in evoking an emotional response?

3. Tearne uses elements of **contrast** within this extract. Identify two of the contrasts made and explain what impact they have.

Activity 2

Think of a place you know well which you would be sad never to see again. Imagine you had to leave this place behind you forever. Follow the steps below to create an imaginative piece of writing describing this.

Planning

Brainstorm your ideas about this place. Select phrases and sentences which are extremely positive about the place. Think about the contrasts you could make to highlight the strength of your feelings about the place.

Drafting

As you write, try to describe your thoughts and feelings in detail. Remember to use emotive language to add impact to your writing. Try to weave the positive statements about the place into your writing to contrast with the negative emotions you describe.

Reviewing

Re-read each sentence to check that it makes sense and is creating the effects you want to achieve.

Key terms

emotive language words and phrases used to arouse a reader's emotions

contrast a difference clearly seen when things are compared or seen together

Tip

Use words such as 'accentuate', 'highlight' and 'enhance' when talking or writing about the impact created by specific techniques or devices.

Extract from *Brixton Beach* by Roma Tearne

Alice Fonseka and her mother Sita are leaving their beloved family and home in Sri Lanka, which is on the brink of civil war, to seek a new life in England with Alice's father who has already emigrated there. At the time, many people who were citizens of the British Empire were emigrating in the hope of finding greater security in the UK.

And that too was it; once again the swiftness of departure was what they remembered. All around them people were crying. Sita watched impassively; she could not cry. Not even when they were on the launch, moving unsteadily across the bay, not even when May waved and called her name was she able to respond. The small motor boat took them out to the furthest tip of the sun-washed harbour, close to the breakwater. Then the boatman helped them, one by one, on to the narrow gangway. Children screamed as they stood up and the boat rocked madly. Before them, thin and insubstantial, was the rope ladder, each rung seeming higher than their legs could ever reach. Would it hold their weight? The sun beat relentlessly on Sita's back and her head throbbed as she followed Alice higher and higher up the gangway. Reaching, it seemed, for the sky.

'Hold tight, Alice', she said faintly. 'Hold tight.'

Everything happened too quickly. I wasn't ready to leave; there were things I forgot to say. And now, she thought, it will last forever. They reached the top of the gangway. Below was a mass of swaying, varied women, their oiled heads bent in concentration, their voices a sad chant of farewell. In front of them were the neat dark ankles, the bright patterned silk of an unknown sari, fluttering like a useless flag in the breeze. And far beneath them was the sea, turquoise and restless. There was no going back.

Hands reached out to help them up the last steep step and she saw humanity hanging out of every porthole, from every deck. Ribbons floated down into the sea, someone was flying a kite. The strange unfamiliar smell of diesel mixed with the salty air made Sita nauseous. From somewhere inside the ship they heard the faint strains of the national anthem, its sad sweet melody, haunting and full of all that they loved, all they were leaving. The music, heard only at state funerals and other such occasions, drenched them in sorrow.

Home and belonging

A recurring theme in literature is that of belonging to a particular place.

Learning objective

- To explore how writers use pathetic fallacy and other figurative language to create meaning

Key term

pathetic fallacy giving human feelings to inanimate things or animals

6 Pathetic fallacy

Writers can use landscapes and weather to reflect the way a character is feeling. When an element of nature is presented as being in harmony with a character's emotions, this is called **pathetic fallacy**. Pathetic fallacy uses personification to reflect or mirror a character's mood or situation as shown in the following example:

Cast out from society, she wandered across the lonely moor.

Here, the moor is personified but also reflects the loneliness the woman feels.

Read Source text H from the novel *Jamaica Inn* by Daphne Du Maurier, and then complete the activities below.

Activity 1

1. Describe Mary's mood in this extract. Support your description with textual details.

2. Identify three elements of the natural world which seem to reflect Mary's mood. Explain how they reflect her mood and what impact the use of pathetic fallacy has.

3. How does Du Maurier use the natural world to create contrast between the life Mary has left behind and the one she is travelling towards? Discuss why she might be doing this.

Activity 2

Describe a journey to a place using pathetic fallacy to reflect the character's mood. Follow the steps below to help you to plan, draft and review your writing.

Planning

Think about who your character is and where they are travelling to. Note down the different moods you might want to convey, and think about how you could use elements of the natural world to reflect these.

Drafting

As you write, think about how you can suggest that the weather and surroundings are in harmony with your character's emotions. Try to use other techniques such as personification to add impact to your writing.

Reviewing

Re-read each sentence to check that it makes sense and is creating the effects you want to achieve.

Extract from *Jamaica Inn* by Daphne Du Maurier

Here, Mary Yellan has left behind her beloved home and is travelling to Jamaica Inn, an isolated smugglers' haunt on Bodmin Moor owned by her uncle and aunt, where she plans to live.

Mary Yellan sat in the opposite corner, where the trickle of rain oozed through the crack in the roof. Sometimes a cold drip of moisture fell upon her shoulder, which she brushed away with impatient fingers.

She sat with her chin cupped in her hands, her eyes fixed on the window splashed with mud and rain, hoping with a sort of desperate interest that some ray of light would break the heavy blanket of sky, and but a momentary trace of that lost blue heaven that had **mantled** Helford yesterday shine for an instant as a forerunner of fortune.

Already, though barely forty miles by road from what had been her home for three-and-twenty years, the hope within her heart had tired, and that rather **gallant** courage which was so large a part of her, and had stood her in such stead during the long agony of her mother's illness and death, was now shaken by this first fall of rain and the nagging wind.

The country was alien to her, which was a defeat in itself. As she peered through the misty window of the coach she looked out upon a different world from the one she had known only a day's journey back. How remote now and hidden perhaps for ever were the shining waters of Helford, the green hills and the sloping valleys, the white cluster of cottages at the water's edge. It was a gentle rain that fell at Helford, a rain that pattered in the many trees and lost itself in the lush grass, formed into brooks and rivulets that emptied into the broad river, sank into the grateful soil which gave back flowers in payment.

This was a lashing, pitiless rain that stung the windows of the coach, and it soaked into a hard and **barren** soil. No trees here, save one or two that stretched bare branches to the four winds, bent and twisted from centuries of storm, and so blackened were they by time and tempest that, even if spring did breathe on such a place, no buds would dare to come to leaf for fear that the late frost should kill them. It was a scrubby land, without hedgerow or meadow; a country of stones, black heather, and stunted **broom**.

mantled cloaked

gallant brave, heroic

barren too poor to produce plants

broom a type of shrub

7 Analysing language

Learning objectives

- To analyse and compare writers' use of language to evoke sensory experiences

Key term

descriptive detail the inclusion of specific details to add to the vividness of the description

Writers can use language to evoke different sensory experiences and help readers to share these. Read Source text I from the novel *Chocolat* by Joanne Harris, and then complete the activities below.

SPAG

Activity 1

1. What does the imagery Harris uses in the opening paragraph suggest about the bakery? How does this help to show Vianne and Anouk's feelings about this place?

2. What do Vianne and Anouk do in the text? Identify the verbs Harris uses to convey their actions and effects of their actions. What do these verbs add to the atmosphere she creates?

3. Source text I contains images which use some unusual and powerful adjectives. Choose one which strikes you as particularly effective and explain why.

4a. Imagery is used in the extract to appeal to each of the five senses: taste, touch, smell, sound and sight. For each of the senses, identify a quotation that uses imagery and explain why you think it is effective.

4b. Which sense, in your opinion, is strongest in this piece of writing? Why do you think this is?

Activity 2

Write a description of a disused or abandoned building. Follow the steps below to help you to plan, draft and review your writing.

Planning

Think about the building you will describe. Note down any images you could use to convey its abandoned state.

Drafting

As you write, remember to include **descriptive details** that evoke different senses such as sight, hearing, smell and touch. Think about how your choice of verbs and adjectives can add to the atmosphere you wish to create.

Reviewing

Re-read each sentence to check that it makes sense and is creating the effects you want to achieve.

Extract from *Chocolat* by Joanne Harris

Here, Vianne and her daughter, Anouk, have just arrived in a tiny French village where they are moving into a disused bakery. Anouk has an imaginary companion, a rabbit called Pantoufle.

The smell is like daylight trapped for years until it has gone sour and rancid, of mouse-droppings and the ghosts of things unremembered and unmourned. It echoes like a cave, the small heat of our presence only serving to **accentuate** every shadow. Paint and sunlight and soapy water will rid us of the grime, but the sadness is another matter, the forlorn resonance of a house where no-one has laughed for years. Anouk's face looked pale and large-eyed in the candlelight, her hand tightening in mine.

"Do we have to sleep here?" she asked. "Pantoufle doesn't like it. He's afraid."

I smiled and kissed her solemn golden cheek. "Pantoufle is going to help us."

We lit a candle for every room, gold and red and white and orange. I prefer to make my own incense, but in a crisis the bought sticks are good enough for our purposes, lavender and cedar and lemongrass. We each held a candle, Anouk blowing her toy trumpet and I rattling a metal spoon in an old saucepan, and for ten minutes we stamped around every room, shouting and singing at the top of our voices – *Out! Out! Out!* – until the walls shook and the outraged ghosts fled, leaving in their wake a faint scent of scorching and a good deal of fallen plaster. Look behind the cracked and blackened paintwork, behind the sadness of things abandoned, and begin to see faint outlines, like the after-image of a sparkler held in the hand – here a wall adazzle with golden paint, there an armchair, a little shabby, but coloured a triumphant orange, the old awning suddenly glowing as half-hidden colours slide out from beneath the layers of grime. *Out! Out! Out!* Anouk and Pantoufle stamped and sang and the faint images seemed to grow brighter – a red stool beside the vinyl counter, a string of bells against the front door. Of course, I know it's only a game. Glamours to comfort a frightened child. There'll have to be work done, hard work, before any of this becomes real. And yet for the moment it is enough to know that the house welcomes us, as we welcome it. Rock salt and bread by the doorstep to **placate** any resident gods. Sandalwood on our pillow, to sweeten our dreams.

Later Anouk told me Pantoufle wasn't frightened any more, so that was all right. We slept together in our clothes on the floury mattress in the bedroom with all the candles burning, and when we awoke it was morning.

accentuate emphasize

placate make someone less angry

Sometimes a particular memory can be evoked suddenly by one of our senses. Our sense of smell is particularly powerful at doing this because it is created by a part of our brain closely associated with memory and feeling. Read Source text J where the journalist Ziauddin Sardar describes walking through an area of Birmingham known as the 'Balti Triangle', and then complete the activities below.

Activity 3

SPAG

1. Which smells does Sardar describe particularly positively? What places and people does he associate with each of these?

2. Identify the vocabulary used to convey smell in Source text J and place these words on a scale from most positive to most negative.

3. Rewrite the description of one of the smells Sardar describes to give the opposite effect, for example, something he describes positively becomes negative and vice versa.

Support

You could draw on some of the following vocabulary in your description:

sickly	nauseating	pervasive	unbearable
appetizing	enticing	seductive	energizing

4. Identify two adjectives Sardar uses to reflect how the ingredients make him feel and explain what they suggest about his feelings.

Stretch

Sardar describes the area he is walking through as an 'olfactory playground'. Explain why you think he has chosen this metaphor.

5. Think about the similarities and differences between Source text I from *Chocolat* on page 121 and Source text J from *Balti Britain* on page 123. What techniques do both writers use to evoke a sensory experience?

Activity 4

1. Think about a food which always generates a reaction in you by its smell. Without naming the food, talk about this smell to a partner and see if they can guess what it is from the adjectives you use.

2. Write a description of this food and its aroma. In your description, think carefully about the following:

   • Vocabulary choices – aim to be specific in the words that you use to identify and describe things.

   • Imagery – include some unexpected comparisons.

   • Sentence structure – vary the length and structure of your sentences and include some well-constructed relative clauses.

Source text J

Extract from *Balti Britain* by Ziauddin Sardar

I tried to distinguish the different fragrances, to savour the associations stirred by each particular spice, vegetable or **sweetmeat** I could isolate as I wandered through this **olfactory** playground. There was the invigorating smell of fresh coriander, which is guaranteed to drive me wild. Then I detected the warm musky scent of turmeric, which always evokes deep memories of my childhood in Pakistan. The aromas of cardamom, clove, nutmeg and camphor wafted by – these I always sense collectively because they are the ingredients of *paan*, the kingly assemblage of **condiments** that comes wrapped in **betel** leaf. *Paan* is usually taken after a meal to stimulate saliva and gastric flow; it is also an **auspicious** symbol of hospitality and nourishment. Often it is **proffered** as a moral commitment to bring people closer together, to bind friendships, to demonstrate family bonds. It always reminds me of my infant days with my grandfather. Then, my eyes became moist: the strong, hot and strangely sweet smell of *hari mirch*, the slim, long green chilli, which my mother used to cook as a vegetable and affects not just the nose but the eyes. It never fails to rekindle the bitter-sweet memories of my youthful days in East London. Finally, my mouth began to water. First I picked out the whiff of *biryani*, the standard fare of all Asian weddings. It reminds me of my own wedding and summons images of all future weddings, those of my nephews and nieces, my daughter and sons. Next, I feel – yes, *feel* – the unmistakable bitter stink of bitter gourd (surely the ugliest vegetable in the world), which invokes a whole range of complex emotions, of racism and multi-culturalism, loss and exile, home and belonging. Underneath it all, the rich, sweet, delicious aroma of *barfi*, the fudge sweet made from milk, which I always associate with my crazy, madcap uncle, Waheed.

Glossary

sweetmeat food rich in sugar

olfactory relating to the sense of smell

condiments seasoning or relish for food

betel an Asian climbing plant

auspicious favourable

proffer to offer as a gift

123

8 Structure and symbolism

Learning objectives

- To explore how writers use symbolism to create specific effects

- To analyse how writers use structure to achieve effects and influence readers

Symbolism is the use of an object, image, place or idea to represent or suggest something else. It is not a comparison like a metaphor. An object described in a text may become a symbol when it seems to represent something about a character's thoughts and feelings. For example, if a character is feeling restless, the writer might describe a clock ticking in the background. Symbols rely on association and we have thousands of such associations to draw on, meaning that our interpretations of texts are all the richer and more varied.

Read Source text K from Maggie O'Farrell's novel *Instructions for a Heatwave*. Here, Aoife (pronounced Ee-fa) is returning to her childhood home in London after three years of living away from her family. Before she left, a rift had developed between her and her sister and she chose to leave suddenly and cut all contact with them.

Activity 1

1. How does Aoife feel about returning home to Gillerton Road? Support your response with words or phrases which you think convey her feelings most clearly.

2. What one word would you use to describe Gillerton Road as it is presented in the text?

3. Re-read Source text K, and then copy and complete the table below to explore the symbols included in the text. Aim to develop your own interpretations of the symbols.

Symbol	Idea, feeling or experience it represents or suggests	Explanation of why you think this
Train		
Earring		
Baby		
Tricycle		
Wall		

Stretch

Source text K starts with a fox running away and disappearing. How might the fox symbolize aspects of Aoife's behaviour?

Extract from *Instructions for a Heatwave* by Maggie O'Farrell

A fox skitters out from behind a parked van, pauses in the middle of Gillerton Road, then disappears over a garden wall with a circular flourish of tail. An early tube train shudders beneath the paving stones, the reverberation is felt in the houses' brickwork, their window frames, the floorboards and plasterwork. A **percussive**, trembling hum travels along the street, passing from one end of the terrace to the other. But the houses are used to it and so are the occupants. Tumblers judder together on kitchen shelves, a carriage clock on a mantelpiece in number four makes a half-strike, an earring left on a bedside table across the street rolls to the floor. Further down the row a woman turns over in bed; a baby wakes and finds itself inside the ribcage bars of its cot and wonders, what is this, and, where is everyone, and calls out for someone to come, now, please.

Aoife Riordan, walking down the middle of the road, hears the child's cry. It makes her turn her head. Her gaze passes over the shut curtains, the limp-blossomed hydrangea bush in the front garden, the tricycle abandoned halfway up the path, but she doesn't see these things, doesn't register their existence. She is barely even aware of the child still crying, or what made her look that way.

It is the most **disconcerting** sensation for Aoife, walking down this road. She is at once conscious of its utter familiarity – the way the sight of her own hand, the boned row of knuckles, the flat fingernails, are familiar – and its disquieting strangeness. It has the upsetting **surreality** of a dream, this walk down Gillerton Road at six a.m. in the middle of summer. What is she doing here? How did she come, in the space of a night, from the apartment in New York, where she and Gabe had been together for the first time in weeks, to this – a road she has walked down a thousand thousand times, to and from school, back from the corner shop carrying her mother's cigarettes and a pound of flour, from those awful dance lessons, from her chess club after school, from the tube station? She feels light-headed and small waves of nausea keep breaking over her. She has thought, in the last three years, that she might never come back, might never walk down Gillerton Road again. And yet here she is. Here is the row of trees, roots nurturing the paving slabs. Here are the tiled front paths. Here is the triangular-capped concrete wall that runs along the fronts of five houses. She knows without putting her hand on it the exact rasping, grainy texture of the concrete, how it would feel to try to sit on its **unyielding**, unfriendly ridge, the way the inevitable slide off it would catch and mark the fabric of your **serge** school skirt. The adult Aoife suddenly sees that its shape is specifically designed to stop people – children – sitting on it and she is filled with disgust for the people in these houses who would put up such a wall. What kind of human being denies a rest to a child coming home from school?

Aoife gives the wall a kick.

percussive drum-like

disconcerting unsettling

surreality disorientating strangeness

unyielding unwilling to give

serge hardwearing fabric

125

The structural features of a text can be used to create different effects, for example, to contribute significantly to the sense of place a writer is trying to create.

Activity 2 SPAG

Read the following sentence and then look at the different interpretations of its structure.

> 'We wandered through the narrow, cobbled streets, feeling a little lost but nevertheless content in this labyrinth that formed a city – a city where we felt as if we could stay forever and never tire of its magical ways and fascinating architecture.'

- The writer's use of a long, complex sentence almost makes us feel that we are wandering along with the narrator.

- The long, complex sentence seems to reflect the long, complicated 'labyrinth' of streets.

- This long, complex sentence reflects the narrator's feelings about staying forever in this place.

Which interpretation do you agree with? Discuss your ideas.

Activity 3 SPAG

How does Maggie O'Farrell use structure to convey a sense of character and place? Identify the different structural features she uses and explore the effects these create. You should think about:

- sentence types
- sentence structures
- repetition
- punctuation.

Support

Discuss and develop the following student's comment:

With her inclusion of rhetorical questions such as 'What is she doing here?', Maggie O'Farrell creates a sense of Aoife's uncertainty...

Activity 4

Write a journal entry in which you describe the last part of your journey home from school. Follow the steps below to help you plan, draft and review your writing.

Planning

Think about the last part of your journey. Make notes about the places you pass and the things you see. You might be able to use online map tools such as Google Streetview to help you to visualize your journey.

Drafting

Think about how you can convey your feelings about this journey to the reader. You could:

- include references to one or two small details which are symbolic of some larger feeling or idea

- think about how you can use structural features to convey a sense of your journey.

Reviewing

Re-read each sentence to check that it makes sense and is creating the effects you want to achieve.

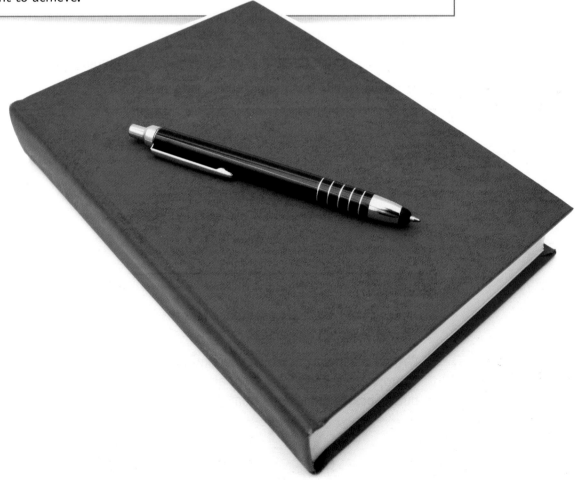

Assessment

Reading

In this section you will have the chance to apply what you have learned in this chapter about reading for meaning and effects and writing imaginatively and creatively as you complete the reading and writing activities. The activities are organized by assessment objective, so think carefully about the specific skills required by each assessment objective and demonstrate these skills in your response to the activities.

Read Source text L from *I'm the King of the Castle* by Susan Hill, and then complete the activities below.

Exam link

In Section A of Component 02: Exploring effects and impact, you will have one hour to read two unseen prose texts and answer questions about the texts. One text may be literary non-fiction.

A01

- Identify and interpret explicit and implicit information and ideas

Activity 1

1. What can you infer about the man who had this house built?

2. Why is the place important to Joseph Hooper? Explain what the following quotations suggest about his personality:
   - 'he had come to admire its solidity and the gloom'
   - 'have it lend both importance and support'

A02

- Explain, comment on and analyse how writers use language and structure to achieve effects and influence readers, using relevant subject terminology to support your views

Activity 2

1. How do the contrasting sentence lengths in the last paragraph help to convey Hooper's character?

2. Write a paragraph in which you explain why this house seems like an appropriate setting for a story about a teenaged boy who becomes a bully. Include quotations from the text to support your ideas.

Extract from *I'm the King of the Castle* by Susan Hill

Here, Susan Hill describes the house where her bullying protagonist Edmund lives with his father, Joseph Hooper.

Warings was ugly. It was entirely graceless, rather tall and badly angled, built of dark red brick. At the front, and on both sides, there was the lawn, sloping downwards to a gravelled drive, and then into the lane, and without any tree or flower-bed to relieve the bald greenness. Up the drive, and at the back of the house, bunched between the yew trees, were the great bushes of rhododendron.

The yew trees had stood here before the house, Warings, had been built around them, for the first Joseph Hooper had admired their solidity and denseness, the fact that they grew so slowly and were the longest lived of all trees. He had planted the rhododendrons too, not at all for their brief, dramatic show of colour in May and June, but for their dark green, leathery leaves and toughness of stem, their substantial look. He liked their gathered shapes, seen from the end of the drive.

Inside the house, everything was predictable, the high-ceilinged rooms, with heavy, sashed windows, the oak wall panelling and the oak doors, and the oak staircase, the massive furniture. Little had been changed since the beginning.

Joseph Hooper had spent that part of his childhood before school, and between terms, in this house, and he did not like it, he had unhappy memories of Warings. Yet now, at the age of fifty one, he admitted that he was a Hooper, his father's son, and so he had come to admire the solidity and the gloom. He thought, it is a prepossessing house.

For he knew himself to be an ineffectual man, without any strength or imposing qualities, a man who was liked and humoured but little regarded, a man who had failed – but not dramatically, as one falling from a great height, who attracts attention. He was a dull man, a man who got by. He thought, I know myself and am depressed by what I know. But now, with his father gone, he could stand before this house, and have it lend him both importance and support, he could speak of "Warings – my place in the country", and it would make up for a good deal.

Now read Source text M, taken from the novel *On the Black Hill* by Bruce Chatwin, and then complete the activities below.

AO1

- Identify and interpret explicit and implicit information and ideas

---

Activity 3

1. Identify three pieces of explicit information that are given about the farm.

2. What impressions of the farm does the reader get from this description?

AO2

- Explain, comment on and analyse how writers use language and structure to achieve effects and influence readers, using relevant subject terminology to support your views

---

Activity 4

1. Identify three examples of imagery and explain how these help to convey a sense of atmosphere.

2. Present your interpretation of what the 'old rag doll' and 'beehives' symbolize.

AO4

- Evaluate texts critically and support this with appropriate textual references

---

Activity 5

1. Explain how the writer presents a sense of place. You should comment on:
   - the language used to convey an impression of the farm
   - how the structure helps to develop this
   - the impact of the text on the reader.

   Refer to evidence from the text to support your analysis, using relevant subject terminology.

Extract from *On the Black Hill* by Bruce Chatwin

This novel is set at the start of the 20th century. Here, Amos and Mary, who plan to marry, go to view a derelict farm which they might rent. Mary has just returned from living in India.

The tenant had died in 1896, leaving an old unmarried sister who had carried on alone until they fetched her to a madhouse. In the yard, a young ash-tree reared its trunk through the boards of a hay-waggon. The roofs of the buildings were yellow with stonecrop; and the dungheap was overgrown with grass. At the end of the garden stood a brick-built privy. Amos slashed down the nettles to clear a path to the porch.

A broken hinge prevented the door from opening properly and, as he lifted it, a gust of fetid air flew in their faces.

They went into the kitchen and saw a bundle of the old woman's possessions, rotting away in a corner. The plaster was flaking and the flagstones had grown a film of slime. Twigs from a jackdaw's nest up the chimney were choking the grate. The table was still laid, with two places, for tea; but the cups were covered with spiders' webs, and the cloth was in shreds.

Amos took a napkin and flicked away the mouse-droppings.

'And rats!' said Mary cheerfully, as they heard the scuttle of feet in the rafters. 'But I'm used to rats. In India you have to get used to rats.'

In one of the bedrooms she found an old rag doll and handed it to him, laughing. He made a move to chuck it from the window; but she stayed his hand and said, 'No, I shall keep it.'

They went outside to inspect the buildings and the orchard. There'd be a good crop of damsons, he said, but the apple trees would have to be replanted. Peering through the brambles, she saw a row of mouldering beehives.

'And I,' she said, 'shall learn the secrets of the bee.'

He helped her over a stile and they walked uphill across two fields overgrown with gorse and blackthorn. The sun had dropped behind the escarpment, and swirls of coppery cloud were trailing over the rim. The thorns bit her ankles and tiny beads of blood burst through the white of her stockings. She said, 'I can manage,' when he offered to carry her.

The moon was up by the time they came back to the horses. The moonlight caught the curve of her neck, and a nightingale flung liquid notes into the darkness. He slipped an arm around her waist and said, 'Could you live in this?'

'I could,' she said, turning to face him, as he knotted his hands in the small of her back.

AO3

- Compare writers' ideas and perspectives, as well as how these are conveyed, across two texts

---

Activity 6

Compare the ways in which Source texts L and M use settings as a way of conveying characters' personalities and attitudes. In your answer you should comment on:

- similarities and differences between the settings described
- the techniques used by the writers to convey atmosphere.

Writing

AO5

- Communicate clearly, effectively and imaginatively, selecting and adapting tone, style and register for different forms, purposes and audiences
- Organize information and ideas, using structural and grammatical features to support coherence and cohesion of texts

AO6

- Use a range of vocabulary and sentence structures for clarity, purpose and effect, with accurate spelling and punctuation

Activity 7

Write a story or a description written from a particular viewpoint with the title 'The Joke Shop'. Look at the suggestions below or use your own idea.

Story ideas

A prank bought from The Joke Shop that goes wrong.

A mystery that begins or ends in The Joke Shop.

Description ideas

A successful magician, reminiscing about a childhood visit to The Joke Shop.

The shop owner who is about to go out of business, describing how changing times have affected the shop.

In your writing, aim to:

- engage your reader by establishing and maintaining a convincing voice
- convey a strong sense of setting and atmosphere
- use language and structure, including some of the techniques you have explored in this chapter, to create specific effects.

Exam link

In Section B of Component 02: Exploring effects and impact, you will have one hour to complete a creative writing task, selecting this from a choice of two. You will be assessed on the quality of your extended response.

5 WAR AND CONFLICT

'War is what happens when language fails.'

Margaret Atwood, writer

'They wrote in the old days that it is sweet and fitting to die for one's country. But in modern war, there is nothing sweet nor fitting in your dying. You will die like a dog for no good reason.'

Ernest Hemingway, writer

'War was always here. Before man was, war waited for him. The ultimate trade, awaiting its ultimate practitioner.'

Cormac McCarthy, writer

'War does not determine who is right – only who is left.'

Bertrand Russell, philosopher

Introduction

War and conflict is a constant feature of today's news. Whether online, on TV or in the newspapers, there are constant reminders that in certain situations the human race has not been able to find a way to settle its differences by any means other than by going to war. As people naturally write about their experiences, it is of no surprise that war, such a life-changing experience, features so often in all forms of writing, from fiction to non-fiction.

Exam link

The activities in this chapter are designed to help you develop the skills needed for success in the two exam papers you will sit at the end of your course: Component 01: Communicating information and ideas and Component 02: Exploring effects and impact, where you will have to demonstrate the ability to evaluate and compare unseen texts.

Activity 1

1. Write down as many words as you can in one minute which you associate with 'war'. Compare your list with a partner. How many words did you both write down? How many words are different?

2. Read and discuss the quotations on the facing page. Explain what you think the meaning of each quotation is. Which do you agree with most, and why?

3. Choose a quotation and make a list of arguments for or against it. Present your ideas in a speech to your class.

Memories and reflections

Many people turn to writing as a way of coping with the powerful experiences they go through during war.

Learning objectives

- To identify and interpret key ideas in order to develop an overview of a text

- To select textual examples that are apt, convincing and persuasive

Key term

dialogue the words spoken by characters in a play, film, or story

narrator the person or character who recounts the events of a story

Tip

The right quotation will illustrate and reinforce the point you are making and also provide a springboard for other skills, like analysing language choices.

1 Developing a critical overview

As a critical reader, you need to be able to develop an overview of the texts you encounter. This is the ability to stand back from a text, discuss it clearly, and neatly summarize how it works, demonstrating your appreciation that it is something that has been very deliberately constructed. You need to be able to support your critical evaluation of a text with evidence. This may be in the form of a reference to a specific aspect of the text to successfully demonstrate your understanding, or it may mean the careful selection of quotations to support and strengthen your ideas.

Read Source text A, which is taken from a memoir written by John Cook, and then complete the activities below.

Activity 1

1. Summarize why John Cook decides to join the army.

2. How does the information you are told about the mother affect your response to her? Use supporting quotations to back up your interpretation.

3. How does the writer use language to emphasize the effect of the mother's death on:

   - the father   • the son?

4. Discuss how the form of Source text A and the inclusion of **dialogue** influence the reader's response to this family and how they are portrayed?

Activity 2

1a. Below, a student begins to evaluate Source text A. Read it carefully and identify the things it does which make it successful.

   The extract contextualizes the reasons for the man joining up. The memoir's first-person narration is effective as it brings the reader close to the narrator and his family which makes it easier to feel sympathy for them. Although his loss is tragic, the passage of time means that the narrator reflects on those tragic events in a clear, detailed and informative way.

1b. Select two quotations to support the points made in the paragraph above. Compare these with a partner. If you have different ones, debate which one you think works best and why.

Activity 3

'This text successfully creates sympathy for the **narrator** and his family.'

How far do you agree with this statement? In your evaluation you should discuss how sympathy is created and explain the impact of this on you as a reader.

Extract from *Joining Up* by John Cook

Here, John Cook describes why he decided to fight in the Second World War.

My mother, Lily Rose Cook, to do an old friend (crippled and unable to do housework) a favour, would visit her every Thursday and help out for three hours. She would return by dinner time, 1pm, when my father and I would also be home. But this particular week for some reason the day had been changed to a Wednesday. So my mother was in someone else's house and my father at work in a big chemical factory – less than a quarter of a mile from each other.

It was the chemical plant the German bombers were after and they hit it while my father was inside. The factory was next to some allotments, separated from them by a high wall.

As the string of bombs dropped the first one fell on the house next to the one where my mother was. That house was completely destroyed and along with it half the house adjoining. My mother was killed instantly. She was 42. The second bomb fell in the allotments within feet of my father, but the separating wall withstood the blast and he was uninjured except for shock.

I arrived home first for dinner just after 1pm, as did father, and the first obvious question was, 'Where's Mother?'

We waited a few minutes, then my father said, 'You lay the table and I'll go and see if Mum's on the way.'

He returned about half an hour later. At first he was evasive, telling me that Mum was seriously injured and in hospital, but I could tell by the expression on his face that he was not telling the truth and finally forced him to admit that she had been killed. As he slumped into a chair he added, almost as an afterthought, that he had no wish to live any longer.

He had his wish fulfilled a few months later when he died on 14th July 1941 of shock and a broken heart.

From the moment my mother was killed my sole aim was to avenge her death and I vowed I would join the services. So on May 3rd 1942 I went to the recruiting office at Romford, Essex. My 17th birthday had fallen on the day before and I knew you had to be 18 to join the Royal Marines.

'Birth Certificate,' the sergeant said, holding out his hand.

'Sorry, sergeant,' I replied. 'Lost in the bombing.'

He looked at me consideringly for a moment, then nodded and I was in. I still have my service documents and they show my date of birth as 1924 instead of 1925.

2 Purpose and form

Learning objective

- To evaluate and compare how texts achieve their purpose

Every writer who puts pen to paper does so with a specific **purpose** in mind. This could be to persuade, advise, instruct, describe or inform. It is important that you can identify what a writer wants to achieve and evaluate how effectively they do this. You should consider the ways in which writers use language, form and structure to achieve their purpose.

Source text B is from a 19th-century English newspaper article about a famous attack by British forces on Russians during the Crimean War.

Key terms

purpose something that you intend to do or achieve, and intended result

bias an opinion or feeling that strongly favours one side in preference to another

propaganda biased or misleading publicity that is intended to promote a political point of view

Activity 1

1. What information is included about the British and Russian armies? How does it influence your attitude to both?

2a. How does the article in Source text B include the typical features of a newspaper article?

2b. In what ways is this article not like a typical newspaper article? Discuss your ideas.

2c. Who is the audience for this newspaper article? How might this influence the purpose?

3. The writer says the British forces had 'a halo of flashing steel above their heads'. Why does he say this?

4. Look carefully at the language used to describe both the British and Russian forces. Select three quotations which indicate **bias** and suggest that the purpose of the article is **propaganda**.

Glossary

luster a brilliant brightness

Source text B

Extract from *The Times* newspaper, dated 14 November, 1854

If the exhibition of the most brilliant valor, of the excess of courage, and of a daring which would have reflected **luster** on the best days of chivalry can afford full consolation for the disaster of today, we can have no reason to regret the melancholy loss which we sustained in a contest with a savage and barbarian enemy.

I shall proceed to describe, to the best of my power, what occurred under my own eyes...

At 11:00 our Light Cavalry Brigade rushed to the front...

They swept proudly past, glittering in the morning sun in all the pride and splendor of war. We could hardly believe the evidence of our senses. Surely that handful of men were not going to charge an army in position?

Source text B (continued)

They advanced in two lines, quickening the pace as they closed towards the enemy. A more fearful spectacle was never witnessed than by those who, without the power to aid, beheld their heroic countrymen rushing to the arms of sudden death. At the distance of 1200 yards the whole line of the enemy belched forth, from thirty iron mouths, a flood of smoke and flame through which hissed the deadly balls. Their flight was marked by instant gaps in our ranks, the dead men and horses, by steeds flying wounded or riderless across the plain. The first line was broken – it was joined by the second, they never halted or checked their speed an instant.

With diminished ranks, thinned by those thirty guns, which the Russians had laid with the most deadly accuracy, with a halo of flashing steel above their heads, and with a cheer which was many a noble fellow's death cry, they flew into the smoke of the batteries; but **ere** they were lost from view, the plain was strewed with their bodies and with the carcasses of horses. They were exposed to an **oblique** fire from the **batteries** on the hills on both sides, as well as to a direct fire of musketry.

Through the clouds of smoke we could see their sabers flashing as they rode up to the guns and dashed between them, cutting down the gunners as they stood... To our delight, we saw them returning, after breaking through a column of Russian infantry and scattering them like chaff, when the flank fire of the battery on the hill swept them down, scattered and broken as they were. Wounded men and dismounted troopers flying towards us told the sad tale – **demigods** could not have done what they had failed to do. At the very moment when they were about to retreat, a regiment of lancers was hurled upon their flank. Colonel Shewell, of the 8th Hussars, saw the danger and rode his men straight at them, cutting his way through with fearful loss. The other regiments turned and engaged in a desperate encounter. With courage too great almost for **credence**, they were breaking their way through the columns which enveloped them, where there took place an act of atrocity without parallel in modern warfare of civilized nations. The Russian gunners, when the storm of cavalry passed, returned to their guns. They saw their own cavalry mingled with the troopers who had just ridden over them, and to the eternal disgrace of the Russian name, the miscreants poured a murderous volley of grape and canister on the mass of struggling men and horses, mingling friend and foe in one common ruin...

At 11:35 not a British soldier, except the dead and dying, was left in front of those bloody Muscovite guns...

Glossary

ere before

oblique at an angle

batteries a group of artillery guns fired together

demigods divine or supernatural beings

credence belief

Now read Source text C where a soldier reflects on his experience during the infamous Battle of Passchendale in the First World War.

Tip

Use phrases like, 'This suggests...', 'This conveys...', 'This implies' and 'This emphasizes...' to move into deeper analysis of the quotations you select to support your points.

Activity 2

1a. The writer says 'The whole place exuded evil'. Choose a supporting quotation from the first paragraph which you think best supports this point and analyse why you think it is effective.

1b. Choose and analyse another quotation, from elsewhere in Source text C, which you think works well in conveying this idea.

The two texts you have read can be compared in terms of their purpose and form. For example, one similarity is that they both describe war from first-hand experience. An obvious difference, however, is that one of the narrators is an active participant in the war while the other is a reporter merely observing it.

Activity 3

Identify other similarities and differences between Source texts B and C and explain how effectively each text achieves its purpose.

SPAG

Activity 4

Write an article for your school magazine in which you persuade readers that war is either a good or a bad thing. Follow the steps below to help you to plan and draft your article.

Planning

Think about how you can select and organize the information and ideas you present in a logical and coherent way to influence your reader. You could use the following structure:

• An interesting, short opening paragraph making clear your point of view.

• First main argument and supporting ideas and information.

• Second argument and supporting ideas and information.

• Third argument and supporting ideas and information.

• A short but powerful conclusion.

Drafting

As you write, remember to consider who you are writing for and how this will affect the language you use. Use connectives such as 'firstly', 'moreover', and 'in addition' to introduce your arguments and rhetorical devices to persuade your readers to support your point of view.

Extract from *A Period on the Passchendale Ridge* by Don J. Price

The earth had been churned into a sea of mud and water beneath the constant shelling and shell-holes, large and small, had totally obliterated what had once been rich vegetation. All that remained of the magnificent trees was the occasional stump, the majority of which leaned drunkenly this way and that. **Very lights** floating down along the ridge turned them into weird and awesome shapes. The whole place exuded evil.

We were being shelled continually and our casualties were mounting. Cries for stretcher-bearers were heard repeatedly, though the chances of rescue were dim.

We continued to make our way up, though our progress was slow and deliberate over the duckboards laid across the broken land. Heavily laden with thick overcoats, equipment, rifles, ammunition and rations as we were, falling off the duckboards could prove fatal. We were wet through and cold, and the shelling did not help, but eventually we arrived at our destination.

There was no trench. The line consisted of a series of shell-holes joined together and mostly half full of water. Two of us were allocated one which was reasonably dry. This was to be our 'home' for the next two days and nights. It was deep enough for us to dig a sleeping hole in the side – assuming we ever reached a stage of resting, which was rare indeed.

Covered in lice, big fat rats were our constant companions, nosing and squeaking about and finding more than they could ever need to eat. The smell of rotting flesh and mustard gas was nauseating, though oddly one grew used to it. The bloated bodies of mules and horses littered the landscape, along with various items of equipment and dud unexploded shells. Hereabouts, the Germans were no more than 200 yards away, but as their conditions were no doubt the same as ours they kept very quiet, even moderating their shelling.

Glossary

very lights lights created by a flare gun

3 Comparing texts

Learning objective

- To understand how to structure a comparison of two texts

When you compare texts as a reader, you need to be able to identify similarities and differences and evaluate how these create an impact on the reader. In particular, you should consider how different writers present attitudes and ideas and also how they use form, grammatical features and language to successfully convey these.

Read Source text D, which is taken from a soldier's letter home sent during the First World War, and then complete the activities on the facing page.

Glossary

kismet fate

Hun the name given to German soldiers by British troops

kultur German civilization (sometimes used in a derogatory way)

oracles those who make wise, important announcements

omen a sign that something good or evil is coming

Haig the commander in chief of British troops in France from 1915–1918

Source text D

Extract from a letter from Captain McKerrow, sent 19 July, 1916

We have now been under shell-fire (not, fortunately, continuous) for a fortnight and are becoming hardened. As a battalion we have had amazing luck. Two or three officers wounded, and, so far, none killed. We have not yet, however, had to make an unsuccessful attack, which is where the losses occur. The other Battalions in our Brigade have lost much more heavily. Twice we were to have stormed strong points, and both times the battalion ahead of us was cut up, and we had to dig in and wait. No doubt, our turn will come.

This will not affect me except that I shall lose some friends, and be very busy. Where I am, and where we are likely to be, the cover is not at all bad, and I do not neglect it. I have a strong feeling of **Kismet**, but nevertheless, do not go out trying to be hit. The weather is perfect, and all our aeroplanes are up, nosing round to see what they can discover. Between you and me, the **Hun** is having a rotten time. We fairly smother him with shells. In spite of that, he puts up a plucky fight though his methods are abominable. Of them I shall talk later. Never ask me to know or write to or think of anyone who is German, in the future. They are – one and all – the most vile, loathsome, crawling reptiles that **kultur** could produce. As a matter of fact, they are all brains and very little soul. They talk much of the latter and of their various virtues. They have only one virtue and that is courage. After all, the stoat and the rat are about the bravest of animals.

I have an idea that we are going into rest very soon now. The **oracles** suggest it. How long a rest, no one knows. The last rest was 3 days, and we were shelled constantly. The Hun resistance is undoubtedly nothing to what it was, and in this one sees a happy **omen**. Many consider the War nearly won. Certainly, this offensive of ours, though slow, is very complete, and must be worrying the Hun quite a lot. **Haig** seems to have found a way to deal with him.

Activity 1

1. Summarize how the writer feels about the following things, selecting a supporting quotation to back up each of your points:

   - his own situation

   - the Germans

   - the war.

2. Write a paragraph evaluating how the writer's language reinforces his attitude towards the Germans. Remember to include the supporting quotations you have selected.

3. How is the form of Source text D related to the writer's attitudes and ideas? Discuss your ideas.

4. How does the content of the text impact on the reader and their attitude to the writer?

Now read Source text E on page 144, which is taken from the author J. G. Ballard's memoir *Memories of Life*.

Activity 2

1. These texts clearly show the writers' opinions of the enemy in wartime.'

   How far do you agree with this statement?

   First, identify as many similarities and differences as you can between Source texts D and E. You should compare:

   - the two writers' attitudes towards the situations they find themselves in and the people that surround them

   - the way both extracts have been written, for example, the form chosen and the type of narrator employed

   - the writers' use of language and how this reflects their backgrounds and views

   - the **tone** created through the language used in both extracts.

   ### Support

   Tone refers to the way a writer expresses their attitudes and feelings and it affects how the reader responds. It can be, for example, angry, sad, joyful or excited. Unlike spoken language, a writer can only rely on the words they use and how they organize them to create a tone.

2. Discuss the impact of each extract on you as a reader. Think about:

   - how the type of narrator influences your reaction

   - what impact the information presented and language used has on you as a reader.

Key term

tone a manner of expression in speaking or writing

Glossary

parlance speech

caricature a picture or description which exaggerates a person's features

feral wild like an animal

kendo a Japanese form of fencing

Source text E

Extract from *Miracles of Life* by J. G. Ballard

The writer reflects on a time during his childhood, when his family was imprisoned in an internment camp in Shanghai during the Second World War.

I thrived in Lunghua, and made the most of my years there, in the school report **parlance** of my childhood. My impression is that, during my first year of internment, life in the camp was tolerable for my parents and most of the other adults. There were very few rows between the internees, despite the cramped space, malaria mosquitoes and meagre rations. Children went regularly to school, and there were packed programmes of sporting and social events, language classes and lectures. All this may have been a necessary illusion, but for a while it worked, and sustained everyone's morale.

Hopes were still high that the war would soon be over, and by the end of 1943 the eventual defeat of Germany seemed almost certain. The commandant, Hyashi, was a civilised man who did his best to meet the internees' demands. Almost a **caricature** short-sighted Japanese with a toothbrush moustache, spectacles and slightly popping eyes, he would cycle around Lunghua on a tandem bicycle with his small son, also in glasses, sitting on the rear saddle. He would smile at the noisy British children, a **feral** tribe if there was one, and struck up close relationships with members of the camp committee. Among the documents Mrs Braidwood sent me was a letter which Mr Hyashi wrote to her husband some time after he had been dismissed as commandant, in which he describes (in English) his horse rides around Shanghai and sends his warm regards. After the war my father flew down to the war-crimes trials in Hong Kong and testified as a witness for Hyashi, who was later acquitted and released.

I also made friendships of a kind with several of the young Japanese guards. When they were off duty I would visit them in staff bungalows fifty yards from G Block, and they would allow me to sit in their hot tubs and then wear their **kendo** armour. After handing me a duelling sword, a fearsome weapon of long wooden segments loosely strung together, they would encourage me to fence with them. Each bout would last twenty seconds and involved me being repeatedly struck about the helmet and face mask, which I could scarcely see through, every dizzying blow being greeted with friendly cheers from the watching Japanese. They too were bored, only a few years older than me, and had little hope of seeing their families again soon, if ever.

Now read the two student responses below. The first evaluates a similarity and the second evaluates a difference between Source texts D and E. Note how both responses are structured in the same way with:

- an opening topic sentence
- discussion of the first extract
- inclusion of a connective of **contrast** or similarity
- discussion of the second extract.

Student response A

Both texts express the writers' opinions of the enemy in wartime situations through first-person narrators, an approach which brings them close to the reader. The letter home during WWI makes clear the soldier's very negative attitudes, towards not just the German soldiers on the frontline but a hatred of all Germans. Similarly, Ballard expresses his, albeit more positive attitudes, towards the Japanese soldiers who guarded him and his family during his childhood in his autobiography.

Student response B

A major difference is how the form contributes to the content and impact of the extracts. The first text is a letter home from the front to family. Letters are private between the sender and receiver and are not intended for public reading as they can contain deeply personal opinions and very strongly expressed views. For this reason, the solider expresses his contempt for the German race in a way he may not have done if he knew it was to have a wider readership. Alternatively, Miracles of Life is an autobiography, which was written to be published so Ballard's ideas and opinions are much more measured and expressed more carefully.

Activity 3

Use this structure to write your own two paragraphs comparing the two texts. The first should evaluate another similarity and the second should evaluate another difference.

Tip

Make clear you are analysing comparisons by using connectives such as 'alternatively', 'in contrast', 'however', 'on the other hand' and 'on the contrary'.

When analysing similarities, use connectives such as 'similarly', 'likewise', 'in the same way', 'comparably', 'equally' to make clear what you are doing.

Key term

contrast a difference clearly seen when things are compared or seen together

4 Layers of meaning

Learning objectives

- To analyse the effects and connotations of specific words
- To understand the layers of meaning in a text

Key term

connotation something implied or suggested in addition to the main meaning

To begin to evaluate a writer's vocabulary you need to consider the **connotations** that the words they choose have. Read Source text F, which is taken from *The Reluctant Tommy*, a memoir by Ronald Skirth who served as a soldier during the First World War.

Activity 1

1. The writer uses the word 'resting' in the first paragraph of Source text F. List the connotations this word has.

2. Look at the connotations the following student has identified. How successfully do you think they have analysed this word?

   The writer describes the German soldier using the verb 'resting'. This is a word with mostly positive connotations. It suggests a pause or break from a tiring activity. At this stage the reader naturally assumes he is 'resting' from the fatigue and exhaustion of battle. It can also imply sleeping and a degree of comfort not associated with the First World War. These positive suggestions are reversed however when the writer reveals that the soldier is actually dead. This revelation gives the word 'resting' a completely new meaning, in the religious sense that he has now met his final 'resting' place.

3. Select three more words and write a paragraph analysing the effect of each word on the reader. Remember to focus on the most relevant connotations in your analysis.

To develop your analysis you need to look beyond the obvious to explore deeper meanings. For example, one longer quotation from Source text F states:

'He had been my enemy, perhaps, but he wasn't now.'

On a surface level, this means that as the German soldier is dead, he can no longer be his enemy. However, this quotation also suggests the following deeper meanings:

- The writer is so disgusted by the horror of war that he no longer hates anyone.

- He now sees beyond the uniform to the human being beneath it.

- This revelation fills him with pity and compassion.

Activity 2

1a. Select three longer quotations which you think suggest deeper meanings.

1b. Write down a surface level reading for each quotation. Then analyse each quotation to explore the deeper meaning suggested.

Source text F

Extract from *The Reluctant Tommy* by Ronald Skirth

Here, the author describes the aftermath of a battle.

What I saw might have been a life-size wax model of a German soldier. He was in a posture I can only describe as half-sitting and half-reclining. Resting his body on the edge of a smaller shell hole he had leaned back against a mound of thrown-up earth. But for his complete **immobility** you would have thought he had assumed that position quite deliberately and, overcome by tiredness, had fallen asleep. Everything about his posture looked perfectly natural and normal, – except that there was a something you don't see, you feel. An **aura** of death.

There was no bloodstain, no bruise visible either on his person or uniform. Leaning back, his helmet had been tilted upwards revealing his face. It was the deathly **pallor** of that face which shocked me beyond my powers of description. Part of a lock of blonde hair was resting on his forehead above the two closed eyes. I thought Germans wore their hair closely cropped, – but not this one. There was the suggestion of a smile on the pale lips, – a smile of contentment.

I fought down my initial revulsion and went closer still. This figure was my enemy. He had been my enemy, perhaps, but he wasn't now. For this man I should feel hatred, not compassion.

This man! He was, or had been, no man. He was a boy who, but for the colour of his hair and uniform, must have looked very like me. I was nineteen, he probably younger still. What could he possibly have done to deserve this?

Whatever killed him, it couldn't have been one of our mines, – otherwise his body would have been inflated till it had burst open to look like those … those other things. No, he must have died of shell shock.

One hand still held the open wallet he had been looking at before death struck. There were two **mica** windows with photographs behind them. One must have been of his parents. The other had '**Mein Hans**' written diagonally across one of the lower corners. It was the picture of a young girl who could have been Ella's twin sister.

I was sick with shame and pity. That was the sight at which but for the first aid treatment I'd given myself, I would have fainted.

Glossary

immobility stillness, unable to move

aura a distinctive atmosphere that surrounds a person

pallor an unhealthy, pale appearance

mica a thin sheet of see-through plastic, like those found in wallets to protect a picture

Mein Hans the German for 'My Hans'

The heat of battle

Writing about the chaos and horror of battle is one way writers try to make sense of it.

Learning objective

- To analyse the impact and effects of structural features

Key term

ellipsis a series of dots used to show the omission of a word or words from speech and writing, usually leaving the meaning still clear

5 Evaluating structure

When critically evaluating a text, you need to be able to analyse the impact that its structure has on the reader. This might include looking at:

- the form of the text you are reading
- how the writer organizes the length of their paragraphs and their sentences
- how the writer uses specific types of punctuation to create deliberate effects.

Read Source text G from the memoir *Some Of It Was Fun* by Hugh Falkus, and then complete the activities below.

Activity 1

1. The shortest paragraph in Source text G is the first one. Discuss why you think this is.
2. Why do you think the writer has chosen to write the first paragraph as a single sentence even though it describes the pilot doing three things?
3. Re-read the second paragraph. Why do you think the first five sentences of this paragraph are written as short sentences? What effect does this create?
4. The final paragraph begins, 'Then I saw a lone bomber'. What impact does this have on you as a reader?

Activity 2

Copy and complete the table below to identify and analyse the effects of the punctuation used in the extract. The first one is done for you.

Punctuation and its effect	Supporting quotation	Further exploration
Use of **ellipsis** to create dramatic tension by forcing the reader to pause	'I fired at the first head-on… and it blew up.'	The ellipsis causes the reader to pause and wonder if the pilot's firing was successful. It engages the reader by making them question the outcome which is then revealed.
Use of an exclamation mark to...		
Use of ellipsis to suggest...		
Use of an exclamation mark to suggest...		
Use of commas to...		

Activity 3

Imagine you are the pilot. Describe your next attack on the lone bomber. Think about how you can use structural features to create tension and capture the pilot's situation.

Extract from *Some Of It Was Fun* by Hugh Falkus

Here, the writer describes an air attack on German bombers when fighting with the RAF during the Second World War.

I twisted the gun-button on the control column to 'Fire', banked in a shallow dive and headed straight at the bomber formation.

The **flak batteries** had stopped firing. German fighters were peeling off to attack. Vapour trails streamed down like ribbons from a maypole. Lines of tracer bullets arced across the sky. A **Messerschmitt** went flashing past me in a steep dive. There was a knot in my stomach, but this was the moment of excitement that overrides fear and sweeps you on with every nerve stretched tight.

The enemy bombers made no attempt at evasion. I fired at the first head-on... and it blew up. The Spitfire shuddered with the blast of the explosion as I swung round in a steep climbing turn. Now the bombers were scattering. One had turned inland just below me and I closed on it from the quarter. I had hardly touched the gun-button when, one after another, the bomber's crew baled out. I stopped firing. White parachutes billowed far beneath. The nose of the doomed aircraft dipped. She went down in a long twisting **aileron** turn... and burst into flames. Dear God! That was two! And I had enough ammunition left to get a third. A third...!

I corkscrewed in a tight figure-of-eight and looked hopefully round the sky. It was strangely empty. A feature of air-fighting is the speed with which the sky seems to clear in battle.

Then I saw a lone bomber. It was two or three thousand feet below me, well in land and heading for home. Immediately, I turned and gave chase. It was probably the silliest thing I ever did. We had done our job. The German bomber attack had split up. Alone, with fuel running low, I should have turned back. But there was that single bomber. I had the speed and the all-too-rare advantage of height. And my blood was racing.

flak batteries anti-aircraft guns

Messerschmitt the name given to a particular type of German fighter aircraft used in the Second World War, named after the man who made it

aileron a flap used to control the plane, found at the back of each wing

6 Comparing narrative voices

Learning objective

- To compare the techniques used by writers to create a narrative voice

Key terms

narrative voice the personality or character of the narrator as it is revealed through dialogue or descriptive and narrative commentary

narrative viewpoint the perspective a story is narrated from, for example, first person, third-person omniscient, third-person limited, second person

When evaluating a work of prose fiction such as a novel or short story, you need to consider the **narrative voice** created by the writer. Narrative voice refers to the person telling the story and the way in which they do this. It is central to the success of any novel because it impacts directly on not just what the reader is told but also how they respond to it. When considering the narrative voice it is important to think about:

- the **narrative viewpoint** chosen
- what the narrator says and how they say it
- the narrator's attitudes and actions and how these are revealed.

Read Source text H, which is taken from the novel *All Quiet on the Western Front* by Erich Maria Remarque, and then complete the activities below.

Activity 1 · SPAG

1. Why does the writer use a first-person narrator? Discuss your ideas.

2. What tense does the narrator use to tell his story? Explain the impact this has on the reader?

Stretch

Rewrite Source text H from a third-person viewpoint. Annotate your writing with comments exploring the effect of this change in narrative perspective.

3. How does the use of abbreviated language contribute to the narrative voice created?

Support

Think about the formality or informality of the language used and the impression this gives you of the narrator.

4. What do the narrator's actions reveal about his views and attitudes? Select quotations which you think best support your answer.

5. How does the description of the French soldier influence your reaction to the narrator?

Activity 2 · SPAG

Write a paragraph evaluating how the writer creates the narrative voice in Source text H and its impact on the reader. You should comment on the techniques the writer uses to create a convincing narrative voice and how they influence your response as a reader.

Extract from *All Quiet on the Western Front* by Erich Maria Remarque

Here, a young German soldier describes waking up to find himself lying in a crater in no-man's-land, after an attack the night before. Beside him lies the French soldier he stabbed in self-defence.

The gurgling still continues. I block my ears, but I quickly have to take my hands away from them because otherwise I won't be able to hear anything else.

The figure opposite me moves. That startles me, and I look across at him, although I don't want to. Now my eyes are riveted on him. A man with a little moustache is lying there, his head hanging lopsidedly, one arm half crooked and the head against it...

He's dead, I tell myself, he must be dead, he can't feel anything any more; that gurgling, it can only be the body. But the head tries to lift itself and for a moment the groaning gets louder, the forehead sinks back on to the arm. The man is not dead. He is dying, but he is not dead. I push myself forward, pause, prop myself on my hands, slip a bit further along, wait – further, a terrible journey of three yards, a long and fearsome journey. At last I am by his side.

Then he opens his eyes. He must have been able to hear me and he looks at me with an expression of absolute terror. His body doesn't move, but in his eyes there is such an incredible desire to get away that I can imagine for a moment that they might summon up enough strength to drag his body with them, carrying him hundreds of miles away, far, far away, at a single leap. The body is still, completely quiet, there is not a single sound, and even the gurgling has stopped, but the eyes are screaming, roaring, all his life has gathered in them and formed itself into an incredible urge to escape, into a terrible fear of death, a fear of me.

My legs give way and I fall down on to my elbows. 'No, no,' I whisper.

The eyes follow me. I am quite incapable of making any movement as long as they are watching me.

Then his hand falls slowly away from his chest, just a little way, dropping only an inch or two. But that movement breaks the spell of the eyes. I lean forward, shake my head and whisper, 'No, no, no' and lift my hand up – I have to show him that I want to help, and I wipe his forehead.

The eyes flinched when my hand came close, but now they lose their fixed gaze, the eyelids sink deeper, the tension eases. I open his collar for him and prop his head a bit more comfortably.

Now read Source text I, which is taken from the novel *The Boy in the Striped Pyjamas* by John Boyne, and then complete the activities below.

Activity 3

1. Discuss what you think is happening in Source text I.

2. What narrative viewpoint has the writer chosen? Discuss how this influences the way you respond to the text as a reader.

3. Bruno says, 'I'm going to catch a cold out here. I have to go home.' What does this reveal about his understanding of the situation and his character?

4a. What words could you use to describe the narrative voice in this text?

4b. Select three quotations that you think most effectively contribute to creating this voice. Give reasons for your choices.

5. Discuss your response to the ending. How did it make you feel?

Activity 4

1. Compare Source text H from *All Quiet on the Western Front* and Source text I from *The Boy in the Striped Pyjamas*. In your comparison you should:

   • identify any similarities and differences between the narrative voices and the techniques used to create these

   • explore how you respond to each narrative voice as a reader

   • evaluate which narrative voice you think is the most successful and why.

Support

Use the following model to help you to develop your analysis:

• Make a point.

• Select evidence to support this point.

• Use terminology to refer to specific techniques or features.

• Develop your explanation of the effects created.

• Relate your point back to the subject of the essay.

Remember to make comparisons between the two texts rather than evaluating each text individually.

Extract from *The Boy in the Striped Pyjamas* by John Boyne

Here, Bruno, the son of the Nazi Commandant of a concentration camp, has sneaked into the concentration camp to play with an imprisoned Jewish boy.

Bruno frowned. He looked up at the sky, and as he did so there was another loud sound, this time the sound of thunder overhead, and just as quickly the sky seemed to grow even darker, almost black, and rain poured down even more heavily than it had in the morning. Bruno closed his eyes for a moment and felt it wash over him. When he opened them again he wasn't so much marching as being swept along by the group of people, and all he could feel was the mud that was caked all over his body and his pyjamas clinging to his skin with all the rain and he longed to be back in his house, watching all this from a distance and not wrapped up in the centre of it.

'That's it,' he said to Shmuel. 'I'm going to catch a cold out here. I have to go home.'

But just as he said this, his feet brought him up a set of steps, and as he marched on he found there was no more rain coming down any more because they were all piling into a long room that was surprisingly warm and must have been very securely built because no rain was getting in anywhere. In fact it felt completely airtight.

'Well, that's something,' he said, glad to be out of the storm for a few minutes at least. 'I expect we'll have to wait here till it eases off and then I'll get to go home.'

Shmuel gathered himself very close to Bruno and looked up at him in fright. 'I'm sorry we didn't find your papa,' said Bruno.

'It's all right,' said Shmuel.

'And I'm sorry we didn't really get to play, but when you come to Berlin, that's what we'll do. And I'll introduce you to ... Oh, what were their names again?' he asked himself, frustrated because they were supposed to be his three best friends for life but they had all vanished from his memory now. He couldn't remember any of their names and he couldn't picture any of their faces.

'Actually,' he said, looking down at Shmuel, 'it doesn't matter whether I do or don't. They're not my best friends any more anyway.' He looked down and did something quite out of character for him: he took hold of Shmuel's tiny hand in his and squeezed it tightly.

'You're my best friend, Shmuel,' he said. 'My best friend for life.'

Shmuel may well have opened his mouth to say something back, but Bruno never heard it because at that moment there was a loud gasp from all the marchers who had filled the room, as the door at the front was suddenly closed and a loud metallic sound rang through from the outside.

Bruno raised an eyebrow, unable to understand the sense of all of this, but he assumed that it had something to do with keeping the rain out and stopping people from catching colds.

And then the room went very dark and somehow, despite the chaos that followed, Bruno found that he was still holding Shmuel's hand in his own and nothing in the world would have persuaded him to let it go.

7 Comparing attitudes and ideas

Learning objective

- To evaluate and compare how ideas and attitudes are conveyed in prose fiction

Whether you are reading fiction or non-fiction, you need to be able to identify the ideas and attitudes presented in a text and evaluate how these are conveyed. In non-fiction a writer can directly state their own attitudes and ideas, but in fiction writers create characters to represent, express and explore specific ideas and reflect different points of view. If a writer depicts a character in a sympathetic way, it may be likely that this character's ideas, attitudes and opinions are close to the writer's own.

Read Source text J, which is taken from the novel *How Many Miles to Babylon?* by Jennifer Johnston, set during the First World War, and then complete the activities below.

Activity 1

1. What is the narrator's attitude to the following? Support your answers with carefully selected supporting quotations.

   - the padre
   - his family
   - himself.
   - the war
   - life

2. What impact do the Captain's views and attitudes have on you as a reader? Explain your answer.

Exploring the tone created can reveal more about a writer's ideas and attitudes. For example, in Source text J, the narrator says, 'There is no place for speculation or hope, or even dreams.' This helps to create a depressing and negative tone and suggests the writer's views about the treatment of deserters during the First World War.

Activity 2

1. Identify two more quotations and explain how they contribute to the tone created.

2. Do you think the speaker's attitudes and ideas about war in this source text are the same as or different to the writer's? Explain your ideas.

3. Write a paragraph analysing and evaluating how the writer presents the narrator's attitudes and ideas and the impact these have on you as a reader.

Support

In your answer you should comment on:

- the narrative viewpoint chosen
- the **context** of the extract
- the tone created
- how the padre is described
- how the narrator talks about the war, his family and himself.

Key term

context the circumstances or background in which something happens

Extract from *How Many Miles to Babylon?* by Jennifer Johnston

Here, the narrator, Jeremiah Crowe, has been arrested for desertion from the front line and sentenced to death by firing squad.

Because I am an officer and a gentleman they have given me my notebooks, pen, ink, and paper. So I write and wait. I am committed to no cause, I love no living person. The fact that I have no future except what you can count in hours doesn't seem to disturb me unduly. After all, the future whether here or there is equally unknown. So for the waiting days I have only the past to play about with. I can juggle with a series of possibly inaccurate memories, my own interpretation, for what it is worth, of events. There is no place for speculation or hope, or even dreams. Strangely enough I think I like it like that.

I have not communicated with either my father or mother. Time enough for others to do that when it is all over. The **fait accompli**. On His Majesty's Service. Why prolong the pain that they will inevitably feel? It may kill him, but then, like me, he may be better off dead. My heart doesn't bleed for her.

They are treating me with the respect apparently due to my class, and with a reserve due, I am sure, to the fear that I may be mad. How alarmed men are by the lurking demons of the mind!...

By now the attack must be on. A hundred yards of mournful earth, a hill topped with a circle of trees, that at home would have belonged exclusively to the fairies, a farm, some roofless cottages, quiet unimportant places, now the centre of the world for tens of thousands of men. The end of the world for many, the heroes and the cowards, the masters and the slaves. It will no doubt be raining on them, a thick and evil February rain.

The **padre** comes to visit me from time to time. He showed me yesterday the gold cross he wears under his **viyella** vest, pressing into the black hairs that seem to ramp over his chest.

'Have you Faith?' he asked me.

He didn't put it quite like that. He had a more sophisticated way of phrasing things, and also a certain embarrassment in asking what he made sound like an almost indecent question.

'I've never really thought about it.'

'Now is perhaps the time to think.'

I wished that he would go away. I was not, nor am I now, in the mood for soul wrestling, that is a pastime for those who have time to spare.

'It's a bit late now I fear, Padre. Faith is to comfort the living. It seems irrelevant for the dead.'

'You are alive.'

'Technically.'

'Comfort perhaps...'

'I am comfortable, thank you. I...I wonder always why you...you know...you...' I put out my hand and touched his dog collar, 'well, representatives, seem to get such satisfaction in making us afraid of death.'

Now read Source text K, which is taken from the novel *Atonement* by Ian McEwan, and then complete the activities below.

Activity 3

1. What are Turner's attitudes towards:
   - the mother and her son
   - the war
   - life in general?

   Support your ideas with carefully selected quotations from the text.

2. What is the impact of Turner's attitudes and ideas on you as the reader? Discuss your ideas.

Activity 4

1. Compare Source texts J and K. Copy and complete the Venn diagram below to identify the similarities and differences in the attitudes and ideas presented and how these are conveyed in both extracts.

2. 'These texts powerfully convey attitudes towards war.'

   How far do you agree with this statement?

   Write a response comparing and evaluating the way attitudes towards war are conveyed in these extracts and their impact on the reader.

   Support

   Decide which points in your Venn diagram you are going to include in your response and how you will order them in your essay. It may be that not every point is relevant to the question you are answering. Remember to:
   - select evidence from each text to support the points you make
   - use terminology to refer to specific techniques or features
   - develop your explanation of the effects created
   - relate your point back to the subject of the essay.

Extract from *Atonement* by Ian McEwan

This extract describes an attack by a German dive bomber on soldiers and civilians during the Second World War.

The rippling thuds of machine-gun fire in the ploughed earth and the engine roar flashed past them. A wounded soldier was screaming. Turner was on his feet. But the woman would not take his hand. She sat on the ground and hugged the boy tightly to her. She was speaking Flemish to him, soothing him, surely telling him that everything was going to be all right. Mama would see to that. Turner didn't know a single word of the language. It would have made no difference. She paid him no attention. The boy was staring at him blankly over his mother's shoulder.

Turner took a step back. Then he ran. As he floundered across the furrows the attack was coming in. The rich soil was clinging to his boots. Only in nightmares were his feet so heavy. A bomb fell on the road, way over in the centre of the village, where the lorries were. But one screech hid another, and it hit the field before he could go down. The blast lifted him forwards several feet and drove him face-first into the soil. When he came to, his mouth and nose and ears were filled with dirt. He was trying to clear his mouth, but he had no saliva. He used his finger, but that was worse. He was gagging on the dirt, then he was gagging on his filthy finger. He blew the dirt from his nose. His snot was mud and it covered his mouth. But the woods were near, there would be streams and waterfalls and lakes in there. He imagined a paradise. When the rising howl of a diving **Stuka** sounded again, he struggled to place the sound. Was it the all–clear? His thoughts too were clogged. He could not spit or swallow, he could not easily breathe, and he could not think. Then, at the sight of the farmer with the dog still waiting patiently under the tree, it came back to him, he remembered everything and he turned to look back. Where the woman and her son had been was a crater. Even as he saw it, he thought he had always known. That was why he had to leave them. His business was to survive, though he had forgotten why. He kept on towards the woods.

Glossary

Stuka a German dive bomber used during the Second World War

Assessment

Reading

In this section, you will have the chance to apply what you have learned about comparing and evaluating texts as you complete the reading activities on page 161. Read the two non-fiction texts which follow carefully and then complete the activities. Source text L is a speech given by Black Hawk, the leader of the Sauk American Indian tribe, following his capture and surrender in 1832. Source text M is written by Winston Churchill, the Prime Minister of Great Britain during the Second World War, and is taken from a speech he made to the House of Commons when the Battle of France was raging and Britain was under threat.

Glossary

squaws young women

papooses children

Source text L

Extract from Black Hawk's surrender speech

Black Hawk is an Indian. He has done nothing for which an Indian ought to be ashamed. He has fought for his countrymen, the **squaws** and **papooses**, against white men, who came, year after year, to cheat them and take away their lands. You know the cause of our making war. It is known to all white men. They ought to be ashamed of it. The white men despise the Indians, and drive them from their homes. But the Indians are not deceitful. The white men speak bad of the Indian, and look at him spitefully. But the Indian does not tell lies; Indians do not steal.

An Indian who is as bad as the white men, could not live in our nation; he would be put to death, and eat up by the wolves. The white men are bad school-masters; they carry false looks, and deal in false actions; they smile in the face of the poor Indian to cheat him; they shake them by the hand to gain their confidence, to make them drunk, to deceive them, and ruin our wives. We told them to let us alone; but they followed on and beset our paths, and they coiled themselves among us like the snake. They poisoned us by their touch. We were not safe. We lived in danger. We were becoming like them, hypocrites and liars, adulterers, lazy drones, all talkers, and no workers.

Source text L (continued)

We looked up to the Great Spirit. We went to our great father. We were encouraged. His great council gave us fair words and big promises, but we got no satisfaction. Things were growing worse. There were no deer in the forest. The **oppossum** and beaver were fled; the springs were drying up, and our squaws and papooses without **victuals** to keep them from starving; we called a great council and built a large fire. The spirit of our fathers arose and spoke to us to avenge our wrongs or die.... We set up the war-whoop, and dug up the tomahawk; our knives were ready, and the heart of Black Hawk swelled high in his bosom when he led his warriors to battle. He is satisfied. He will go to the world of spirits contented. He has done his duty. His father will meet him there, and commend him.

Black Hawk is a true Indian, and disdains to cry like a woman. He feels for his wife, his children and friends. But he does not care for himself. He cares for his nation and the Indians. They will suffer. He laments their fate. The white men do not scalp the head; but they do worse – they poison the heart, it is not pure with them. His countrymen will not be scalped, but they will, in a few years, become like the white men, so that you can't trust them, and there must be, as in the white settlements, nearly as many officers as men, to take care of them and keep them in order.

Farewell, my nation. Black Hawk tried to save you, and avenge your wrongs. He drank the blood of some of the whites. He has been taken prisoner, and his plans are stopped. He can do no more. He is near his end. His sun is setting, and he will rise no more. Farewell to Black Hawk.

Glossary

oppossum an animal, similar to a stoat

victuals food

Source text M

Extract from a speech by Winston Churchill

I have, myself, full confidence that if all do their duty, if nothing is neglected, and if the best arrangements are made, as they are being made, we shall prove ourselves once again able to defend our Island home, to ride out the storm of war, and to outlive the menace of tyranny, if necessary for years, if necessary alone.

At any rate, that is what we are going to try to do. That is the resolve of His Majesty's Government – every man of them. That is the will of Parliament and the nation.

The British Empire and the French Republic, linked together in their cause and in their need, will defend to the death their native soil, aiding each other like good comrades to the utmost of their strength.

Even though large tracts of Europe and many old and famous States have fallen or may fall into the grip of the Gestapo and all the odious apparatus of Nazi rule, we shall not flag or fail.

We shall go on to the end, we shall fight in France, we shall fight on the seas and oceans, we shall fight with growing confidence and growing strength in the air, we shall defend our Island, whatever the cost may be, we shall fight on the beaches, we shall fight on the landing grounds, we shall fight in the fields and in the streets, we shall fight in the hills; we shall never surrender, and even if, which I do not for a moment believe, this Island or a large part of it were subjugated and starving, then our Empire beyond the seas, armed and guarded by the British Fleet, would carry on the struggle, until, in God's good time, the New World, with all its power and might, steps forth to the rescue and the liberation of the old.

A03

- Compare writers' ideas and perspectives, as well as how these are conveyed, across two texts

A04

- Evaluate texts critically and support this with appropriate textual references

---

Activity 1

'These texts powerfully communicate the speakers' views about surrender.'

How far do you agree with this statement?

In your answer you should:

- discuss what you learn about each speaker
- explain the impact of these views on you as a reader
- compare the ways ideas about surrender are presented.

Support your response with quotations from both texts.

Now read Source texts N and O on pages 162 and 163 and then complete the activity below. Source text N is taken from an essay written by the author Alan Bennett about his Uncle Clarence who was killed in the First World War. Source text O is an extract from the novel *Birdsong* by Sebastian Faulks.

Activity 2

'In these texts, war is presented as a pointless endeavour.'

How far do you agree with this statement?

In your answer you should:

- discuss your impressions of the experiences described
- explain what you find interesting about the characters and **viewpoints** presented
- compare the ways the writers present the impact of war.

Key term

viewpoint an opinion or point of view

Glossary

Bodleian Library the main library of the University of Oxford

ingenuous innocent

Mirage jet a fighter aircraft

Blomfield, Baker and Lutyens the architects who designed the cemeteries

Extract from 'Uncle Clarence' by Alan Bennett

Here, Alan Bennett describes his visit to his Uncle Clarence's grave at the war cemetery near Ypres in Belgium.

There is a plan of the graves, drawn up like an order of battle, these soldiers laid in the earth still in military formation, with the graves set in files and groups and at slight angles to one another, as if they were companies waiting for some last advance. All face east, the direction of the enemy and only incidentally of God.

I sit in the little brick pavilion looking at this register. The book is neat (so much is neat now when nothing was neat then); it is unfingermarked, not even dog-eared. It might be drawn from the **Bodleian Library**, not from a cupboard in a wall in the middle of a field. Of course if this foreign field were forever England the bronze door would long since have been wrenched off, the gates nicked, 'Skins' and 'Chelsea' sprayed over all. The notion of a register so freely available would in England seem **ingenuous** nonsense. I sit there, wondering about this, never knowing if our barbarism denotes vigour or decay. Across the hedgeless fields are the rebuilt towers of Ypres, looking, behind a line of willows, oddly like Oxford. At which point, with a heavy symbolism that in a film would elicit a sophisticated groan, a **Mirage jet** scorches low over the fields.

For all the dead who lie here and the filthy, futile deaths they died, it is still hard to suppress a twinge of imperial pride, partly to be put down to the design of these silent cities: the work of **Blomfield, Baker and Lutyens**, the last architects of Empire. The other feeling, less ambiguous here than it would be in a cemetery of the Second War, is anger. Nobody could say now why these men died.

Extract from *Birdsong* by Sebastian Faulks.

Here, Lieutenant Stephen Wraysford leads his forces into battle during the First World War.

His feet pressed onwards gingerly over the broken ground. After twenty or thirty yards there came a feeling that he was floating above his body, that it had taken an automatic life of its own over which he had no power. It was as though he had become detached, in a dream, from the metal air through which his flesh was walking. In this trance there was a kind of relief, something close to hilarity.

Ten yards ahead of him and to the right was Colonel Barclay, he was carrying a sword.

Stephen went down. Some force had blown him. He was in a dip in the ground with a bleeding man, shivering. The barrage was too far ahead. Now the German guns were placing a curtain of their own. Shrapnel was blasting its jagged cones through any air space not filled by the machine guns.

All that metal will not find room enough, Stephen thought. It must crash and strike sparks above them. The man with him was screaming inaudibly. Stephen wrapped his dressing round the man's leg, then looked at himself. There was no wound. He crawled to the rim of the shellhole. There were others ahead of him. He stood up and began to walk again.

Perhaps with them he would be safer. He felt nothing as he crossed the pitted land on which humps of khaki lay every few yards. The load on his back was heavy. He looked behind and saw a second line walking into the barrage of no-man's-land. They were hurled up like waves breaking backwards into the sea. Bodies were starting to pile up and clog the progress.

There was a man beside him missing part of his face, but walking in the same dreamlike state, his rifle pressing forward. His nose dangled and Stephen could see his teeth through the missing cheek. The noise was unlike anything Stephen had ever heard before. It lay against his skin, shaking his bones.

6 REFLECT AND REVIEW

'A book is made from a tree. One glance at it and you can hear the voice of another person, perhaps someone dead for thousands of years. Across the millennia, the author is speaking, clearly and silently, inside your head, directly to you. Writing is perhaps the greatest of human inventions, binding together people, citizens of distant epochs, who never knew one another. Books break the shackles of time – proof that humans can work magic.'

   Carl Sagan, astronomer

'Don't say it was delightful; make us say delightful when we've read the description. You see, all those words (horrifying, wonderful, hideous, exquisite) are only like saying to your readers please will you do the job for me.'

   C. S. Lewis, writer

'Start telling stories that only you can tell, because there'll always be better writers than you and there'll always be smarter writers than you. There will always be people who are much better at doing this or that – but you are the only you.'

   Neil Gaiman, writer

Introduction

'Writing is perhaps the greatest of human inventions' not only because it enables people to share their knowledge, ideas, stories and experiences, but also because it creates readers who can access this 'magic'. The more widely you read, the more you will learn and the better your own writing will be. Reading and writing are far more than skills you learn at school in order to pass exams: they are life skills which will help you to understand the world, give you pleasure and empower you to express your ideas, thoughts and feelings for the rest of your life.

Exam link

The activities in this chapter are designed to help you develop the reading and writing skills needed for success in both Component 01: Communicating information and ideas and Component 02: Exploring effects and impact. Each section focuses on one or more learning objectives, linked to the assessment objectives which will be assessed in your two GCSE English Language papers. You will have the opportunity to practise the skills you have learned so far and check that you understand the kinds of responses required to meet each of the objectives.

Activity 1

1. Read and discuss the quotations on the facing page. Which do you find most interesting and why? Which do you agree with or disagree with and why?

2. Think about yourself as a reader and as a writer. Discuss:

   • what you enjoy about reading and writing

   • what you think are your strengths as a reader and a writer

   • what skills you want to develop further.

1 Identifying information

Learning objective

- To identify and interpret explicit and implicit information and ideas

When you read any text, you need to be aware of the information and ideas the writer is conveying, both those which are explicit and those which are implicit. Explicit information and ideas are stated directly, while implicit ideas are implied or suggested by what the writer has written. When you identify and interpret information and ideas, you should be able to support the points you make with evidence from the text, such as quotations.

Malala Yousafzai is a teenaged girl who was living in Pakistan, who spoke out about the importance of education for girls and was shot by the Taliban in 2012. Read Source text A from her autobiography *I Am Malala*, and then complete the activities below.

Tip

Questions 1 and 2 are asking you to identify explicit information from the extract, although in question 2 you have to infer what might be a difference between Malala's home in the Swat Valley and the UK.

Activity 1

1. What time of day was Malala shot and who was responsible?

2. Identify one difference between Malala's home in the Swat Valley in Pakistan and the UK.

When selecting evidence from the text to support the points you make, you need to find precise quotations. This means choosing the exact words or phrases that help you answer the question. Don't copy out overly long quotations.

Tip

Question 1 asks you to find two quotations but you have to make inferences about which parts of the text *reveal* Malala's feelings about Pakistan as this information isn't spelt out directly.

Activity 2

1. Identify two quotations which show how Malala feels about Pakistan and being away from her home.

2. Explain the impression you get of Malala's feelings in this section of the extract. Support your ideas by referring to the text.

Source text A

Glossary

bazaar market

Extract from *I am Malala* by Malala Yousafzai

Here, Malala reflects on the events that brought her from her home in the Swat Valley in Pakistan to Birmingham, England.

I come from a country which was created at midnight. When I almost died it was just after midday.

One year ago I left my home for school and never returned. I was shot by a Taliban bullet and was flown out of Pakistan unconscious. Some people say I will never return home but I believe firmly in my heart that I will. To be torn from the country that you love is not something to wish on anyone.

Now, every morning when I open my eyes, I long to see my old room full of my things, my clothes all over the floor and my school prizes on the shelves. Instead I am in a country which is five hours behind my beloved homeland Pakistan and my home in the Swat Valley. But my country is centuries behind this one. Here there is any convenience you can imagine. Water running from every tap, hot or cold as you wish; lights at the flick of a switch, day and night, no need for oil lamps; ovens to cook on that don't need anyone to go and fetch gas cylinders from the **bazaar**. Here everything is so modern one can even find food ready cooked in packets.

When I stand in front of my window and look out, I see tall buildings, long roads full of vehicles moving in orderly lines, neat green hedges and lawns, and tidy pavements to walk on. I close my eyes and for a moment I am back in my valley – the high snow-topped mountains, green waving fields and fresh blue rivers – and my heart smiles when it looks at the people of Swat. My mind transports me back to my school and there I am reunited with my friends and teachers. I meet my best friend Moniba and we sit together, talking and joking as if I had never left.

Then I remember I am in Birmingham.

Now read the next section of Malala's autobiography and complete the activities that follow.

Source text A (continued)

Extract from *I am Malala* by Malala Yousazfai

Here, Malala describes what led up to the moment when she was shot.

When our bus was called, we ran down the steps. The other girls all covered their heads before emerging from the door and climbing up into the back. The bus was actually what we call a *dyna*, a white Toyota TownAce truck with three parallel benches, one along either side and one in the middle. It was cramped with twenty girls and three teachers. I was sitting on the left between Moniba and a girl from the year below called Shazia Ramzan, holding our exam folders to our chests and our school bags under our feet.

After that it is all a bit hazy. I remember that inside the *dyna* it was hot and sticky. The cooler days were late coming and only the faraway mountains of the **Hindu Kush** had a frosting of snow. The back where we sat had no windows, just thick plastic sheeting at the sides which flapped and was too yellowed and dusty to see through. All we could see was a little stamp of open sky out of the back and glimpses of the sun, at that time of day a yellow orb floating in the dust that streamed over everything.

I remember that the bus turned right off the main road at the army checkpoint as always and rounded the corner past the deserted cricket ground. I don't remember any more.

In my dreams about the shooting my father is also in the bus and he is shot with me, and then there are men everywhere and I am searching for my father.

In reality what happened was we suddenly stopped. On our left was the tomb of Sher Mohammed Khan, the finance minister of the first ruler of Swat, all overgrown with grass, and on our right the snack factory. We must have been less than 200 metres from the checkpoint.

We couldn't see in front, but a young bearded man in light-coloured clothes had stepped into the road and waved the van down.

'Is this the Khushal School bus?' he asked our driver. Usman Bhai Jan thought this was a stupid question as the name was painted on the side. 'Yes,' he said.

'I need information about some children,' said the man.

'You should go to the office,' said Usman Bhai Jan.

As he was speaking another young man in white approached the back of the van. 'Look, it's one of those journalists coming to ask for an interview,' said Moniba. Since I'd started speaking at events with my father to campaign for girls' education and against those like the Taliban who want to hide us away, journalists often came, though not like this in the road.

The man was wearing a peaked cap and looked like a college student. He swung himself onto the tailboard at the back and leaned in right over us.

'Who is Malala?' he demanded.

No-one said anything but several of the girls looked at me. I was the only girl with my face not covered.

That's when he lifted up a black pistol. I later learned it was a Colt 45. Some of the girls screamed. Moniba tells me I squeezed her hand.

My friends say he fired three shots, one after another. The first went through my left eye socket and out under my left shoulder. I slumped forward onto Moniba, blood coming from my left ear, so the other two bullets hit the girls next to me. One bullet went into Shazia's left hand. The third went through her left shoulder and into the upper right arm of Kainat Riaz.

My friends later told me the gunman's hand was shaking as he fired.

By the time we got to the hospital my long hair and Moniba's lap were full of blood.

Who is Malala? I am Malala and this is my story.

Activity 3

1. In your own words, explain what it was like for the girls on the bus before the shooting. Support your ideas by referring to the text.

2. Read the beginning of the following student's explanation and discuss how effectively it uses quotations from the text.

   The bus was not really a bus but a truck, and it sounds rather uncomfortable, with three basic 'benches' for the girls to sit on. It was 'cramped' which shows they were all squashed in…

Activity 4

1. Give two ways the behaviour of the man who stops the bus seems unusual to the girls.

2. How did the assassin know which of the girls was Malala?

3. How does Malala suggest that the assassin may have been young and unused to killing? Select two quotations to support your ideas.

Tip

Use your own words as far as possible. Select key words or phrases from the text that help to answer the question and then explain what each of them suggests.

2 Synthesizing information

Learning objective

- To select and synthesize information from two different texts

Exam link

You could be asked to synthesize information from the two unseen texts you read in Component 01: Communicating information and ideas of your GCSE English Language exam. A reading question that asks you to find 'similarities' between the two texts is asking you to synthesize information.

Selecting and synthesizing information means identifying points of information and ideas which are similar from different texts, drawing them together and commenting on them, with supporting evidence.

Read Source text B, which is an account of the assassination of President Kennedy in 1963. It is written by Jim Garrison who was the district attorney of New Orleans at the time.

Activity 1

1. Identify two quotations from the first two paragraphs of Source text B and explain how each one shows just how shocked Jim and his assistant, Frank, were when they heard the news of Kennedy's death.

2. How does the writer show the reactions of Jim and Frank and the other people in the restaurant in the next three paragraphs of the text? Support your ideas by referring to the text.

Source text B and the extracts from Malala's autobiography on pages 167–169 describe incidents which shook the world.

Activity 2

What other similarities do the extracts from Source texts A and B share? Draw on evidence from both texts to support your answer.

Support

You could draw a Venn diagram identifying points of similarity between the two texts. Think about the similarities in what happened but also the similarities in the ideas and emotions conveyed.

Stretch

Look at the last paragraph of Source text B about the assassination of President Kennedy. Explore how the image of the bomb and the structure of the paragraph build up to the last sentence and add to the impact of this section.

Source text B

'The assassination of President Kennedy' by Jim Garrison

I was working at my desk in Criminal Court, as **district attorney** of New Orleans, when the doors flew open and my chief assistant rushed in. 'The president has been shot!' he yelled. It was just past 12.30 pm, Friday, November 22, 1963.

Today, a quarter of a century later, I remember my shock, my disbelief. After I grasped what Frank Klein was telling me, I clung to the hope that perhaps Kennedy had merely been wounded and would survive.

Frank and I headed for Tortorich's on Royal Street in the French Quarter. It was a quiet, uncrowded place where they kept a television set in the dining room. On the way, the car radio announced that John Kennedy had been killed. The remainder of that trip was spent in absolute silence.

At the restaurant the midday customers were staring solemnly at the television set mounted high in the corner of the room. I felt a sense of unreality as the unending reportage flooded in from Dallas. There was very little conversation at the tables. A waiter came up, and we ordered something for lunch. When it arrived we toyed with our food, but neither of us ate anything.

The information coming from the television was inconclusive. Although the Secret Service, the F.B.I., and the Dallas police, along with an enormous crowd of onlookers, had all been at the assassination scene in Dallas, for at least two hours the crisp voices of the newscasters provided no real facts about who the rifleman or riflemen had been. However, we were hypnotised by the confusion, the unending snippets of trivia, the magic of the communications spectacle. Concerned with what had happened to the President and with our own hurt, no one left the restaurant that afternoon. The business and professional men who had come for lunch cancelled their appointments. Frank and I made our calls to the office and returned to the television set.

Then, well into the middle of the afternoon, the arrest of the accused assassin suddenly was announced. Approximately 15 Dallas police officers had caught him while he was seated in a movie theatre a considerable distance from the assassination scene. The delayed arrest burst like a bomb on the television screen, and the long silence in the restaurant ended. You could feel the sudden explosion of fury, the outburst of hate against this previously unknown young man. His name was Lee Harvey Oswald.

3 Analysing language

Learning objectives

- To analyse the effects and connotations of language
- To use linguistic terminology effectively when writing about texts

Key terms

connotation something implied or suggested in addition to the main meaning

Analysing the effects and **connotations** of language means exploring the words and phrases a writer has used and explaining their associations and impact. Using the correct terminology to refer to the different techniques used can support and enhance your analysis.

Read Source text C which is taken from *This is Not About Me*, an autobiography written by Janice Galloway who was born in Scotland in the 1950s, and presents a vivid portrait of her family, particularly her sister.

Activity 1

SPAG

1. In the first five paragraphs, Janice Galloway describes Cora through her physical appearance and through her actions. Select two aspects of her physical appearance and two of her actions and explain what each one suggests about Cora.

2. Cora is described as being a '*presence*'. What does this word suggest about her?

3. Choose two quotations and explain what each one shows about Cora's mother's view of Cora. What do you notice about the language Cora's mother uses?

4. Look at the final paragraph and explain what the choice of language conveys about Cora.

   In your answer you should:

   - explore the connotations of specific vocabulary
   - analyse the effects of different sentence structures
   - relate your points to the impression of Cora that is conveyed
   - support your ideas with relevant quotations.

   #### Support

   You could start by analysing the first sentence of the final paragraph. Use the following questions to help you:

   - Which is the main clause in this sentence? Where does it come in the sentence and what is the effect of its position?
   - What is the impact of the verb 'clawed' and the phrase 'sprung like a steel trap'?
   - Why is the word 'Life' written in italics and with a capital letter?

Extract from *This is Not About Me* by Janice Galloway

Here, Janice describes her sister, Cora, who has left her husband and baby to return home and live with her mother and Janice, who was five at the time.

He's your husband. You canny just *leave*. Are you even going to tell him where you are?

Cora ignored her. She ignored most things my mother said. Dolled up for work, her nails slick and her stilettos sharp, Cora had her mind on other things, most of them in the mirror.

How's that for *gorgeous*? she'd say, a deliberate interruption so my mother gave up. Pouting, flicking her hair, she got into character, you had to hand it to her. For gorgeous, she was good. *Pretty* was not an adjective to which she aspired and she was constitutionally incapable of **winsome**. If Cora laughed, it was out loud with all her fillings on show, a big **guttural**, dirty laugh like she meant it. Her other laugh, a smirk, had nothing to do with humour. Delight to spite took seconds: there was no middle ground. How she dealt with being a waitress and dealing with the general public was anybody's guess.

She'll be found dead up a close with her stockings round her neck one of these days, my mother said. Too bloody cheeky by half.

Cora barely registered that anyone had spoken. Voices she chose not to hear didn't exist. She could do the same trick with people, stepping firmly in front of anyone else at the mirror or the kitchen sink as though they had no substance at all. Cora, on the other hand, was a *presence*. Every morning, she painted on eyebrows like gull wings, curled her thick black hair and set it rigid with whole cans of hairspray. She put on a dress with a sticky-out skirt, a clasp belt as wide as a man's forearm, seamed nylons and a too-wee cardi with buttons open at the neck to show the dress material and low-cut neck beneath. Her lipstick was red or coral and patted down with powder. Cora's lipstick did not wander to her teeth or come off. It wouldn't have dared. Ladders in her stockings was neither here nor there: people noticed my sister in the street and some of them smiled. Whether they did or not was of no consequence to Cora. She was apparently self-contained.

I like a good time, me, she said. I do what I bloody well like.

Twenty one, just clawed herself free from motherhood and sprung like a steel trap for what she imagined might be *Life*, she never sat still. She read four books a week, knitted like a wild thing and watched anything that moved on TV, sometimes all three together with added fags. Stillness was not in her nature. Even wedged into a chair, Cora charged the air with electricity. Something around her crackled fit to kill flies and drop them at her feet in crispy little packets. I couldn't take my eyes off her.

4 Analysing structure

Learning objective

- To analyse how writers use structure to achieve effects and influence readers

Tip

In non-fiction, writers can use structure to control the flow of information to the reader, whilst in fiction, structure can be used to alter the pace of the narrative or create a particular mood or atmosphere.

Glossary

ratiocination process of thinking logically

Analysing structure means exploring how a text has been organized and shaped to create particular effects. Read Source text D from the novel *Ordinary Thunderstorms* by William Boyd, and then complete the activities below.

Activity 1

SPAG

How does the way the text is structured help build a sense of tension for the reader? Discuss:

- the impact of the first paragraph
- how the sequence of events and Adam's thoughts create a sense of tension for the reader
- the use of punctuation, sentence lengths and structures and the effects these create
- how the ending of the extract contrasts with the opening.

Refer to evidence from the text to support your ideas.

Source text D

Extract from *Ordinary Thunderstorms* by William Boyd

Adam is in London for an interview. He goes to return a lost folder to a man he met briefly in a restaurant and finds him stabbed in his flat. He runs away in horror and has just returned to his hotel, Grafton Lodge, and is wondering what to do next.

He stood in the dark mews at the back of Grafton Lodge and looked at the back of the hotel for the window of his room and duly found it: dark, the curtains half-drawn as he had left them that morning for his interview at Imperial College. What world was that, he thought? Everything was still in order, nothing out of the ordinary, at all. He was a fool to be acting so suspic—

'Adam Kindred?'

Later, Adam found it hard to explain to himself why he had reacted so violently to hearing his name. Perhaps he was more traumatised than he thought; perhaps the levels of recent stress he had been experiencing had made him a creature of reflex rather than **ratiocination**. In the event, on hearing this man's voice so close, uttering his name, he had gripped the handle of his new, solid briefcase and had swung it in a backhanded arc, full force, behind him. The immediate unseen impact had jarred his entire arm and shoulder. The man made a noise halfway between a sigh and a moan and Adam heard him fall to the ground with a thud and a clatter.

Adam swivelled round – he now felt a surge of absurd concern: Jesus Christ, what had he done? – and he crouched by the man's semi-conscious body. The man was moving – just – and blood was flowing from his mouth and nose. The right-angled, heavy brass trim at the bottom corner of Adam's briefcase had connected with the man's right temple and in the dim glow of the mews' street lighting he could see a clear, red, L-shaped welt already forming there as if placed by a branding iron. The man groaned and stirred and his hands stretched out as if reaching for something. Adam, following the gesture, saw he was trying to take hold of an automatic pistol (with silencer, he realised, a milli-second later) lying on the cobbles beside him.

Adam stood, fear and alarm now replacing his guilty concern, and then, almost immediately, he heard the approaching yips and yelps of a police car's siren. But this man, he knew, lying at his feet was no policeman. The police, as far as he was aware, didn't issue automatic pistols with silencers to their plain-clothes officers. He tried to stay calm as the logical thought processes made themselves plain – somebody else was also after him, now: this man had been sent to find and kill him. Adam felt a **bolus** of nausea rise in his throat. He was experiencing pure fear, he realised, like an animal, like a trapped animal. He looked down to see that the man had groggily hauled himself up into a sitting position and was managing to hold himself upright there, swaying uncertainly like a baby, before he spat out a tooth. Adam kicked his gun away, sending it sliding and clattering across the cobbled roadway of the mews and stepped back a few paces. This man wasn't a policeman but the real police were coming closer – he could hear another siren some streets away in clamorous dissonance with the first. The man was now beginning to crawl erratically across the cobbles towards his gun. All right: this man was looking for him and so were the police – he heard the first car stop outside the hotel and the urgent slam of doors – the night had clearly gone wrong in ways he couldn't even imagine. He looked around to see that the crawling man had nearly reached his gun and was stretching out an uncertain hand to grab it, as if his vision was defective in some crucial way and he could barely focus. The man keeled over and laboriously righted himself. Adam knew he had to make a decision now, in the next second or two, and with that knowledge came the unwelcome realisation that it would probably be one of the most important decisions of his life. Should he surrender himself to the police – or not? But some unspecified fear in him screamed – NO! NO! RUN! And he knew that his life was about to take a turning he could never reverse – he couldn't surrender himself, now, he wouldn't surrender himself: he needed some time. He was terrified, he realised, of how bad circumstances looked for him, terrified of what complicated, disastrous trouble the baleful, awful implications of the story he would tell – the true story – would land him in. So, time was key, time was his only possible friend and ally at this moment. If he had a little time then things could be sorted out in an orderly way. So he made his decision, one of the most important decisions of his life. It wasn't a question of whether he had chosen the right course of action or the wrong one. He simply had to follow his instincts – he had to be true to himself. He turned and ran away, at a steady pace, up the mews and into the anonymous streets of Pimlico.

5 Comparing ideas

Learning objectives

- To compare the viewpoints and ideas presented in two texts
- To compare how language and structure are used to convey ideas and viewpoints

When you are making comparisons, you need to identify the key features of each text before you line them up against each other. You should think about:

- the main ideas in the text
- the **purpose** of the text
- the **viewpoint** of the writer.

Remember, the viewpoint of the writer may be presented explicitly or may be suggested in a more implicit way.

You are going to read two texts about an incident involving factory workers who make cheap clothes. Source text E is a newspaper article reporting the incident. Source text F on page 178 is an opinion column presenting a writer's response to this incident. Read both articles and complete the activities below.

Key terms

purpose something that you intend to do or achieve, an intended result

viewpoint an opinion or point of view

Activity 1

1. Summarize the news story that Source text E reports.

2. Discuss your views about this news story. Would it change the way you buy clothes?

3. Identify the different viewpoints presented in the text.

4. Explain the different ways Source text E presents Primark in a negative light. Support your ideas with quotations from the text.

5. Do you think that Source text E reports the news story in a balanced way? Think about how language and structure are used to convey the ideas and viewpoints in the text.

Primark shopper finds 'cry for help' stitched into her £10 dress

Primark is poised to investigate after a shopper claimed that she found a label stitched inside a dress drawing attention to exploitative work conditions.

Rebecca Gallagher, 25, claims that a £10 dress that she purchased from a Primark store in Swansea contained a label reading "forced to work exhausting hours". The mother said that the message was written on one of a number of stitched labels which gave Primark addresses in Spain and Ireland along with washing instructions.

"You hear all sorts of stories about people working in sweatshops abroad – it made me so guilty that I can never wear that dress again," she told *The South Wales Evening Post*. Ms Gallagher claims that she attempted to call the retailing giant and was "put on hold for 15 minutes before being cut off". She added: "I dread to think that my summer top may be made by some exhausted person toiling away for hours in some sweatshop abroad."

A spokesman for Primark said: "We would be grateful if the customer would give us the dress, so we can investigate how the additional label became attached and whether there are issues which need to be looked into.

"Primark's Code of Conduct sets out the core principles that suppliers and factories must follow to ensure products are made in good working conditions, and that the people making them are treated decently and paid a fair wage."

It is the latest ethical setback for the retailer since the Rana Plaza factory disaster in 2013, in which more than 1,000 people died in Bangladesh in a tragedy that raised questions about labourers who make the cut-price clothing for Primark and other Western clothing retailers.

The Primark 'cry for help' won't change my shopping habits.

conglomerates companies that own a number of different businesses

It's time to confess – I've got some skeletons in my closet. I buy dresses, trousers, t-shirts and sweaters that have been made in factories with terrible working conditions. It's unethical, irresponsible, and I'm not proud of it. But like many in the UK, I can't afford to do otherwise.

Ethical clothing isn't a financially viable option for me. But why shouldn't it be?

It's hard not be moved by the news today that a "cry for help" label has been found stitched into a Primark dress which reads "'forced to work exhausting hours". The woman who bought it said she dreaded to think "that my summer top may be made by some exhausted person toiling away for hours in some sweatshop abroad." And, of course, I agree.

I shop at low-price high street chains, like Primark, so when I read about the story I immediately felt ashamed. But any guilt was quickly replaced with indignation.

I'm not an evil person. I do not relish the thought of men and women being forced to endure hideous and life-threatening conditions to make the clothes I wear. I was shocked and outraged by the collapse of a clothing factory in Bangladesh last year, which at the time supplied two low-price UK retailers among other brands.

But calling for an outright ban like Katharine Hamnett, the fashion designer famous for staging a protest against nuclear weapons in Downing Street, ignores an inconvenient truth.

Hamnett thinks that by refusing to buy cheap clothes, we can change the way the industry works. Rather than being something extra we pay for, it should be a standard feature of all our attire.

However, most people cannot afford to pay for Hamnett's alternative – a £35 t-shirt. One carries the slogan "No More Fashion Victims", but with fuel and housing costs soaring in the UK we can't all get behind such a sentiment.

What's more, in the past year over a million people have had to use food banks. When it's a choice between being able to put food on the table and ethical clothing, can you blame someone for choosing dinner?

There are other cheaper options than Katharine Hamnett. People Tree also sell ethically made t-shirts, but they're still £20. It's a tall order to expect when many high street chains offer similar items for less than a quarter of the price.

This all makes demonising those who continue to buy from low-price brands incredibly unfair. A more productive approach would be to focus upon making ethical fashion more affordable, and putting pressure on brands that fail to demand safe working conditions and a living wage for workers employed by their suppliers.

So I call on all fellow consumers to hear my confession, and join me in putting the spotlight on the brands, and not the buyer. It should be big **conglomerates** on the catwalk of shame, and not those stitched up by today's cost of living.

Activity 2

1. Summarize the viewpoint presented in Source text F.

2. Discuss your own views about the writer's viewpoint. Are you convinced by the arguments she presents?

3. How does the writer use figurative language to present her views?

Support

Explain why you think the writer has included the following phrases:

- 'I've got some skeletons in my closet'

- 'putting the spotlight on'

- 'It should be big conglomerates on the catwalk of shame, and not those stitched up by today's cost of living.'

Try to link your analysis of the language used to the topic of the article.

4. How does the writer sequence and structure her points in Source text F in order to develop her argument? You should comment on:

- how the opening tries to engage the reader's interest

- the impact of the single-sentence paragraph

- the way each paragraph begins and how this links back to the previous paragraph

- the last paragraph and how it rounds off the article.

When comparing texts you need to explore the connections between them. Think about the ideas and viewpoints presented in each text and how language and structure are used to convey these.

Activity 3

Write a comparison of how Source texts E and F explore the same issue. Support your response with quotations from both texts.

6 Comparing perspectives

Learning objectives

- To understand how to structure an effective comparison of two texts

When you compare two texts it is important to give equal weight to both texts, structuring your writing to explore points of similarity and difference and not simply writing about one text and then the other. A helpful way to approach this is by identifying key topics, **themes** or features on which to base each section of your comparison.

Read Source text G. This is an extract from a speech by Barack Obama, the US President, in which he argues that the minimum wage in America should be raised.

Key term

theme the subject about which a person speaks, writes, or thinks

personal pronoun each of the pronouns (I, me, we, us, you, he, him, she, her, it, they, them) that indicate person, gender, number, and case

- **first-person pronouns** such as 'I' and 'we' refer to the speaker or to the speaker and others

- **second-person pronouns** such as 'you' refers to the person or people being addressed

- **third-person pronouns** such as 'she', 'it' and 'they' refer to third parties other than the speaker or the person being addressed.

Activity 1

1. Discuss your response to the arguments presented and explain how convincing you find them.

2. How effectively do you think President Obama argues his case? Analyse the different techniques he uses and the effects these create. You could explore his use of:

   - anecdotes
   - statistics
   - abstract nouns
   - **personal pronouns**
   - colloquialisms
   - any other techniques.

3. How does Obama structure this section of the speech to make it more persuasive?

Support

You should consider:

- how Obama draws the audience in at the beginning of Source text G
- the way he sequences his arguments and the supporting evidence he puts forward
- how the last paragraph builds up to the final sentence, focusing particularly on the kinds of sentences he uses and the effect they have.

Tip

Think about how the different techniques help President Obama to connect with his audience.

Source text G

Extract from a speech by President Obama

This is an extract from a speech given by President Obama in the USA in February 2014 about wages for lowest paid workers.

The bottom line is, **Michelle** and I want every child to have the same chance this country gave us. But we know our opportunity agenda won't be complete – and too many young people entering the workforce today will see the American Dream as an empty promise – unless we do more to make

Source text G (continued)

sure our economy honours the dignity of work, and hard work pays off for every single American.

Today, women make up about half our workforce. But they still make 77 cents for every dollar a man earns. That is wrong, and in 2014, it's an embarrassment. A woman deserves equal pay for equal work. She deserves to have a baby without sacrificing her job. A mother deserves a day off to care for a sick child or sick parent without running into hardship – and you know what, a father does, too. It's time to do away with workplace policies that belong in a **"Mad Men"** episode. This year, let's all come together – Congress, the White House, and businesses from Wall Street to Main Street – to give every woman the opportunity she deserves. Because I firmly believe when women succeed, America succeeds.

Now, women hold a majority of lower-wage jobs – but they're not the only ones stifled by stagnant wages. Americans understand that some people will earn more than others, and we don't resent those who, by virtue of their efforts, achieve incredible success. But Americans overwhelmingly agree that no one who works full time should ever have to raise a family in poverty.

In the year since I asked this Congress to raise the minimum wage, five states have passed laws to raise theirs. Many businesses have done it on their own. Nick Chute is here tonight with his boss, John Soranno. John's an owner of Punch Pizza in Minneapolis, and Nick helps make the dough. Only now he makes more of it: John just gave his employees a raise, to ten bucks an hour – a decision that eased their financial stress and boosted their morale.

Tonight, I ask more of America's business leaders to follow John's lead and do what you can to raise your employees' wages. To every mayor, governor, and state legislator in America, I say, you don't have to wait for Congress to act; Americans will support you if you take this on. And as a chief executive, I intend to lead by example. Profitable corporations like Costco see higher wages as the smart way to boost productivity and reduce turnover. We should too. In the coming weeks, I will issue an Executive Order requiring federal contractors to pay their federally-funded employees a fair wage of at least $10.10 an hour – because if you cook our troops' meals or wash their dishes, you shouldn't have to live in poverty.

Of course, to reach millions more, Congress needs to get on board. Today, the federal minimum wage is worth about twenty percent less than it was when Ronald Reagan first stood here. Tom Harkin and George Miller have a bill to fix that by lifting the minimum wage to $10.10. This will help families. It will give businesses customers with more money to spend. It doesn't involve any new bureaucratic program. So join the rest of the country. Say yes. Give America a raise.

Glossary

Michelle Michelle Obama, the President's wife

Mad Men a TV drama set in 1960s America

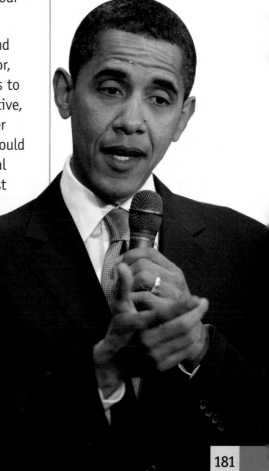

Read Source text H. This is a newspaper article about a proposal to raise the minimum wage in the UK.

Activity 2

1. Discuss your response to the arguments presented and explain how convincing you find them.

2. Prepare a spoken presentation arguing for or against raising the minimum wage. In your presentation you should:

   - refer to information and ideas from the texts you have read

   - sequence and structure the points you make in order to develop your argument

   - express your ideas using Standard English.

Now look back at Harriet Brignall's opinion column in Source text F on page 178. Both Harriet Brignall and President Obama are trying to argue a case and convince the audience.

Activity 3

Compare the ways Harriet Brignall and President Obama present their arguments and explain which one you find more convincing and why.

Support

You could use the following plan to help you structure your comparison:

- Introduction: identify the main similarities and differences in content, purpose and viewpoint, for example:

Both texts are about the wages paid to workers, both are trying to make a case or persuade the reader and in both there is a clear personal viewpoint. However, Obama is speaking from the position of President about the responsibility of those in power in relation to a national issue, while Brignall is giving a personal viewpoint of an individual, representing the ordinary person, who, she believes, should not have to feel responsibility for these kinds of issues.

- Topic: fair pay for all.

- Themes: power, responsibility, fairness.

- Features: explore the structural and stylistic features and the effects these create.

- Personal and critical response: which text you found more persuasive and why.

Source text H

Extract from newspaper article

This newspaper article reports on the response from business groups to a Labour party proposal to raise the minimum wage.

Labour's minimum wage plan 'puts jobs at risk'

Job creation could take a hammering under Labour's plans to increase the minimum wage to £8 an hour by 2020, business groups have warned, as they told party leader Ed Miliband to steer clear of the issue.

In a fierce backlash against the pledge, unveiled on Sunday, Katja Hall, CBI deputy director general, said the minimum wage is already at the "highest rate it can be without putting job creation at risk".

"Raising wages in this way would put serious strain on businesses, particularly hard-pressed smaller firms with tight margins, which would end up employing fewer people," she said.

John Longworth, director general of the British Chambers of Commerce, added that while the minimum wage must rise, forcing an increase from Westminster would be detrimental.

"Businesses are in favour of an evidence-based approach to the minimum wage rather than political parties using it to gain support from voters," he said...

The pair also warned against politicians meddling with the minimum wage, saying that it would hurt economic growth in the long term.

"The national minimum wage has enjoyed broad business support and a move to a politicised US-style system is not in the interest of companies or workers," said Ms Hall.

Mr Longworth meanwhile said the government "should not intervene in such matters, unless there is market failure". He added: "Politicians should instead focus on implementing policies to raise productivity and improve skills in the workplace, which are the keys to higher wages for all."

The pair stressed that the Low Pay Commission, a Labour invention, was already tasked with balancing the minimum wage with job creation and long-term economic growth.

"The Low Pay Commission is one of the biggest success stories of the last Labour Government and makes its judgements based on considerable independent expertise," said Ms Hall, adding that it is "not for politicians to play politics with".

7 Evaluating texts

Learning objective

- To evaluate texts critically

Exam link

Question 4 in both Component 01 and Component 02 will ask you to evaluate and compare the two unseen texts you have read in the exam paper.

Key term

symbolism the use of symbols to represent things

To evaluate a text, you have to give a personal and critical view in relation to a particular focus. You might need to explore how texts convey ideas or explore a theme, and reflect a personal and considered response in your analysis.

You are going to read two texts which look at the importance and impact of places on people. Source text I is an extract from the autobiography of Jackie Kay, *Red Dust Road*, in which she describes going to Africa to find her 'homeland'. Source text J presents two extracts from the novel *Stoner* by John Williams, and in these, William Stoner returns to the place where he was born to bury his parents. Read both texts and then complete the activities.

Activity 1

1. Find evidence from each text to support or disprove the following statements:

   - Jackie Kay is overjoyed to see the land of her ancestors for the first time.

   - William Stoner has a negative view of the place he came from.

In order to evaluate a text effectively, you need to show you can identify and analyse the literary techniques and language features used. Think about the focus of your evaluation and explore how specific techniques help to convey the particular idea or theme you have been asked to consider. One literary technique used in the extracts from *Red Dust Road* and *Stoner* is **symbolism**.

Activity 2

1a. Identify all the references to earth in Source texts I and J. You could make a list of relevant quotations.

1b. What do you notice about how earth is described and the connotations of the description in each text?

1c. What do you think earth symbolizes in each text? Does it symbolize the same thing in both texts or does it symbolize something different? Discuss your ideas.

Extract from *Red Dust Road* by Jackie Kay

Here, Jackie Kay is returning to her ancestral village in Nigeria, hoping to meet some of her family. She is travelling with Kachi and Pious.

September 27th, 2009

The road up to the Niger is smooth and lovely and when we turn the corner and see the metal structure that is the Niger Bridge, something in me lifts. I feel so full of excitement just to be crossing the Niger. It's a bigger bridge than I imagined, not as big as the Forth Bridge in Scotland or the Golden Gate in California, but still impressive. It's difficult to judge the length of bridges when you are on them. There's hundreds of cars cramming and queuing as if everyone is desperate to cross over into a new life entirely. It's thrilling because the River Niger is just something I learnt about and now it has suddenly leapt into life, and is running underneath me, like it would still have been running when I was doing my geography lessons at school years ago. The River Niger, we learnt, roughly bisects Nigeria, entering from the north-west to the country's centre, then flowing due south to the Bight of Biafra. It strikes me how timeless rivers are, how placid they can be, until sometimes their banks swell and they feel as if that is their only way of expressing rage or grief.

September 28th, 2009

We turn into a road that takes my breath away. The whole time I've been in Nigeria, I've never come across a red-dust road exactly like the one in my imagination until I come to my own village. I ask Pious to stop so that I can get out and walk on it. I take off my shoes so the red earth can touch my bare soles. It's as if my footprints were already on the road before I even got there. I walk into them, my waiting footprints. The earth is so copper warm and beautiful and the green of the long elephant grasses so lushly green they make me want to weep. I feel such a strong sense of affinity with the colours and the landscape, a strong sense of recognition. There's a feeling of liberation, and exhilaration, that at last, at last I'm here. It feels a million miles away from Glasgow, from my lovely Fintry Hills, but surprisingly, it also feels like home. I feel shy with the landscape too, like I might be meeting a new blood relation. I almost feel like talking to it and whispering sweet nothings into its listening ear. The road welcomes me: it is benevolent, warm, friendly, accepting and for now feels enough, the red, red of it, the vivid green against it, the long and winding red-dust road. It doesn't matter now that my father turned out to be the Wizard of Oz, a smaller man than the one in my head, and a frightened man at that. What matters is that I've found my village. **Matthew** had asked me how I could feel anything for a place without the people, and I'd wondered whether I might feel nothing. But I feel overwhelmed just to be here.

Glossary

Matthew Jackie Kay's son

Extracts from *Stoner* by John Williams

Here, William Stoner has returned home because his father has died. This novel is set in the USA and these events happen in 1927.

Booneville had changed little during the years he had not seen it. A few new buildings had gone up, a few old ones had been torn down; but the town still retained its bareness and flimsiness, and looked still as if it were only a temporary arrangement that could be dispensed with at any moment. Though most of the streets had been paved in the last few years, a thin haze of dust hung about the town, and a few horse-drawn, steel-tired wagons were still around, the wheels sometimes giving off sparks as they scraped against the concrete paving of street and curb.

Nor had the house changed substantially. It was perhaps drier and grayer than it had been; not even a fleck of paint remained on the clapboards, and the unpainted timber of the porch sagged a bit nearer to the bare earth...

They buried his father in a small plot on the outskirts of Booneville, and William returned to the farm with his mother. That night he could not sleep. He dressed and walked into the field that his father had worked year after year, to the end that he now had found. He tried to remember his father, but the face he had known in his youth would not come to him. He knelt in the field and took a dry clod of earth in his hand. He broke it and watched the grains, dark in the moonlight, crumble and flow through his fingers. He brushed his hand on his trouser leg and got up and went back into the house. He did not sleep; he lay on the bed and looked out the single window until the dawn came, until there were no shadows upon the land, until it stretched gray and barren and infinite before him.

*   *   *

This extract is taken from later in the novel when William Stoner buries his mother.

He buried her beside her husband. After the services were over and the few mourners had gone, he stood alone in a cold November wind and looked at the two graves, one open to its burden and the other mounded and covered by a thin fuzz of grass. He turned on the bare, treeless little plot that held others like his mother and father and looked across the flat land in the direction of the farm where he had been born, where his mother and father had spent their years. He thought of the cost exacted, year after year, by the soil; and it remained as it had been – a little more barren, perhaps, a little more frugal of increase. Nothing had changed. Their lives had been expended in cheerless labor, their wills broken, their intelligences numbed. Now they were in the earth to which they had given their lives; and slowly, year by year, the earth would take them. Slowly the damp and rot would infest the pine boxes which held their bodies, and slowly it would touch their flesh, and finally it would consume the last vestiges of their substances. And they would become a meaningless part of that stubborn earth to which they had long given themselves.

Exam link

Question 4 in both Component 01 and Component 02 will present you with a statement and ask you to evaluate how far you agree with this statement.

Activity 3

'These texts are moving because they show the powerful importance of 'home' to men and women.'

How far do you agree with this statement?

In your answer you should:

- discuss the perspectives and feelings of the people in the two texts
- compare the way language is used to create impact
- explain which text you found more moving and why.

Support your ideas by referring to both texts.

Support

You could copy and complete the table below to help you to develop a critical overview of each text.

	Source text H *Red Dust Road*	Source text I *Stoner*
Type of text		
Place described		
First experience or a return visit		
The effect of the text being written in first or third person		
Impression created of place		
Mood of person experiencing the place		
Key words or phrases		
Notable language features or literary techniques		

Tip

When evaluating these texts, it may be helpful to use the following words and phrases in your response:

- Both texts are about/ focus on...
- In the first text..., while in the second text...
- Jackie Kay creates the impression that... In contrast, John Williams...
- In the same way/ Similarly...
- However/On the other hand...

8 Non-fiction writing

Learning objectives

- To select appropriate tone, style and register for form, purpose and audience
- To use vocabulary and sentence structure for purpose and effect
- To use structural and grammatical features to support coherence and cohesion

Exam link

In Section B of Component 01: Communicating information and ideas, you will be asked to produce your own piece of original non-fiction writing. You will have a choice of two writing tasks which are designed to assess your ability to produce a piece of extended writing for audience, impact and purpose. These writing tasks might be linked by theme or form to the unseen texts you have read in the reading section of the exam paper and you will have one hour to complete your chosen writing task.

When writing non-fiction, you need to keep in mind the purpose of your writing and the audience you are writing for. For example, if you were writing a travel guide to persuade young people to visit your local area, you would select different ideas and information than if you were writing a letter of complaint to your local paper about the lack of facilities for young people in your area.

Activity 1

Choose one of the following topics to write an article about. The article is for the magazine of a broadsheet newspaper.

1. It's more important to enjoy your job than to earn lots of money. Do you agree?

2. Some people are paid too much and some people are paid too little. Do you agree?

Once you have selected your topic, use the steps on pages 189–191 to help you to plan, draft and review your article.

Planning

Whatever topic you are writing about, you need to present the reader with relevant and interesting content. Generating ideas and selecting the information you want to include is an important first stage of the planning process.

Activity 2

1. Think about your own views on your chosen topic. Do you agree or disagree with the statement? List the points you could make to support your views.

2. Discuss your chosen topic with others and make a note of any alternative views. Think about how you could present and counter these views in your own writing.

3. Research and collect further information that you could include in your article. This might include:

   - statistics

   - anecdotes

   - quotations.

   Make sure that the information you collect is relevant to the topic you are writing about.

You now need to decide how you are going to organize the information and ideas you want to present. What are the main points you want to make? How can you develop each idea? How do your ideas connect to each other?

SPAG

Activity 3

Choose a planning format to plan your article. As you complete your plan, make sure you consider:

- the main points you want to make

- the opening paragraph: how you will introduce your main ideas or line of argument

- how you are going to organize your main ideas into paragraphs or sections

- how you are going to link your ideas

- how you are going to develop and support your views

- the closing paragraph: how you will end your article in a way that reinforces your main point.

Activity 4

Think about the style and tone of your article. Make notes on your plan of any different techniques you think will help you to create your chosen style and tone and where you could include these.

Drafting

One of the most important parts of your writing is the opening, as this is your first chance to capture the reader's attention. Here are some different ways of opening an article:

- Historical review: providing some background historical information about the topic in focus.

- Anecdote: a short interesting story taken from personal experience which relates to the topic in some way.

- Surprising or controversial statement: a statement about the topic which will shock or surprise the reader.

- Quotation: an apt quotation from someone well known, an expert or a historical figure.

- Facts: an interesting and relevant piece of information that could be presented as a statistic or framed as a 'did you know' question.

- Question: posing a question related to the topic that will interest or intrigue the reader.

- Specific, recognizable detail: including something that people can identify with.

Activity 5

Read the opening paragraphs of three different magazine articles below and discuss the approach each writer uses. Which do you think is the most effective opening? Which do you think is the least effective?

1. Why us? It's a simple question. Why are humans the only creatures on the planet who have mastered language? It's a puzzle that has engaged some of the best brains from linguists to evolutionary anthropologists. And yet we still don't have an answer.

2. It's 6.30 a.m. and the first rays of sunlight glint on the surf at Peron Point, a remote peninsula in Shark bay at the western tip of Australia. Dolphin biologist Janet Mann is already at her lookout. Below her, 2km of deserted beach sweeps in an arc to Skipjack Point.

3. Ask anyone to guess which age group is least likely to be meeting recommended physical activity guidelines, and they'll opt for children. So here's a statistic that may surprise you: in 2007, 72% of boys and 63% of girls aged 2–15 met the '60 minutes a day, every day' target.

Activity 6

1a. Now look at this opening paragraph from an article arguing there should be a minimum and maximum wage. How effective do you think this is as an opening paragraph? Discuss any ways you think it could be improved.

1b. Rewrite this paragraph to create a more engaging opening for the reader.

Everyone should be paid a good wage. Footballers earn way too much. Just for kicking a ball around, then again they do bring in a lot of money, but it's wrong at the same time, the same goes for TV personalities. It can't be that hard to read the news, more than be a nurse or a bus driver, it's wrong.

When writing your article, you need to think about how you are going to convey your ideas to the reader. The most important decision you need to make is to decide what style and **tone** you are going to adopt. Will this be a formal style with a thoughtful, considered and measured tone? Or will you choose a more informal style and attempt to create a more playful, **ironic** or humorous tone?

Keep your purpose and audience in mind as you write and remember to maintain a consistent style and tone throughout.

Reviewing

When you have completed your draft, you should read the whole article through to check that:

- your opening effectively introduces the article
- each paragraph is clearly developed and links with the next one
- the ending closes the article in an effective way.

Progress check

Re-read your article using the following checklist to help you to review and revise your draft:

- Have you maintained a consistent style, tone and viewpoint?
- Are there edits you want to make? Do you need to add or delete any ideas or sections in order to improve the article?
- Have you expressed your ideas in the clearest way? Are there unnecessary words and phrases that could be deleted? Do you need to rewrite any sections in order to make your points more clearly or further develop your ideas?
- Check that your sentences are clearly and accurately constructed with the correct punctuation.
- Proofread your writing to make sure it is written in Standard English, with accurate spelling and punctuation. Check especially for any errors you know you tend to make, for example, the correct use of apostrophes, spelling of particular words, etc.

Key term

tone a manner of expression in speaking or writing

ironic where the intended meaning differs from the expected one

Tip

Reading what you have written out loud will help you to spot any sections that aren't clear, don't follow logically or need correcting. Reading to someone else and getting their feedback will also help you to identify what could be improved.

9 Creative writing

Learning objectives

- To maintain a consistent narrative viewpoint

- To effectively organize and structure ideas in a narrative

- To use language creatively, making considered choices of vocabulary and sentence structures to create deliberate effects

Narrative writing can often be based on memories, observations and reflections or influenced by the stories and novels you have read. As with non-fiction writing, you can borrow techniques from other writers, but you should try to develop your own style and voice.

Exam link

In Section B of Component 02: Exploring effects and impact, you will be asked to produce your own piece of original creative writing. You will have a choice of two writing tasks which are designed to assess your ability to produce a piece of extended narrative writing, such as a short story or piece of autobiographical writing. These writing tasks might be linked by theme or form to the unseen texts you have read in the reading section of the exam paper and you will have one hour to complete your chosen writing task.

Activity 1

Choose either the title or opening below to write a short story about.

1. Escape

2. I thought I would only ever see that place again in my dreams but I was wrong...

Once you have selected the title or opening, use the steps on the following pages to help you to plan, draft and review your short story.

Planning

When writing a short story, think about what this form allows you to do. Don't fall into the trap of developing a long and complicated plot. In a story of about 400–600 words, it is better to use one or two settings and two or three main characters. In your writing you should focus on developing a sense of place, a character or relationship and building up a particular mood or **atmosphere**.

Key term

interior monologue a piece of writing that represents the thoughts of a character

atmosphere a feeling or tone conveyed by something

Activity 2

SPAG

1. Brainstorm some ideas for stories related to your chosen title or opening. Think about what you can use from your own experience, for example, something that happened to you, a place you know or a real event you have read about.

2. Choose a planning format to plan your short story. As you complete your plan, make sure you consider:

   • what will happen in your story

   • whose viewpoint you are writing from

   • whether you are going to tell the story in the first or third person

   • whether you are going to write in the past or present tense

   • what kind of mood or atmosphere you want to create for the reader

   • how you are going to start and end your story.

3. As you plan your story, use the following checklist to help you to experiment with different approaches.

Structure

Decide at what point in the story you want to start. Do you want to start at the beginning, the end or with a reflection on the experience? You could start at the most exciting point to draw the reader in and then go back and explain what led up to this moment.

Viewpoint

Write your opening sentence and then rewrite it as a different person written from a different point of view. Which version do you prefer? You can write from the viewpoint of a character in the first person, but also in the third person by using **interior monologue**.

Tense

Try writing your first sentence in a different tense. Past tense is the most usual narrative tense, but using the present tense can create a feeling of immediacy and tension for the reader. Take care though – using the present tense can be difficult to sustain.

Drafting

As you draft your short story, think about the different decisions you need to make to create the impact you want on your reader. The choice of style, voice and tense is yours – but it is important to sustain it successfully throughout the story – or if you make a shift, it should be conscious and deliberate.

Thinking about your language choices can help you to create an appropriate mood in your writing without having to explain explicitly what it is.

Tip

Avoid clichés, that is, overused and over-familiar expressions which have lost their impact, and instead try to use language in a precise and imaginative way. You might want to focus on your choice of specific nouns and verbs and use adjectives and adverbs sparingly.

Activity 3

Write a paragraph about someone arriving somewhere and feeling very lonely and miserable. Try to convey the impression that your character feels lonely and miserable without stating this explicitly. You could imply this through the way you describe the place and the movements, actions and reactions of the person.

Activity 4

1a. Read the following paragraph and discuss how effective you think this description is.

It was the most miserable hotel room he had ever seen. Jackson sighed with dismay as he wheeled his suitcase across the worn and threadbare carpet. A single yellow bulb threw an atmosphere of gloom across the room illuminating an unmade bed, the torn and tattered sheets left in disarray. It looked more like a prison cell than the five-star accommodation he had been promised.

1b. Rewrite this paragraph experimenting with different ways of showing Jackson's emotions.

Reviewing

When you have completed your draft, read the whole story through to check that:

- the plot makes sense and the sequence of events is clear

- you have successfully sustained your choice of style, voice and tense

- your choices of vocabulary, grammar and narrative techniques create the effects you intended.

Progress check

Re-read your short story using the following checklist to help you to review and revise your draft:

- Have you sustained a consistent style, voice and viewpoint?

- Are there edits you want to make? Do you need to add or delete any ideas or sections in order to improve the short story?

- Have you expressed your ideas in the clearest way? Are there unnecessary words and phrases that could be deleted? Do you need to rewrite any sections in order to convey the action more clearly or further develop the narrative?

- Check that your sentences are clearly and accurately constructed with the correct punctuation.

- Proofread your writing to make sure it is written in Standard English, with accurate spelling and punctuation. Check especially for any errors you know you tend to make, for example, the correct use of apostrophes, spelling of particular words, etc.

Tip

When asked for advice about writing stories, many authors say 'show, don't tell'. This means writing in a way that lets the reader interpret the details of the story rather than telling the reader information directly. You could use the following techniques to help you to do this:

- Don't explain how a character is feeling, but show this emotion through their actions and dialogue. Avoid using adverbs unless these are the most effective way of describing what you mean.

- Include specific details to help your reader imagine the scene you are describing.

- Delete any unnecessary words and phrases, strings of adjectives and passive sentences to make your writing sharper and more effective.

Component 01: Communicating information and ideas

Section A
Reading information and ideas

Answer all the questions in Section A.
You are advised to spend **one** hour on this section.

Question 1 is about **Text 1**, *A Guide through the District of the Lakes.*

1 a) Look again at lines 1–11. Give two quotations which show William Wordsworth's
       reactions to his surroundings.   **[2]**

   b) Explain the way William Wordsworth's mood changes in lines 11–20.   **[2]**

Question 2 is about **Text 1,** *A Guide through the District of the Lakes* and **Text 2**, *Get Ready
for Summer: The Lake District.*

2   Both texts are taken from guides to the Lake District.

    What other similarities and differences can you identify between the two texts. Draw on
    evidence from **both** texts to support your answer.   **[6]**

Question 3 is about **Text 2**, *Get Ready for Summer: The Lake District.*

3   Explore how the writer uses language and structure in this extract to present information
    about the Lake District.

    Support your ideas by referring to the text, using relevant subject terminology.   **[12]**

Question 4 is about **Text 1**, *A Guide through the District of the Lakes* and **Text 2**, *Get Ready
for Summer: The Lake District.*

4   'These texts show the beauty and appeal of the Lake District for visitors.'

    How far do you agree with this statement?

    In your answer you should:

    • discuss what you learn about the beauty and appeal of the Lake District
    • explain the impact of these ideas on you as a reader
    • compare the ways information and ideas about the Lake District are presented.

    Support your response with quotations from **both** texts.   **[18]**

Text 1

This is an extract from A Guide through the District of the Lakes *by William Wordsworth. Born in 1770, William Wordsworth was a Romantic poet who lived in the Lake District, a mountainous region in north-west England. In 1810, he published a traveller's guidebook to this area and in this extract he describes a journey he and his companions made from Grasmere Vale to Ullswater.*

On the 7th of November, on a damp and gloomy morning, we left **Grasmere Vale**, intending to pass a few days on the banks of **Ullswater**. A mild and dry autumn had been unusually favourable to the preservation and beauty of foliage; and, far advanced as the season was, the trees on the larger Island of **Rydal-mere** retained a splendour which did
5   not need the heightening of sunshine. We noticed, as we passed, that the line of the grey rocky shore of that island, shaggy with bushes and shrubs, and spotted and striped with purplish brown heath, indistinguishably blending with its image reflected in the still water, produced a curious resemblance, both in form and colour, to a richly-coated caterpillar, as it might appear through a magnifying glass of extraordinary power. The mists gathered
10 as we went along: but, when we reached the top of **Kirkstone**, we were glad we had not been discouraged by the apprehension of bad weather. Though not able to see a hundred yards before us, we were more than contented. At such a time, and in such a place, every scattered stone the size of one's head becomes a companion. Near the top of the Pass is the remnant of an old wall, which (magnified, though obscured, by the vapour) might
15 have been taken for a fragment of some monument of ancient grandeur,—yet that same pile of stones we had never before even observed. This situation, it must be allowed, is not favourable to **gaiety**; but a pleasing hurry of spirits accompanies the surprise occasioned by objects transformed, dilated, or distorted, as they are when seen through such a medium. Many of the fragments of rock on the top and slopes of Kirkstone, and of similar places, are
20 fantastic enough in themselves; but the full effect of such impressions can only be had in a state of weather when they are not likely to be *sought* for. It was not till we had descended considerably that the fields of **Hartshope** were seen, like a lake tinged by the reflection of sunny clouds: I mistook them for **Brotherswater**, but, soon after, we saw that lake gleaming faintly with a steely brightness,—then, as we continued to descend, appeared the brown
25 oaks, and the birches of lively yellow—and the cottages—and the lowly Hall of Hartshope, with its long roof and ancient chimneys. During a great part of our way, we had rain, or rather drizzling vapour; for there was never a drop upon our hair or clothes larger than the smallest pearls upon a lady's ring.

Glossary

Grasmere Vale a village in the Lake District
Ullswater a lake in the Lake District
Rydal-mere a lake in the Lake District
Kirkstone a mountain pass in the Lake District
gaiety cheerfulness
Hartshope a village in the Lake District
Brotherswater a lake in the Lake District

Text 2

This is an extract from Get Ready for Summer: The Lake District, *an article first published in the Travel section of* The Independent *newspaper on 24 April, 2011.*

Get Ready for Summer: The Lake District

Big-sky scenery, a ready-to-go infrastructure and something for all budgets – no wonder the Lake District remains a perennial favourite for holidays at home.

The region first inspired the Romantic poets to wander lonely as a cloud in the early 19th century. It has since reinvented itself as a hub for families, foodies and walkers with a slew

5   of great places to stay, eat and visit. While honey-pot towns within the Lake District National Park remain the favourite hangouts, think about venturing beyond the central Lakes this summer to Kirkby Lonsdale, Ulverston or Carlisle. You'll find all of the scenery – but less of the crowds.

The Great Outdoors

Grizedale Forest Park, the Forestry Commission estate west of Windermere, is the place to

10   dodge high-season traffic jams. The estate recently added Signs of Adventure, a series of offbeat road signs, to its excellent al-fresco art trail through the forest. Pick up a map at the newly re-opened visitor centre and follow the trail on foot or by bike.

For wildlife fans, Piel Island is a little-known gem off the Cumbrian coast near Barrow-in-Furness. The self-appointed King of Piel reigns over his fauna-rich fiefdom from the Ship

15   Inn and arranges wildlife-watching excursions. A new visitor centre and smart new B&B just opened – expect an influx of loyal new subjects.

The History Trail

William Wordsworth remains Cumbria's literary poster boy. His life story can be traced across the Lakes from his old grammar school in Hawkshead to the family home at Dove Cottage. But it's Wordworth House in his boyhood hometown of Cockermouth that really

20   brings his story to life. Walk through the house with costumed interpreters and dress the kids up in period costume.

The Retail Therapy

Local goodies remain the souvenir du jour with Grasmere gingerbread and Kendal mint cake perennially popular. The humble Cumberland sausage is even a protected species now, thanks to new Protected Geographical Indication (PGI) status under EU law. Local produce

25   and farmers' markets on Saturdays in Keswick, Kendal and Ulverston are prime hunting ground. But the Holy Grail remains the Cartmel Village Shop for a sugar-hit fix of traditional Lakeland sticky toffee pudding.

The Places to Eat and Drink

The Lakes remains a hotspot on the foodie radar with four Michelin-starred eateries: Holbeck Ghyll, Sharrow Bay, The Samling and, most notably, L'Enclume in Cartmel.

30   More affordable, Cumbria's gastropubs combine the best of regional produce, such as fell-bred lamb and Cartmel Valley kippers, with a pint of local ale – mine's a pint of Lakeland Gold. The latest addition to the gastro scene is The Crown at High Newton, which also just unveiled four stylish new B&B rooms.

And no visit is complete without a stop at the Good Taste Café in Keswick, which still

35   serves the best coffee and muffins in the Lakes.

Section B
Writing for audience, impact and purpose

Choose **one** of the following writing tasks.
You are advised to spend **one** hour on this section.

In this section you will be assessed on the quality of your extended response. You are advised to plan and check your work carefully.

EITHER

5   Write a section of a travel guidebook for teenagers which gives advice on how to deal with any problems they might encounter when travelling.

   In your writing you should:

   • identify some of the problems that young travellers could face

   • suggest why these problems may be difficult to deal with

   • explain some of the ways in which these problems can be resolved.   **[40]**

OR

6   Write an article for a national newspaper in which you argue that places of natural beauty should be protected from developments such as new housing to ensure that they remain unspoilt.

   In your article you should:

   • explain why you think places of natural beauty should be protected

   • give some examples to support your argument

   • convince your readers that it is important to protect places of natural beauty.   **[40]**

Component 02: Exploring effects and impact

Section A
Reading meaning and effects

Answer all the questions in Section A.
You are advised to spend **one** hour on this section.

Question 1 is about **Text 1**, *The Shrimp and the Anemone* by L. P. Hartley.

1 Look again at lines 1–12.

   a) Give **two** quotations which show Eustace's reaction to his discovery of the shrimp and the anemone. **[2]**

   b) What do these suggest about Eustace's character? **[2]**

Question 2 is about **Text 1**, *The Shrimp and the Anemone* by L. P. Hartley.

2 Look again at lines 40–53.

   How does L. P. Hartley use language and structure to emphasize the differences between Eustace and Hilda?

   You should use relevant subject terminology to support your answer. **[6]**

Question 3 is about **Text 2**, 'Dossy' by Janet Frame.

3 Look again at lines 10–37.

   Explore how the writer presents Dossy and how this influences readers' views about the character.

   Support your ideas by referring to the language and structure of this section, using relevant subject terminology. **[12]**

Question 4 is about **Text 1**, *The Shrimp and the Anemone* and **Text 2**, 'Dossy'.

4 'These texts show childhood innocence.' How far do you agree with this statement?

   In your answer you should:

   • discuss your impressions of the childhood experiences presented

   • explain what you find interesting or unusual about the characters depicted

   • compare the ways the writers present the theme of innocence.

Support your response with quotations from **both** texts. **[18]**

Text 1

This is an extract from the novel The Shrimp and the Anemone, *by L. P. Hartley, published in 1944.*

Set in 1907, the extract, from the opening of the novel, describes nine-year-old Eustace and his older sister, Hilda, playing in rock pools at the seaside in Norfolk.

"EUSTACE! Eustace!" Hilda's tones were always urgent; it might not be anything very serious. Eustace bent over the pool. His feet sank in its soggy edge, so he drew back, for he must not get them wet. But he could still see the anemone. Its base was fastened to a boulder, just above the water-line. From the middle of the other end, which was below,
5   something stuck out, quivering. It was a shrimp, Eustace decided, and the anemone was eating it, sucking it in. A tumult arose in Eustace's breast. His heart bled for the shrimp, he longed to rescue it; but, on the other hand, how could he bear to rob the anemone of its dinner? The anemone was more beautiful than the shrimp, more interesting and much rarer. It was a 'plumose' anemone; he recognised it from the picture in his Natural History, and the
10 lovely feathery **epithet** stroked the fringes of his mind like a caress. If he took the shrimp away, the anemone might never catch another, and die of hunger. But while he debated the unswallowed part of the shrimp grew perceptibly smaller.

Once more, mingled with the cries of the **seamews** and pitched even higher than theirs, came Hilda's voice.

15 "Eustace! Eustace! Come here! The bank's breaking! It's your fault! You never mended your side!"

Here was another complication. Ought he not perhaps to go to Hilda and help her build up the bank? It was true he had scamped his side, partly because he was **piqued** with her for always taking more than her fair share. But then she was a girl and older than he and she did
20 it for his good, as she had often told him, and in order that he might not overstrain himself. He leaned on his wooden spade and, looking doubtfully round, saw Hilda signalling with her iron one. An ancient jealousy invaded his heart. Why should *she* have an iron spade? He tried to fix his mind on the anemone. The shrimp's tail was still visible but wriggling more feebly. Horror at its plight began to swamp all other considerations. He made up his mind to release
25 it. But how? If he waded into water he would get his socks wet, which would be bad enough; if he climbed on to the rock he might fall in and get wet all over, which would be worse. There was only one thing to do.

Turn over

"Hilda," he cried, "come here."

30   His low soft voice was whirled away by the wind; it could not compete with the elements, as Hilda's could.

He called again. It was an effort for him to call: he screwed his face up: the cry was unmelodious now that he forced it, more like a squeak than a summons.

But directly she heard him Hilda came, as he knew she would. Eustace put the situation before her, weighing the pros and cons. Which was to be sacrificed, the anemone or the
35   shrimp? Eustace stated the case for each with unflinching impartiality and began to enlarge on the **felicity** that would attend their after-lives, once this situation was straightened out – forgetting, in his enthusiasm, that the well-being of the one depended on the misfortune of the other. But Hilda cut him short.

"Here, catch hold of my feet," she said.

40   She climbed on to the boulder, and flung herself face down on the sea-weedy slope. Eustace followed her more slowly, showing respect for the inequalities of the rock. Then he lowered himself, sprawling uncertainly and rather timidly, and grasped his sister's thin ankles with hands that in spite of his nine years still retained some of the chubbiness of infancy. Once assumed, the position was not uncomfortable. Eustace's thoughts wandered, while his
45   body automatically accommodated itself to the movements of Hilda, who was wriggling ever nearer the edge.

"I've got it," said Hilda at last in a stifled voice. There was no elation, only satisfaction in her tone, and Eustace knew that something had gone wrong.

"Let me look!" he cried, and they struggled up from the rock.

50   The shrimp lay in the palm of Hilda's hand, a sad, disappointing sight. Its reprieve had come too late; its head was mangled and there was no vibration in its tail. The horrible appearance fascinated Eustace for a moment, then upset him so much that he turned away with trembling lips.

Glossary

epithet name or descriptive term
seamews seagulls
piqued irritated
felicity great happiness

Text 2

This is a short story 'Dossy' by Janet Frame, published in 1952.

Set in New Zealand in the 1950s, this story describes a girl called Dossy who is playing with her imaginary friend on the street outside a convent.

Only on the shadows sang out Dossy, and the little girl with fair straight hair sang out answering, only on the shadows, and the two of them went hopping and skipping very carefully for three blocks, and then they got tired and they forgot, and they stopped to pick marigolds through the crack in the corner fence, but only Dossy could reach them because
5 she was bigger. Pick me a marigold, Dossy, to put in my hair, said the little girl and Dossy picked a big yellow flower and she had to bend down to stick it in the little girl's hair. 'Race you to the convent gate,' she said, and together the two of them tore along the footpath and Dossy won, Dossy won easily.

'I'm bigger,' she said.

10 And the little girl looked up at Dossy's bigness and supposed that Dossy must live in a big house to match. Everything matched thought the little girl. Mother and Father. Mother singing and Father singing. Mother washing the dishes and Father drying. Mother in her blue dress and Father in his black suit.

And when you were small you did things that small people did, Grandma said, and when you
15 were big like Dossy you did things the grownup way. And the little girl thought that Dossy must live in a big house to match her bigness. A big house at the end of a long street. With a garden. And a plum tree. And a piano in the front room. And a piano stool to go round and round on. And lollies in a blue tin on the mantelpiece for Father to reach up to and say have a striped one, chicken, they last longer.

20 The little girl put her hand in Dossy's and said Can I come to live with you, Dossy. Can I live in your house.

And Dossy looked down at the little girl with her shiny new shoes on and her neat blue dress and her thick hair ribbon, and then she looked down at her own dirty shoes and turned up dress from her aunties, and she drew away her hand that was dirty and sticky and said
25 nothing but went over to the fence to peep through at the nuns. The little girl followed her and together they looked through to the nuns. They watched them walking up and down with their hands folded in front and their eyes staring straight ahead, and the little girl thought I'll be a nun some day and wear black and white and have a black and white nightie, and I'll pray all day and sit under a plum tree and perhaps God won't mind if I get hungry and eat two or
30 three plums, and every night I'll comb out my mother's long golden hair with a gold comb and I'll have a black and white bed.

Dossy, said the little girl, will you be a nun with me?

Dossy giggled and giggled. I don't think so, she said.

The nuns heard someone laughing and they stopped at the gate to see who it was. They saw
35 a little girl playing ball by herself on the footpath.

It's little Dossy Park, they said. With no mother and living in that poky little house in Hart Street and playing by herself all the time, goodness knows what she'll turn out to be.

203

Section B
Writing imaginatively and creatively

Choose **one** of the following writing tasks.
You are advised to spend **one** hour on this section.

In this section you will be assessed on the quality of your extended response. You are advised to plan and check your work carefully.

EITHER

5   Imagine you are writing your autobiography. Describe **your** experiences of a time when you needed help from someone.

You could write about:

- why you needed help and how this made you feel

- how the person tried to help you and the ways in which you behaved

- the way that you feel about this experience now.   **[40]**

OR

6   *My imaginary friend*. Use this as a title for a story or piece of personal writing.

In your writing you should:

- choose a clear viewpoint

- describe the setting

- explore what having an 'imaginary friend' could be like.   **[40]**

Key terms

Anaphora the use of a short word (e.g. a pronoun such as 'it' or a verb such as 'do') to refer back to a word or phrase used earlier

Anecdote a short entertaining story about a real person or event

Atmosphere a feeling or tone conveyed by something

Bias an opinion or feeling that strongly favours one side in preference to another

Chronologically arranged in the order in which things occurred

Cliché a phrase or idea that is used so often that it has little meaning

Cohesive devices words or phrases which link paragraphs together and link points within paragraphs

Colloquial language informal language used in everyday situations

Connotation something implied or suggested in addition to the main meaning

Context the circumstances or background in which something happens

Contrast a difference clearly seen when things are compared or seen together

Descriptive detail the inclusion of specific details to add to the vividness of the description

Diacope repetition of a word or phrase broken up by one or more intervening words

Dialogue the words spoken by characters in a play, film, or story

Direct speech when the words a person has spoken are relayed to the reader exactly, using speech marks, for example, *She said, 'It's cold'.*

Emotive language words and phrases used to arouse a reader's emotions

Empathizing to understand and share in someone else's feelings, to feel empathy

Extended metaphor a metaphor which is continued through a series of lines or sentences in a text

First-person narration when the story is told from the point of view of the narrator – 'I'/'We'

Foreshadow to be a sign of something that is likely to happen

Hyperbole a deliberately exaggerated statement that is not meant to be taken literally

Imagery the use of figurative or other special language to convey an idea to readers or hearers

Imperative expressing a command

Inference something that you infer; a conclusion reached by reasoning

Informal language language used in everyday speech

Interior monologue a piece of writing that represents the thoughts of a character

Inverted sentence where the normal word order of a sentence is changed for emphasis, for example, 'Whatever you want, you can have.'

Ironic where the intended meaning differs from the expected one

Irony the use of words that mean the opposite of what you really intend, done either for emphasis or for humour

Juxtaposition putting things side by side or close together

Lexical field (or semantic field) words used in a text which have an element of shared meaning

Metaphor the use of a word or phrase in a special meaning that provides an image

Motif a distinctive theme in a literary work or piece of music

Narrator the person or character who recounts the events of a story

Narrative hook a literary technique used in the opening of a story to engage readers so that they will keep reading

Narrative viewpoint the perspective a story is narrated from, for example, first-person, third-person omniscient, third-person limited, second-person

Narrative voice the personality or character of the narrator as it is revealed through dialogue or descriptive and narrative commentary

Pathetic fallacy giving human feelings to inanimate things or animals

Pejorative language words and phrases that express contempt or disapproval

Personal pronoun each of the pronouns (I, me, we, us, you, he, him, she, her, it, they, them) that indicate person, gender, number, and case

- **first-person pronouns** such as 'I' and 'we' refer to the speaker or to the speaker and others

- **second-person pronouns** such as 'you' refer to the person or people being addressed

- **third-person pronouns** such as 'she', 'it' and 'they' refer to third parties other than the speaker or the person being addressed.

Personification representing an idea in human form or a thing as having human characteristics

Polyptoton repetition of words of the same root with different endings, for example, 'strong', 'strength', etc.

Propaganda biased or misleading publicity that is intended to promote a political point of view

Purpose something that you intend to do or achieve, an intended result

Recount to give an account of something

Reference chains different words or phrases used for the same idea, person or thing many times in a piece of writing, like links in a chain

Repetition repeating, or being repeated

Reported speech a speaker's words as reported by another person and put into the tense of the reporting verb (such as 'said' or 'replied')

Rhetorical question a question asked for dramatic effect and not intended to get an answer

Rule of three (also called tricolon) linking three points or features, for example, adjectives, for impact

Setting the way or place in which something is set

Sibilance a literary device where strongly stressed consonants create a hissing sound

Simile where one thing is compared to another thing, using a connective word such as 'like' or 'as'

Stereotype an over-simplified image or idea of a type of person or thing that has become fixed through being widely held

Stream of consciousness a narrative mode that attempts to reflect the narrator's thought processes

Symbol a thing thought of as representing or standing for something else

Symbolism the use of symbols to represent things

Theme the subject about which a person speaks, writes, or thinks

Tone a manner of expression in speaking or writing

Viewpoint an opinion or point of view

Acknowledgements

The authors and publisher are grateful for permission to reprint extracts from the following copyright material:

Kate Atkinson: 'Dissonance' in *Not the End of the World* (Doubleday, 2002), copyright © Kate Atkinson 2002, reprinted by permission of The Random House Group Ltd, and the author c/o Rogers Coleridge & White, 20 Powis Mews, London W11 `JN.

J G Ballard: *Miracles of Life: Shanghai to Shepperton: An autobiography* (HarperPerennial, 2008), reprinted by permission of HarperCollins Publishers UK.

Alan Bennett: 'Uncle Clarence' from *Writing Home* (Faber, 2014), copyright © Alan Bennett 1994, reprinted by permission of Faber & Faber Ltd.

William Boyd: *Ordinary Thunderstorms* (Bloomsbury, 2009), copyright © William Boyd 2009, reprinted by permission of Bloomsbury Publishing Plc and Curtis Brown Group Ltd, London on behalf of William Boyd.

John Boyne: *The Boy in Striped Pyjamas* (David Fickling Books, 2005), copyright © John Boyne 2005, reprinted by permission of The Random House Group Ltd.

Derren Brown: *Confessions of a Conjuror* (Channel 4 Books, 2010), copyright © Derren Brown 2010, reprinted by permission of The Random House Group Ltd.

Bill Bryson: *The Life and Times of The Thunderbolt Kid* (Doubleday, 2006), reprinted by permission of The Random House Group Ltd and of Greene & Heaton for the author.

Bruce Chatwin: *On the Black Hill* (Cape, 1982), copyright © Bruce Chatwin 1982, reprinted by permission of The Random House Group Ltd and Aitken Alexander Associates

Winston Churchill: 'We shall fight them on the beaches', speech given on 4 June 1940, copyright © Winston S Churchill, reprinted by permission of Curtis Brown Group Ltd, London on behalf of the Estate of Sir Winston Churchill.

Roddy Doyle: *The Woman Who Walked Into Doors* (Jonathan Cape, 1996), copyright © Roddy Doyle 1996, reprinted by permission of The Random House Group Ltd and ** John Sutton Management.

Daphne Du Maurier: *Jamaica Inn* (Virago, 2012), copyright © The Estate of Daphne Du Maurier 1936, reprinted by permission of Curtis Brown Group Ltd, London on behalf of The Chichester Partnership.

Hugh Falkus: *Some of it Was Fun* (Medlar Press, 2003), reprinted by permission of Medlar Press, Publishers of Fine Angling Books.

Sebastian Faulks: *Birdsong* (Hutchinson, 1993), copyright © Sebastian Faulks 1993, reprinted by permission of The Random House Group Ltd and Greene & Heaton for the author

E M Forster: *a Room with a View* (Penguin English Library, 2012), reprinted by permission of The Provost and Scholars of King's College, Cambridge, and The Society of Authors as the representatives of the E M Forster Estate.

Stephen Fry: letter to Crystal Nunn, 2006, from *Letters of Note; correspondence deserving a wider audience* compiled by Shaun Usher (Canongate Unbound, 2013)

Neil Gaiman: *The Ocean and the End of the Lane* (Headline, 2013), copyright © Neil Gaiman, 2013, reprinted by permission of Headline Publishing Group, Hachette UK.

Janice Galloway: *This is Not About Me* (Granta, 2008), copyright © Janice Galloway 2008, reprinted by permission of Granta Books.

Jim Garrison: *On the Trail of the Assassins: my investigation and prosecution of the murder of President Kennedy* (Sheridan Square Press, 1988), copyright © Jim Garrison 1988, reprinted by permission of the Lynne Rabinoff Agency.

Mark Haddon: *The Curious Incident of the Dog in the Night-time* (Vintage, 2004), copyright © Mark Haddon 2004, reprinted by permission of The Random House Group Ltd and Aitken Alexander Assocaites.

Joanne Harris: *Chocolat* (Doubleday, 1999), copyright © Joanne Harris 1999, reprinted by permission of The Random House Group Ltd.

Fiona Harrold: *The 10 Minute Life Coach: fast wroking strategies for a brand new you* (Hodder Mobius, 2003), copyright © Fiona Harrold 2002, reprinted by permission of the publishers.

Susan Hill: *I'm the King of the Castle* (Hamish Hamilton, 1970), copyright © Susan Hill 1970, 1989, reprinted by permission of Sheil Land Associates Ltd.

Victoria Hislop: 'Red Pins on a Map', copyright © Victoria Hislop 2012, from *Red: The Waterstones Anthology* (Waterstones, 2012), reprinted by permission of the author c/o Rogers, Coleridge & White, 20 Powis Mews, London 2014 1JN.

Nick Hornby: *High Fidelity* (Penguin, 2014), copyright © Nick Hornby 1995, reprinted by permission of Penguin Books Ltd

Candace Jackson: 'Living the High Life', *Wall Street Journal online*, 20 Sept 2012, © 2012 Dow Jones and Company, Inc, reprinted by permission of the Wall Street Journal. All rights reserved worldwide. Licence Number 3542551265237.

Jennifer Johnston: *How Many Miles to Babylon?* (Penguin, 2010), copyright © Jennifer Johnston 1974, reprinted by permission of Penguin Books Ltd.

Jackie Kay: *Red Dust Road* (Picador, 2010), copyright © Jackie Kay 2010, reprinted by permission of Macmillan Publishers Ltd.

Patrick McCabe: *The Butcher Boy* (Picador, 2002), copyright © Patrick McCabe 2002, reprinted by permission of Macmillan Publishers Ltd.

Frank McCourt: *Angela's Ashes* (HarperPerennial, 2005), copyright © Frank McCourt 1996, reprinted by permission of HarperCollins Publishers UK.

Ian McEwan: *Atonement* (Vintage, 2007), copyright © Ian Mc Ewan 2007, reprinted by permission of The Random House Group Ltd and the author author c/o Rogers, Coleridge & White, 20 Powis Mews, London W11 1JN.

Lucy Mangan: 'How to be a columnist' from *My Family and Other Disasters* (Guardian Books, 2009), copyright © Lucy Mangan 2009, reprinted by permission of the author.

Caitlin Moran: 'Cutting to the heart of the welfare state', *The Times Magazine*, 28 Jan 2012, copyright © Caitlin Moran/News Syndication 2012, rerpinted by permission of News Syndication.

Maggie O'Farrell: *Instructions for a Heatwave* (Tinder Press, 2013), copyright © Maggie O'Farrell 2013, reprinted by permission of the publishers, an imprint of Headline Publishing

George Orwell: *The Road to Wigan Pier* (Penguin, 2001), copyright © George Orwell 1937, reprinted by permission of A M Heath & Co Ltd on behalf of Bill Hamilton as the Literary Executor of the Estate of the Late Sonia Brownell Orwell.

Sylvia Plath: 'Superman and Paula Brown's New Snowsuit' from *Johnny Panic and the Bible of Dreams and other prose writings* (Faber, 1979), copyright © Sylvia Plath 1979, reprinted by permission of Faber & Faber Ltd.

Erich Maria Remarque: All *Quiet on the Western Front* translated by Brian Jonathan Cape, 1994), translation copyright Brian Murdoch 1994, reprinted by permission of The Random House Group Ltd.

Meg Rosoff: *How I Live Now* (Penguin, 2004), copyright © Meg Rosoff 2004, reprinted by permission of Penguin Books Ltd.

Ziauddin Sardar: *Balti Britain: a journey through the British Asian experience* (Granta, 2009), copyright © Ziauddin Sardar 2009, reprinted by permission of Granta Books.

Ronald Skirth: *The Reluctant Tommy* (Macmillan, 2010), copyright © Ronald Skirth 2010, reprinted by permission of Macmillan Publishers Ltd.

Zadie Smith: 'Joy', *New York Review of Books*, 10 January 2013, copyright © Zadie Smith 2013, reprinted by permission of the author c/o Rogers, Coleridge & White, 20 Powis Mews, London W11 1JN.

Meera Syall: *Anita and Me* (HarperPerennial, 1996), copyright © Meera Syall 1996, reprinted by permission of HarperCollins Publishers UK.

Arthur Symons: *London: A Book of Aspects* (Privately printed in 1909), reprinted by permission of the Literary Estate of Arthur Symons.

Roma Tearne: *Brixton Beach* (HarperPress, 2009), copyright © Roma Tearne 2009, reprinted by permission of HarperCollins Publishers UK.

Rose Tremain: *The Colour* (Chatto & Windus, 2003), copyright © Rose Tremain 2003 reprinted by permission of The Random House Group Ltd.

Ruby Wax: *Sane New World; taming the mind* (Hodder, 2013), copyright © Ruby Wax 2013, reprinted by permision of **Hodder & Stoughton Ltd

John Williams: *Stoner* (Vintage, 2013), copyright © John Williams 1965, reprinted by permission of The Random House Group Ltd and Frances Collins Literary Agent for the author.

Jeanette Winterson: *Why Be Happy When You Could Be Normal?* (Jonathan Cape, 2011), copyright © Jeanette Winterson 2011, reprinted by permission of The Random House Group Ltd.

Meg Wolitzer: *The Interestings* (Chatto, 2013), copyright © Meg Wolitzer 2013, reprinted by permission of the publishers, The Random House Group Ltd, and Riverhead, an imprint of Penguin Publishing Group, a division of Penguin Random House LLC

Malala Yousafzai with Christina Lamb: *I Am Malala: the girl who stood up for education and was shot by the Taliban* (Weidenfeld & Nicholson/ Little Brown, 2013), copyright © Salarzai 2013 Ltd, reprinted by permission of The Orion Publishing Group, London and Little Brown & Company, Hachette Book Group, Inc.

and to the following for permission to reprint copyright texts:

Guardian News and Media for extracts from 'Child Geniuses: What happens when they grow up?' by Patrick Barkham, *The Guardian*, 15 May 2010, copyright © Guardian News and Media 2010; and Fyfe Dangerfield in 'Top artists reveal how to find creative inspiration', *The Guardian*, 2 Jan 2012, copyright © Guardian News and Media 2012.

Trustees of the Imperial War Museum for extract from a letter from Captain C K McKerrow, 1916, Private Papers of Captain C K McKerrow, Documents and Sound Section (2386).

The Independent, www.independent.co.uk for 'The Primark cry for help won't change my shopping habits' by Harriet Bignell, *The Independent*, 24 June 2014, copyright © The Independent 2014; and 'Primark shopper finds 'cry for help' stitched into her £10 dress' by Kunal Dutta, *The Independent*, 24 June 2014, copyright © The Independent 2014.

Kinleigh Folkard & Hayward for extract from 'Living the High Life' on *Completely London*, 8 May 2013.

Telegraph Media Group Ltd for extracts from 'How to learn boring facts' by Ed Cooke, *The Telegraph*, 26 Jan 2013, copyright © Telegraph Media Group Ltd 2013; 'The tower block was a disastrous low point in British urban life' by Harry Mount, *The Telegraph*, 24 Jan 2012, copyright © Telegraph Media Group Ltd 2012; and 'Labour's minimum wage plan puts jobs at risk' by Denise Roland, *The Telegraph*, 21 Sept 2014, copyright © Telegraph Media Group Ltd 2014.

Cover image by DrAfter123/Getty Images

p4-5: DrAfter123/Getty Images; **p13:** spyx/Shutterstock; **p14-15:** SCOTT CAMAZINE/Getty Images; **p17:** 9nong/Shutterstock; **p18:** © Norimages/Alamy; **p21:** ROYALTYSTOCKPHOTO/ SCIENCE PHOTO LIBRARY; **p22:** pisaphotography/Shutterstock; **p27:** (l) Anton Gvozdikov/ Shutterstock, (r) Yuriy Chertok/Shutterstock; **p29:** © ClassicStock/Alamy; **p31:** Olesya Feketa/Shutterstock; **p32:** Andy Sheppard/Getty Images; **p34:** © Hulton-Deutsch Collection/ CORBIS; **p37:** Aigars Reinholds/Shutterstock; **p40:** mangpor2004/Shutterstock; **p44:** Alberto Stocco/Shutterstock; **p45:** niepo/Shutterstock; **p47:** Featureflash/Shutterstock; **p48:** J A Hampton/Getty Images; **p51:** Mary Evans Picture Library/MARGARET MONCK; **p52:** Mary Evans/Peter Higginbotham Collection; **p57:** stocker1970/Shutterstock; **p61:** © Darren Lehane/Alamy; **p62:** vipflash/Shutterstock; **p67:** Thomas Owen Jenkins/Shutterstock; **p69:** © David Cole/Alamy; **p71:** © Everett Collection Historical/Alamy; **p74-75:** YanLev/ Shutterstock; **p77:** © AF archive/Alamy; **p79:** © Aladdin Color, Inc./Aladdin Color, Inc./ Corbis; **p81:** © FogStock/Alamy; **p83:** © CBW/Alamy; **p87:** © AF archive/Alamy; **p89:** Veronica Louro/Shutterstock; **p91:** © Moviestore collection Ltd/Alamy; **p93:** Jacqueline Abromeit/Shutterstock; **p95:** © Peter Horree/Alamy; **p99:** makar/Shutterstock; **p101:** © Moviestore collection Ltd/Alamy; **p103:** (t) Goodluz/Shutterstock, (m) Dubova/Shutterstock, (b) michaeljung/Shutterstock; **p104-105:** Galyna Andrushko/Shutterstock; **p107:** Claudio Giovanni Colombo/Shutterstock; **p109:** N K/Shutterstock; **p111:** Mary Evans/Grenville Collins Postcard Collection; **p112:** © Accent Alaska.com/Alamy; **p115:** Mary Evans Picture Library; p119: © Cephas Picture Library/Alamy; **p121:** design36/Shutterstock; **p122-123:** aboikis/Shutterstock; **p125:** © Marc Tielemans/Alamy; **p126:** © Dmitry Rukhlenko/Corbis; **p127:** Binh Thanh Bui/Shutterstock; **p129:** Mariusz Niedzwiedzki/Shutterstock; **p131:** Andrew Fletcher/Shutterstock; **p133:** © f8 images/Alamy; **p134-135:** US Army Photo/Alamy; **p137:** PVDE/Epic/Mary Evans; **p138-139:** © Lebrecht Music and Arts Photo Library/Alamy; **p141:** Mary Evans/Robert Hunt Collection; **p142:** © Elena Rachkovskaya/Alamy; **p144:** © CORBIS; **p146-147:** © CORBIS; **p149:** © Photos 12/ Alamy; **p151:** © World History Archive/Alamy; **p152-153:** © Moviestore collection Ltd/ Alamy; **p155:** © Bettmann/CORBIS; **p157:** © Moviestore collection Ltd/Alamy; **p159:** © North Wind Picture Archives/Alamy; **p160:** © Bettmann/CORBIS; **p162-163:** Annavee/ Shutterstock; **p164-165:** JEREMY WALKER/SCIENCE PHOTO LIBRARY; **p167:** © WENN Ltd/ Alamy; **p168:** © Xinhua/Alamy; **p171:** © Bettmann/CORBIS; **p173:** Kuznechik/Shutterstock; **p175:** © Ron Bailey/Alamy; **p176:** Binh Thanh Bui/Shutterstock; **p177:** © Joerg Boethling/ Alamy; **p181:** Everett Collection/Shutterstock; **p183:** © David Warren/Alamy; **p184-185:** ERIC FEFERBERG/Getty Images; **p186-187:** photoneye/Shutterstock; **p188:** © Janine Wiedel Photolibrary/Alamy; **p192:** George N/Shutterstock; **p194:** Kichigin/Shutterstock

Although we have made every effort to trace and contact all copyright holders before publication this has not been possible in all cases. If notified, the publisher will rectify any errors or omissions at the earliest opportunity.